An Ottoman Tragedy

STUDIES ON THE HISTORY OF SOCIETY AND CULTURE

Victoria E. Bonnell and Lynn Hunt, Editors

An Ottoman Tragedy
History and Historiography at Play

GABRIEL PITERBERG

University of California Press
BERKELEY   LOS ANGELES   LONDON

University of California Press
Berkeley and Los Angeles, California

University of California Press, Ltd.
London, England

© 2003 by the Regents of the University of California

Library of Congress Cataloging-in-Publication Data

Piterberg, Gabriel, 1955–
   An Ottoman tragedy : history and historiography at play / Gabriel Piterberg.
      p.   cm.—(Studies on the history of society and culture ; 50)
   Includes bibliographical references and index.
   ISBN 0-520-23836-2 (cloth)
   1. Turkey—History.   2. Historiography—Turkey.   I. Title.
II. Series.
DR438.8   .P58 2003
956'.015—dc21   2002152983

Manufactured in the United States of America
12 11 10 09 08 07 06 05 04 03
10 9 8 7 6 5 4 3 2 1

The paper used in this publication meets the minimum requirements of ANSI/NISO Z39.48–1992 (R 1997) *(Permanence of Paper)*. ⊗

*For Uri, who puts things in perspective,
and to my parents*

Soon as I beheld thee, mazed and wildered grew
        my sad heart;
How shall I my love disclose to thee who
        tyrant dread art?
How shall I hold straight upon my road,
        when yonder Torment
Smitten hath my breast with deadly wounds by her
        eyelash-dart?
Face, a rose; and mouth, a rosebud; form,
        a slender sapling—
How shall I not be the slave of Princess such
        as thou art?
Ne'er hath heart a beauty seen like her of graceful
        figure;
Joyous would I for yon charmer's eyebrow with
        my life part.
Farisi, what can you do but love that peerless
        beauty?
Ah! this aged Sphere hath made me lover of
        yon sweetheart.

        A *Gazel* written in 1622 by Farisi (Sultan Osman II's *mahlas* or pseudonym), published and translated by E. J. W. Gibb. Was it dedicated to Sultan Osman's beloved, Akile, daughter of the *Sheyhülislam* Esad Efendi?

The skeptical theses based on the reduction of historiography to its narrative or rhetorical dimension have been in circulation for a few decades, even if their roots, as we shall see, are more ancient. In general, the theoreticians of historiography who propose them care little for the concrete work of historians. But even historians, aside from some token homage to a "linguistic turn" or "rhetorical turn" currently in vogue, are scarcely inclined to reflect on the theoretical implications of their own profession. Rarely has the chasm between methodological reflection and actual historiographical practice been as pronounced as in the last few decades. It seems that the only way to overcome it is to take the challenge of the skeptics seriously and attempt to articulate the point of view of those who work in contact with documents, in the broadest sense of the term. My solution transfers to the actuality of research the tensions between narration and documentation. It does not propose a rapprochement between theoreticians and historians, and probably will displease them both.

CARLO GINZBURG, *History, Rhetoric, and Proof*

In the preceding tale, I have tried to narrate the process of failure, the process of defeat. I thought first of that archbishop of Canterbury who set himself the task of proving that God exists; then I thought of the alchemists who sought the philosopher's stone; then of the vain trisectors of the angle and squarers of the circle. Then I reflected that a more poetic case than these would be a man who sets himself a goal that is not forbidden to other men, but is forbidden to him. I recalled Averroës, who, bounded within the circle of Islam, could never know the meaning of the words *tragedy* and *comedy*. I told his story; as I went on, I felt what that god mentioned by Burton must have felt—the god who set himself the task of creating a bull but turned out a buffalo. I felt that the work mocked me, foiled me, thwarted me. I felt that Averroës, trying to imagine what a play is without ever having suspected what a theater is, was no more absurd than I, trying to |imagine Averroës yet with no more material than a few snatches from Renan, Lane, and Asín Palacios. I felt, on the last page, that my story was a symbol of the man I had been as I was writing it, and that in order to write that story I had had to be that man, and that in order to be that man I had had to write that story, and so on, *ad infinitum*. (And just when I stop believing in him, "Averroës" disappears.)

JORGE LUIS BORGES, "Avërroes' Search"

Contents

Acknowledgments   xi

A Note on Transliteration   xv

Introduction: The Content and Form of This Study   1

PART I. FOUNDATIONS

1. The Plot   9
2. The Formation and Study of Ottoman Historiography   30
3. An Interpretive Framework   50

PART II. HISTORIOGRAPHY

4. Tuği's Representation of the Haile-i Osmaniye: The Perspective of the Imperial Army   71
5. The Formation of Alternative Narratives: Hasanbeyzade and Peçevi   91
6. The Conception of the State Narrative   114

PART III. THE STATE

7. The Early Modern Ottoman State: History and Theory   135
8. The Ottoman State as a Discursively Contested Field   163

Epilogue: Poetics of Ottoman Historiography: Preliminary Notes   185

Glossary	201
Notes	207
Bibliography	233
Index	243

Acknowledgments

I was extremely fortunate to have been taught by outstanding scholars, who have become colleagues and friends. Deeply thanking them is a pleasure. At Tel-Aviv University Ehud R. Toledano introduced me to the historical discipline in general and to the *aja'ib* of the Ottoman world in particular. The role he played in launching my academic career and forming my intellect cannot be overstated. Although substantially rethought and reworked, this study began as a D.Phil. thesis. Richard C. Repp, the Master of St. Cross College, was my D.Phil. advisor at Oxford, but he was much more than that. His insightful and humane guidance was a constant source of inspiration and encouragement. The taxing tutorials with Dr. Repp in reading Ottoman texts at the Oriental Institute and at St. Cross College were an experience I cherish and sorely miss. The gist of Dr. Repp's guidance was his comment on a rather pompous paper I had submitted on the theory of historiography, in which "to ponder, "pondering," and "ponderous" had been excessively used. "My dear boy," Dr. Repp remarked wryly, "Sir Isaiah Berlin ponders, you consider." If the present book has redeeming qualities, these two teachers ought to be accredited.

Israel Gershoni has been an inspiring teacher and a supportive friend, in whose seminars I became familiar with the attempts to reinvigorate intellectual history and the debates that issued from these attempts. I hope he recognizes his contribution to certain parts of this book. At Oxford I had the privilege of being exposed to the unique method of teaching—that sensitive, subtle, and understated dialogue whose significance one might appreciate weeks if not months later—of the late Albert Hourani and Roger Owen. I cannot forget how through a couple of suggestions for further reading and seemingly ordinary remarks Roger Owen made me think about the state in ways I had never explored.

James Gelvin's friendship and encouragement have meant a lot, and his comments on the manuscript of this book were invaluable. I doubt that apart from myself anyone read that manuscript as thoroughly and frequently as Jim did. The friendship and shared political concerns I have been lucky to have with Joel Beinin, Zachary Lockman, and Ilan Pappé have been a source of solace and hope in hard times.

The period I taught at Ben-Gurion University of the Negev was not an easy one, but I left there friends—faculty, staff, and students—who contributed in ways unknown to them to the writing of this book, friends in whose debt I forever remain. I wish to acknowledge in particular Aref Abu Rabia, Ismail Abu Saad, Muhammad Abu Saad, Debbie Israel, Uri Poznanski, Haggay Ram, Amnon Raz-Krakotzkin, Haya Sasportas-Bombaji, Tal Shuval, Aliza Uzan-Swissa, and Dror Ze'evi.

The welcome extended to me by UCLA as a whole and the History Department in particular offered, for the first time in my academic career, a perfect environment for completing the writing of this book. For this I am deeply grateful to the chair, Brenda Stevenson, and to the whole department. The weekly Colloquium of European History and Culture at UCLA became my intellectual home in which I was invited to present the gist of the present book and received numerous helpful comments and suggestions. I am indebted to the regular participants of the colloquium, Patrick Geary, Lynn Hunt, Margaret Jacob, Teofilo Ruiz, David Sabean, Debora Silverman, and Geoffrey Symcox, and to the graduate students and guest speakers. Lynn Hunt and Geoffrey Symcox additionally read drafts of the manuscript and offered both kind encouragement and helpful criticism, for which I am very grateful. The colloquium also made it clear to me that there are eminent scholars in other fields who are genuinely interested in what Ottoman historians have to say.

The two readers of the University of California Press wrote encouraging reports and offered extremely helpful comments. I also thank Lynne E. Withey, Director of the Press, for her advice and wisdom, and Lynn Hunt, for her suggestion to include this book in the University of California Press series of which she is the editor, Social and Cultural History. Elisabeth Magnus, the copy editor, and Kate Warne, the production editor, substantially improved the final product.

As it is customary to state, all the above-mentioned and others are not responsible for the flaws of this book, for which I alone should be held accountable. It is less customary to acknowledge places. I cannot, however, refrain from mentioning two cities that had a substantial impact on the book and on me. Oxford taught me, among many things, to take delight in feeling—to use the title and content of Edward Said's memoir—"out of place." I cannot imagine myself wanting too much belonging. Despite the trials and tribulations of a megapolis, Istanbul remains a breathtakingly beautiful and magic city that has not lost its imperial—Byzantine and Ottoman—aura. To a considerable degree, enjoying Istanbul has become synonymous with enjoying the company of my friends there, Selim Deringil, Hakan Erdem, and Şevket Pamuk, all of Boğaziçi University, and Halil Berktay of Sabancı University. The willingness of these friends to share with me their fondness of *Asitane-i Saadet* is deeply appreciated.

In one of my visits to the city, I went to Yedikule. My colleague and guide, Professor Murat Belge, showed me the dungeon where Osman II, one of this book's protagonists, was reportedly strangled. Having been left momentarily alone in that depressing space, I first felt for that sultan. Then the Ottoman histories became as vivid in my mind as if I had actually been there. It must have been Istanbul's magic or *rakı* or both.

This book is dedicated to my parents and my son. My love for them and for my brother and sister and their families is what sustains me. I am deeply grateful to Shlomit, Avishay, and Abigail for showing me that kinship should not necessarily and exclusively be based on biology. Being with Tami Sarfatti has been the most gratifying challenge I have ever faced. The contribution of her wisdom, scholarship, and keen eye to this book is considerable. I hope she accepts it as a modest token of my unalloyed love.

Note on Transliteration

Since it is hoped that this book will be read by not only Ottoman specialists, modern Turkish orthography is preferred over orthography that would reflect Ottoman Turkish more precisely. For those not versed in Middle Eastern languages, a system of transliteration that is faithful to the Ottoman script is bound to be unfriendly, whereas modern Turkish orthography at least conveys the way words and terms sound. The Ottoman specialists will in any case know the correct spelling in the original Ottoman Turkish (or Arabic or Persian), regardless of the particular transliteration.

Words that have a known English form, like *pasha* or *janissary*, are written accordingly. The modern Turkish orthography of words that appear frequently has been compromised for the sake of convenience. Thus I have written padi*sh*ah rather then padişah, except where the Turkish text is cited together with the translation.

PRONUNCIATION OF MODERN TURKISH LETTERS

c   j, as in *journey*
ç   ch, as in *charity*
ğ   unvocalized, lengthens preceding vowel
ı   as i in *bird* or *still*
ö   German ö, as in *schön*
ş   sh, as in *short*
ü   German ü, as in *Führer*

Introduction
The Content and Form of This Study

The month of May in the year 1622 was traumatic and turbulent for the Ottomans. A young ruler, Osman II, paid the heaviest price for an alleged intention to introduce radical reforms. He was deposed and assassinated together with his grand vezir and chief black eunuch. His mad uncle, Mustafa I, who had ruled before him only to be deposed after three months, was re-enthroned and forced to abdicate after four months. Grand vezirs were appointed and dismissed with increasing frequency. In Anatolia the provincial governors and irregular troops, led by Abaza Mehmed Pasha, and the janissaries were at each other's throat.

Katip Çelebi, a foremost Ottoman intellectual of the seventeenth century, aptly inscribed the events of that month in Ottoman collective memory as the *Haile-i Osmaniye*. I chose "Ottoman Tragedy" as the book's title because it is a good title, even though I am aware that "tragedy" for the Ottoman word *haile* is a meaning that did not appear until the very end of the nineteenth century. This is thoroughly explained in the Epilogue. Further, Katip Çelebi's trope seems to have captured that moment so perceptively that I have taken the liberty to apply it to six fascinating—but neglected—years in Ottoman history: in terms of *histoire événementielle*, the reign of Osman II flanked by the two reigns of his uncle, Mustafa I (1617–23). Scholarly considerations aside, the intuitive reason for which this period is worthy of a study is that it constitutes a great story, both historically and historiographically. Despite the tremendous transformations in historical scholarship, historians—at least the present one—may still find great stories and their unfolding irresistible. The uniqueness of a detailed study of the Haile-i Osmaniye in its wider definition is that it may serve as a "historical laboratory" for some of the most significant questions and processes that preoccupy Ottoman scholarship. The events of this period were so dramatic and traumatic for the Ottomans themselves, and their historiography consequently so passionate, that they bring to the fore issues such as the alleged breakdown of the state and cleavages within the ruling elite in a forceful, almost explosive, fashion.

This book is about the interplay between the Hegelian poles that dialectically convey what history is all about: history as the experience of the past *(res gestae)* and history as the recounting and consciousness of that experience *(historia rerum gestarum)*. It is an interpretation of the interplay between a series of highly significant events and their Ottoman historiography. The proximity of these events (1617–23) to their historical representations (the course of the seventeenth century) makes it possible to interpret the interplay as one of the main stories in seventeenth-century Ottoman history, namely the power struggle over the redefinition of the state following the crisis of that century in Eurasia, the drawing of its boundaries vis-à-vis society and, consequently, the determination of who might be included in the state or excluded from it. The underlying argument of this study is that the story of the historiography of the Haile-i Osmaniye up to the point where it was sealed as the state narrative and the story of the Ottoman state in the seventeenth century are in fact inextricably intertwined.

The main subject matter of this study is the works of five Ottoman writers: Hüseyin bin Sefer, better known by his pseudonym, Tuği Çelebi (died during the reign of Murad IV, 1623–40); Hasanbeyzade (d. 1636); Ibrahim Peçevi (d. 1650); Katip Çelebi (d. 1657); and Mustafa Naima (d. 1716). Conveniently, we have the urtext (Tuği's) at one end of the historiographical story and the state narrative (Naima's) at the other.

The analysis of the history/historiography interplay in this study draws on and is informed by two theoretical spheres. One is historiography and, more generally, the hermeneutics of texts; the other might be termed the state as a conceptual and historical problem, with particular attention to its early modern, dynastic appearance. In the first sphere, approaches that undermine and subvert rigid positivist polarities (e.g., content/form, reality/representation, document/text) have been influential and inspiring. Theories and proposals that, first, emphasize historicity as a prerequisite for an adequate understanding of the state and are cognizant of its reification and, second, offer alternatives to Eurocentric models have guided the discussion on the Ottoman state in the seventeenth century.

The book consists of three parts. The first part lays the foundations in three ways. Chapter 1 exhibits the usefulness of the Haile-i Osmaniye as a "historical laboratory" by unfolding the political narrative as a tangible manifestation of the transformation of the royal household in the period 1550–1650. Chapter 2 traces the formation and history of Ottoman historiography, surveys the modern study of this historiography, and offers a sociological portrayal of the Ottoman historians in the seventeenth century. Chapter 3 puts forth a framework within which the historical texts are later interpreted, in the hope that both Ottomanists and students of historiography may find this sort of discussion engaging.

The second part is a rather thorough interpretation of the historiographical story of the Haile-i Osmaniye on the basis of the foundations laid in the first part. The discussion in this part is primarily, to borrow from Paul Ricoeur (see Chapter 3), intertextual. What I deem the ultimate meaning of this historical discourse—that is, how it refers to "the world outside"—is held in suspense until the third part. Each of the chapters (4, 5, and 6) deals with a significant juncture in the evolution of the historiographical story.

The third part brings to the fore what Ricoeur calls the referential quality of the discourse. The two chapters (7 and 8) of this part try to weave together the history of the Ottoman state and that of certain Ottoman historiography in the seventeenth century. They combine three themes: conceptualizations of the state in general and of the Ottoman state in particular; the crisis of the seventeenth century in Eurasia as the proper context for understanding the redefinition of the Ottoman state; and the extent to which the historical discourse in this period simply *is* a significant component of the conflictual process of this redefinition. What underpins the whole discussion is an attempt to take into account the reification of the state and to follow the ways in which the historiography at once reifies the state and reveals the fact of reification.

The Epilogue is a preliminary attempt to stimulate discussions and hopefully more research on the deep structures of Ottoman historiography. It is not a general theory but a suggestion of one possible way to think about the nexus between the manifestly historiographical and political and the deeply poetic and mythic in a concrete corpus of texts.

THE INTERPRETIVE STANCE OF THE STUDY

Within the context of the historical discipline, I have tried to follow the path opened up by scholars of past historiography who, though ill at ease with rigidly authoritative—the oft-used adjective *naive* is too honeyed—positivism, at the same time are wary of being stifled by the rituals of language fetishism. Three historians are especially pertinent to the mood of this book (as distinguished from the interpretive theory proposed in Chapter 3): Cemal Kafadar, who wrote masterfully on early Ottoman historiography and the early Ottoman state; Nancy Partner, whose wry sense of humor concerning postmodernism is as engaging as her work on English medieval historiography; and Gabrielle Spiegel, who combines her interest in theory and medieval French historiography in an original way and whose "Social Logic of the Text" and "Theory of the Middle Ground" are probably the most coherent articulations of the position to which I am alluding. To these should be added, even though his is a different intellectual undertaking, Dominick LaCapra.[1]

What these writers share, at least as far as their impact on this study is concerned, is that in one or another way they seek a middle ground. By *middle ground* I mean an underlying frame of mind that recognizes, is even resigned to, the fact that the postmodernist challenge writ large is too substantial to be dismissed offhandedly or ignored. At the same time, it is a frame of mind that retains the historical discipline's obstinate recalcitrance in the face of the postmodernist threat to deny it *any* access to a real, experienced past existence, lest history becomes a vocation that forsakes moral and political responsibility.

Kafadar's book is a highly successful and coherent account of the Ottoman historians, both the fifteenth-century world in which they lived and worked and the world on which they wrote. The eloquent and perceptive way in which he first deconstructs this historiography, exposing the ideologically and politically conflictual nature of its conception, and then "puts it back together" to show that it also says something about the world that is its referent (the frontier culture and the formation of the imperial state), is simultaneously inspiring and enviable.

I intend the present study to continue Kafadar's in two ways. One is the acceptance that one of the greatest benefits for historians from postmodern theory and suspicion of an easily accessible reality may be in the interpretation of their source material. Instead of tediously disputing whether reality may be at all reconstructed and whether language use is a hermetically sealed world of signs, or (worse) dismissing the postmodernist critique as another fancy French fashion that will vanish in the haze, one may choose to integrate the text and the context, the sources of the past and the world to which they refer, in a coherent interpretive scheme, in one study. Kafadar's success lies precisely in the fact that he collapses the history/historiography distinction so naturally and coherently.

The other way is more concretely Ottoman. The second half of the fifteenth century and the first half of the seventeenth century seem to be two junctures at which the histories of the state and of the historiography are so closely related that they might be indistinguishable. It is more than coincidental, I think, that two scholarly works that deal with these periods and have been written independently of each other resemble each other structurally in that they both begin by discussing the pertinent historiography and end up by discussing the state.

Some of LaCapra's pronouncements have helped to clarify and then remove two hindrances that for an Ottoman historian seem highly pertinent. One pertains to the written record of the past. What LaCapra seeks to undermine here is the untenable classification of the past's record into "documents" (which are putatively informational) and "works" (which are solely "worklike"):

> We usually refer to *The Brothers Karamazov* and *The Phenomenology of the Mind* as works, and to a tax roll, a will, and the register of an inquisition as documents. But . . . both the "document" and the "work" are texts involving an interaction between documentary and worklike components that should be examined in a critical historiography. . . . A register of an inquisition, for example, is itself a textual power structure with links to relations of power in the larger society. How it functions as a text is intimately related to its use for the reconstitution of life in the past.[2]

The other hindrance is the historian's approach—specifically the tyranny of the documentary paradigm of historical knowledge. In this paradigm, the only legitimate purpose of history is reconstruction, and, correspondingly, the only criterion for evaluating a historical source is its factual or referential quality. The consequence is a rigid hierarchy of sources, "whereby a preferential position is accorded to seemingly direct informational documents such as bureaucratic reports, wills, registers, diaries, eyewitness accounts, and so forth. If other texts are treated at all, they are reduced to elements that are either redundant or merely supplementary . . . with respect to privileged 'informational' documents."[3]

LaCapra calls for a history that is metaphorically a dialogue of the historian with the past. In this metaphorical dialogue historians bring to bear "their" present on "their" past, provided that they remain attentive to the past's voices. The existence of the dialogue is a prerequisite for interpretation to take place. LaCapra stresses that the distinction between the documentary and the dialogical should not be taken "as a purely dichotomous opposition," and he recognizes the importance of reconstruction and documentation for "any approach that claims to be historical." What he objects to is the absolute dominance of the documentary paradigm that stifles the historical imagination.[4]

All this must sound rather familiar to an Ottomanist's ear. Although it has been somewhat weakened in recent years and other options have emerged, the field of Ottoman history has been overwhelmed for a long period by, metaphorically speaking, the fetish of the *defter*, literally the register, figuratively the ultimate document. This book is by no means a call to cast aside the defter. It is rather an attempt to redress an imbalanced approach to sources of whatever kind and to look at the whole record left to us by the Ottomans less as an informant and more as an interlocutor.

Finally there is Nancy Partner's essay, strewn with wry remarks on her vocation as a medievalist. I find two features particularly attractive in her consideration of "language and its relation to anything other than itself."[5] One is that the path that leads her to think about this problem is similar to my own: interest in historical texts written in the past and their stance as literary artifacts vis-à-vis the reality to which they refer. The other feature, returning to the middle ground, is that although Partner is well aware that the relationship between words and reality is neither simple nor straightforward, she is constantly—at times intuitively—wary of being drawn into a position in which language would stifle altogether the adventure of writing history.[6]

I end this introduction with Partner's statement on what I keep calling the middle ground. It is where one wishes to be if one does not wish to play the ostrich in the face of postmodernist critique but also does not wish to forsake history, politics, and moral judgment:

> Historians . . . who think history is something (i.e., some "thing") that you "write up" from pieces of a "thing" recorded on cards and in notebooks, live a reductive intellectual life. But to concede that language speaks in its own "language" chiefly about itself must inexorably cut its connection to any past reality and freeze history to death. There is no exhilaration in that, because there is no source of energy. . . . We have to assume that the testimony of others is "evidence," partly because we have to begin everything somewhere, and this is where history begins, and partly because the consequence of doing otherwise is the loss not merely of history but of the independent reality of anything not present to the senses, which does not leave much of the world.[7]

PART I

Foundations

1. The Plot

The present chapter unfolds the story of the Haile-i Osmaniye, in its wider definition, on the basis of an amalgamation of the Ottoman histories considered in this study. It has three aims. The first is to supply the reader with a frame of reference for a series of events with a complicated plot and numerous actors and to make it possible, in the following chapters that interpret and problematize the historiography of this series of events, to refrain from frequent digressions to present this or that episode.

The second aim is to discuss and illustrate the important changes in the sultanic household and the Ottoman state in general in the period 1550–1650. As explained in the Introduction, though this work's chief focus is historiographical, the opening and closing chapters discuss the pertinent contexts of which this historiography is an integral part. The unfolding of the story in the shape of political-narrative historiography requires a few observations on the politics of the royal household and its outstanding protagonists. To attain this second goal, the discussion is in constant dialogue with A. D. Alderson's study of the Ottoman dynasty and, more intensively, with Leslie Peirce's pathbreaking work on the imperial harem (formally) and the whole dynastic household (effectively).[1]

The third aim is to begin a historical study by trying to tell a great story without spoiling it: the challenge is simply irresistible.

Since the Ottoman histories are analyzed in a very detailed manner in the following chapters, and in order not to burden the present discussion with too heavy a scientific apparatus, I have taken a certain liberty in this chapter: references to the Ottoman histories are made only in cases of citations or when one or another particular text warrants it. Otherwise, the aforementioned amalgamation is the basis of the narrative.[2]

THE FIRST ACCESSION AND DEPOSITION OF SULTAN MUSTAFA I (NOVEMBER 1617 – FEBRUARY 1618)

Among the various institutions that underwent changes in the early modern Ottoman state, the ruling dynasty and its household figure prominently. It is difficult to ascertain whether some of these changes were consciously intended, but it is certain that one of them was particularly significant: the ascendancy of the family section within the royal palace and household *(haremlik)* and its prominent personae. Most notable among them were the queen mother *(valide sultan)*, the chief black eunuch *(darüssaade ağası* or *kızlar ağası)*, and, if an anachronism is permitted, the sultan's most significant other *(haseki sultan)*. The concomitant change was the alteration of the succession mechanism from fratricide to seniority *(ekberiyet)*. Underlying all this was the gradual transformation of the empire, in both modus operandi and the self-perception of the ruling elite, from a frontier-oriented state into a sedentary one, whose focal site was an opulent imperial capital.

The first time in which seniority prevailed over fratricide, since fratricide had become "constitutional" in the second half of the fifteenth century, was the accession to the throne of Sultan Mustafa I in 1617. This is where our story begins.

Upon the death of Sultan Ahmed I in November 1617, the grandees of the empire, particularly the *sheyhülislam* (head of the *ulema* hierarchy, or hierarchy of religious officials, and chief jurisconsult) Esad Efendi, decided that since Ahmed's sons were too young, his younger brother Mustafa should become the new *padishah* (an oft-used title for the Ottoman sultan). He ascended the throne as Mustafa I on 22 November 1617. The change in the succession mechanism from fratricide to seniority brought on changes in the accession ceremony. The enthronement of Mustafa I was not only the first occasion on which seniority prevailed over fratricide but also the first time the new coronation ceremony seems to have taken place. Since the strife over the throne among princes positioned in various provinces had ceased to exist, or rather had shifted to the palace and the harem, the tense interval between the death of one sultan and the proclamation of his successor was no longer necessary. The accession ceremonies of the post-fratricide period can be classified into two phases: the first was confined to the boundaries of the Topkapı palace, whereas to perform the second the sultan sailed up the Golden Horn as far as Eyüp and could therefore be seen by his subjects.[3]

The first phase included two parts. First, as soon as a sultan died, his heir was taken out of the *kafes* (the chamber of the Ottoman princes in the harem, sometimes alluded to as a golden cage) by the chief black eunuch and brought to the *Arz Odası* (literally "Chamber of Petition," functionally the sultan's audience chamber). Either there or at the palace's third gate, *Babüssaadet* (Gate of Felicity), the new padishah received the *biat* (oath of allegiance) from the empire's highest officials, who, to affirm their loyalty, kissed the ruler's robe. This was followed by a ceremonial assembly of the Imperial Divan (privy council), in which promotions and gifts were granted, and by the implementation of measures to ensure the change of *sikke ve hutbe* (the sultan's name on coins and in the sermon after the Friday prayer respectively).

The second phase, which could take place five to fifteen days later, included, first, the *kılıç kuşanması* or *taklid-i seyf* (girding of the sword; both terms are in Ottoman, but while the former term is in Turkish, the latter is derived from Arabic). The sultan sailed to the tomb of Abu Ayyub al-Ansari at Eyüp on the Golden Horn, where he was girded with the sword of either the Prophet, Khalid ibn Walid, the Caliph Umar, or Selim I. Thence he went back in procession, visiting the tombs of his forefathers and fulfilling the customs of alms, sacrifice, and an accession-bonus *(cülus akçesi)* for the troops.

As time passed, Mustafa I's reported insanity became evident, whether by the chief black eunuch, Mustafa Ağa, divulging its manifestations or by itself. The accounts of the Ottoman historians on the behavior of the sultan convey a sense of awareness of a political public, at least in Istanbul. Thus Katip Çelebi has the chief black eunuch stressing the severity of this behavior by pointing out its public manifestation: "The state of the padishah has become widely known to the people and well-established among them. There is nothing in [Sultan] Mustafa's state that can be veiled with concealing and covering up."[4] In a similar vein Peçevi observes that from the day the sultan paid the customary visit to his ancestors' tombs "the people disapproved of his behavior and inferred his lightness of mind."[5]

After three months (February 1618), the padishah's behavior grew unbearable, and, with incitement by the chief black eunuch, it was decided to depose him. Mustafa Ağa summoned the troops and assembled the Imperial Divan under the pretext of salary distribution, thus disheartening Mustafa I's supporters. He then locked *Deli* (Mad) Sultan Mustafa in the kafes once again and brought out, through another door, the eldest among the late Sultan Ahmed's sons, Prince Osman. On 26 February, the latter became Sultan Osman II; he would be nicknamed *Genç* (Young), and not only because of his age (fourteen years).

The immediate question that anyone familiar with Ottoman history would raise would probably be: Why was Prince Mustafa not executed after his deposition? Why did he survive the reign of his brother Ahmed I (1603–17)? The complex answer to this question must address a mixture of contingent and structural factors and intentional and accidental actions. The passage to the sedentary state had several manifestations in the first half of the seventeenth century. These were the demise of the princely governorate and career, the increasing tendency of the royal family to remain within the Topkapı palace's third courtyard,[6] the end of fratricide and transition to seniority, the ascendancy of the chief black eunuch, and, especially, the ascendancy of the valide sultan.[7]

Mehmed III's reign (1595–1603) is an instructive turning point in several respects. Mehmed III was the last prince to be assigned a province and the last sultan to father children while a prince. After him, and throughout the period 1603–48 without exceptions, all the dynasty's males spent their lives within the inner part of the palace and came out only if they were enthroned. Upon his accession Mehmed III had his nineteen paternal brothers executed; the trauma of both Ottoman and foreign dignitaries, who attended at the Aya Sofya the funeral of Murad III (1574–95) and a day later that of his nineteen sons, had a significant impact on the changes discussed here. Also, a major incident at the end of Mehmed III's reign suggests the extent to which the exhibition of princely military prowess had ceased being desirable. Prince Mahmud, Ahmed I's older brother, used to urge his father to send him at the head of an army to deal with the Anatolian rebels and the incessant Safavid menace. He was executed shortly before Mehmed III's own death and joined the category of those who were "much loved by the janissaries," an Ottoman way of posthumously describing ambitious princes who did not make it.[8]

The explicit and formal explanations for Mustafa I's survival that are put forth by the Ottoman historians leave the impression that they themselves knew more, an impression shared by Peirce. These explanations are that when Ahmed I ascended the throne Mustafa was only eight years old and insane and was therefore not in a position to endanger his brother's sultanate; that when Ahmed I died, enthroning Mustafa stemmed from the wisdom of avoiding child sultans; and that Mustafa survived Osman II's reign thanks to the difficulty of distinguishing madness and sainthood. All this looks suspiciously unconvincing because, first and foremost, the Ottoman historians present what in effect marked the transformation from fratricide to seniority, and everything this entailed, as a routine state of affairs, as if a sultan being succeeded by his brother because his sons were too young was a familiar event in the Ottoman polity. The explanations are further suspect because in 1617 Prince Osman, the obvious candidate, was thirteen years old, the age when his father (Ahmed I) had ascended the throne in 1603; because the age of princes, according to the system of fratricide, had not hitherto prevented their execution (the small size of many a casket laid at the foot of Murad III's tomb in 1595 accounts for the magnitude of the trauma caused by that particular instance of fratricide); and because although Mustafa's insanity was known in 1617, it did not prevent his accession.[9]

Much will be said in the following chapters about what the Ottoman historians *did* have to say on this issue in ways other than explicit, but at this stage several complementary explanations may be offered for Mustafa I's survival and enthronement. It would seem reasonable to suggest, first, that Mustafa was spared in 1603 as a result of the trauma of 1595 and because he was the only surviving male of the dynasty apart from the new sultan himself. At that stage, the latter's ability to father sons had not yet been proven. In retrospect this anxiety bespeaks sound judgment, for in the first half of the seventeenth century there were few surviving males from among whom the next sultan could be selected. The fact that Ahmed I was not easily resigned to the presence of his brother and the occurrence of four cases of fratricide during that period (perpetrated by Osman II and Murad IV) indicate that the transition from fratricide to seniority was not the result of a constitutional decision, like Mehmed II's *ferman* (edict) that had sanctioned fratricide, but rather the result of what is most appropriately articulated in Arabic as *zuruf* (circumstances) and, correspondingly, ad hoc decisions. At the same time, however, the rather matter-of-fact way that the Ottoman historians comment on Mustafa I's survival and accession might also be interpreted as an indication that seniority was gaining prevalence. The apparent tension is typical of the manner and time span in which complex institutions such as the royal household are transformed. What we have is half a century of transition, at the heart of which the Haile-i Osmaniye is located, through which forces of change and continuity run concurrently; toward the second half of the seventeenth century, however, seniority was clearly seen to prevail.

Another possible explanation for the survival and enthronement of Mustafa is the ascendancy of the valide sultan both in itself and at the expense of the haseki sultan. Peirce convincingly entitles Süleyman's reign (1520–66) the age of the haseki and the period from Süleyman's death to the emergence of the Köprülü grand vezirs (1566–1656) that of the valide.[10] These insightful observations, taken a step further, suggest that the haseki institution was less in congruity with the dynasty's history than the overwhelming dominance of the valide. Also, we seem to have in the period 1520–1656 a historical process in which personalities carry a substantial explanatory force. These are *Kanuni* Sultan Süleyman and his consort and then wife, Hurrem Sultan, at the beginning of the process and Kösem Sultan, haseki of Ahmed I and valide of Murad IV and Ibrahim I, at a crucial juncture. Rather than being the zenith of Ottoman civilization, as the traditional Orientalist narrative of a subsequent decline has framed it, Süleyman's reign seems to have been, in certain respects, strewn with "irregularities," among which the royal household seems to have figured prominently: for example, the unprecedented and never again repeated status of his beloved daughter Mihrimah. I think that the explanation of the rise of the haseki institution and its demise owes much to the particular personalities of Süleyman and Hurrem and to their relationship as the royal couple. At the risk of being simplistic, I would venture that the haseki institution and Hurrem's personality and the influence she wielded on Süleyman were inseparable. In a similar vein, though in a way more typical of the ruling house's history, the explanation for the decline of the haseki and the re-emergence of the valide in the first decades of the seventeenth century has much to do with Kösem's personality and the fact that in 1617 she had ceased being a haseki and, if she were to regain power, could obtain it only from the position of valide sultan.

The woman who might have played a crucial role in Mustafa I's survival was not his mother but his brother's (Ahmed I's) consort, Kösem Sultan. She must have realized the personal gain that might stem from the transition to seniority, coupled with the fact that she was no longer haseki but had sons "in waiting." And indeed, according to the Venetian ambassador, Kösem "lobbied to spare Mustafa the fate of fratricide with the ulterior goal of saving her own sons from the same fate."[11] Mustafa's own valide, an Abkhasian consort of Mehmed III's whose name is unknown, turned out to be, though not at all insignificant, no Kösem. From the revealing use Peirce makes of the privy purse registers to establish the harem's institutional and personal hierarchies, it is evident that she was not one of the outstanding harem personalities of the period, like Nurbanu and Safiye earlier and Turhan later. However, while Mustafa's mother may not have been as instrumental as Kösem in saving her son from fratricide, his mental state allowed her to assume center stage as regent, especially during his second, longer reign. From her location in the Old Palace she was a key figure in the deposition and assassination of Osman II and showed that she was no stranger to the art of *damad* (son-in-law) politics.

As far as the harem women are concerned, what completes the picture is the marginality of Osman II's mother, Mahfiruz. Her gravest problem must have stemmed from the simple but unfortunate fact that she happened to be a consort of Ahmed I's when Kösem was his haseki. Again the Venetian ambassador reports that in 1612 "the sultan had a beating administered to a woman who had irritated Kösem," and Peirce surmises that the woman was probably Mahfiruz. The wretched Mahfiruz was later expelled from the Topkapı to the Old Palace, was most unusually not allowed to return when her son became sultan in 1618, and, when she died in 1620, was buried in Eyüp rather than next to Ahmed I. This marginality, which effectively meant that Prince Osman had no maternal backing at the crucial juncture of November 1617, goes a long toward explaining why seniority prevailed over fratricide at that point and Kösem had her way, and why Osman II was unable to execute his uncle during his reign.[12] The hierarchy within the Ahmed I/Kösem household is retrospectively reiterated in the arrangement of their modest mausoleum, which is adjacent to the Sultan Ahmed, or Blue, Mosque.

In addition to the valide sultan, the other pivotal harem figure who had a hand in shaping the course of events was a very powerful chief black eunuch, Mustafa Ağa. Though it is agreed that he was a powerful person under Ahmed I and was one of Mustafa I's kingmakers, whether he acted as a villain or loyal servant in the latter's first deposition is a serious bone of contention among seventeenth-century Ottoman historians (see Chapter 4). Whatever the judgment passed on him, Mustafa Ağa's involvement highlights another facet of the changes in the royal household at that period: the dramatic ascendancy of the black eunuchs in general and the chief black eunuch in particular, frequently in conjunction and alliance with the valide sultan.

This ascendancy should be understood within the underlying framework of the transformation of the state and the royal household described above. The Ottomans were not the first to recruit and employ eunuchs— black or white—in their households: they were preceded by numerous Mediterranean states all the way back to antiquity. The black eunuchs rose to prominence and relegated the white ones to an inferior position within the household's hierarchy toward the end of the sixteenth century and increasingly in the opening decades of the seventeenth century. By the latter period the black eunuchs took over the harem, and the *kızlar ağası*, or *darüssaade ağası*, was the chief eunuch of the harem. Having a special affinity with Egypt from the moment of their recruitment, the chief black eunuchs' typical career had two phases: first was a term in the harem, followed by banishment to Egypt, where they were prominent actors in the history of the Ottoman Egyptian elite in the seventeenth and eighteenth centuries. Banishment should not be taken in too literal a sense; it was rather a lucrative pension scheme.[13] Despite Sir Humphrey's teasing retort to the Prime Minister's frustrations (in the magnificent BBC satire *Yes Prime Minister*) that "influence without power is a prerogative of the eunuch," the holder of this position in the seventeenth century was one of the most influential *and* powerful individuals in the Ottoman Empire.

Mustafa Ağa was a powerful man under Ahmed I, instrumental in the accession of Mustafa I, and, despite the controversy among Ottoman historians, the key figure in the Mustafa's deposition after three months and Osman II's enthronement. Hasanbeyzade, a most vehement critic of not only Mustafa Ağa but, it would seem, the chief black eunuchship in general, writes that the ulema, headed by the sheyhülislam, appealed to the valide sultan and advised her to banish the chief black eunuch. But, continues Hasanbeyzade, "she was deceived by his sweet tongue and tearful eye."[14] Mustafa Ağa's move from the first stage of his career (the Topkapı) to the second (comfortable retirement in Egypt effectively, banishment officially) occurred in 1619. The Ottoman histories report that at that time the grand vezir, Istanköylü Ali Pasha, attained such proximity to Sultan Osman that he was able to cause the banishment of the chief black eunuch to Egypt.

THE ACCESSION, DEPOSITION, AND ASSASSINATION OF OSMAN II (FEBRUARY 1618 – MAY 1622)

The four-year reign of Genç (Young) Sultan Osman seems congruent with the rest of the period in which it is located, in that it too combines a particular personality with certain historical processes. Sultan Osman attracted the disapproval of the Ottoman historians, with the exception of Peçevi. As this is one of the major themes in the rest of this study, suffice it at this stage briefly to glance at Naima's verdict: "Besides having ascended the throne in the first bloom of his youth, and not having been successful in attaining an experienced, intelligent, and faithful companion, [Osman II] also met only fools who humored his whims." And there is more. Owing to the evil ways of the aforementioned Istanköylü Ali Pasha (grand vezir 1619–21), "The world-adorning padishah was puffed up, and entirely abandoned the path of good harmony and diplomacy that are necessary for the conduct of the kingdom." If this were not enough, his ignorance in politics was exacerbated by "kingly vanity" (*nahvet-i mulukane*).[15]

Sultan Osman was a nonconformist to an extent that, judging by his fate and the way he was treated and seen by contemporaries and by later generations, his society and polity could not tolerate. This nonconformism was articulated in a mode of representing sultanic sovereignty he attempted to carve for himself, one that ran against the grain of Ottoman protocol and the self-image of the Ottoman state. To put it more simply, Osman II tried to revive the image of the *gazi*- or warrior-sultan—the ruler of a frontier-oriented state who not only conducted raids across the Islamic border but more generally left the palace frequently and exposed himself to personal contact with his subjects. Concomitantly, he tried to rid himself of the by-then prevalent image of the sedentary sultan who resides in his sumptuous imperial capital, spends most of his life within the third courtyard of the palace, and to his subjects is more a persona than a person.[16]

In his recent study on Ottoman warfare, Rhoads Murphey plays down—even rejects as simplistic—two distinctions: between sultans who personally led war campaigns (up to and including Mehmed III) and those who did not; and between "sultanically-led" and vezirial campaigns.[17] Murphey's argument might weaken my contention that Sultan Osman's attempt to revive the gazi-sultan image became obsolete and was therefore rejected by the Ottoman polity. But Murphey is more concerned with the excessive attributed influence of the presence or absence of the sultan on the motivation and performance of the troops than with the issue of the present discussion.

The magnitude of Sultan Osman's attempt to invoke an obsolete image of sovereignty and correspondingly the depth of his failure were substantial. Although as Peirce convincingly shows, the actual, multidimensional transition occurred in the period 1550–1650, the dissociation from the gazi-sultan as a mode of sovereignty had begun earlier. Cemal Kafadar, who masterfully captures the tension between the ethos of the frontier (*uc*) and the sultan as gazi on the one hand, and the enterprise of building a sedentary, dynastic state on the other, highlights a quintessential incident:

> The most succinct expression of that transformation may be Mehmed the Conqueror's decision not to stand up at the sound of martial music, as he well knew his ancestors used to do. He was thus abandoning one of the hallowed traditions of earlier Ottomans as frontier warriors, who would show their respect for the call of gaza [raiding at the frontier of Islam] through this practice. This was not an abandonment of the devo-

tion to the principle of gaza, since martial music as a reminder of the
Ottoman duty to struggle for the faith would still be regularly played
at the gates of the palace; it was rather the expression of a fundamental
change in the relationship of the House of Osman and of the Ottoman
state to that principle and its representatives. Being a gazi was not the
primary component of the Ottoman ruler's multiple identity anymore;
he was first and foremost a sultan, a khan, and a caesar, "the ruler of
two seas and two continents," as Mehmed the Conqueror called himself
on the inscription at the gate of his new palace in his new capital.[18]

The basic and exceptional weakness from which Osman II suffered was
the conspicuous absence of a female power basis in the harem. Mahfiruz's
unusual marginality has already been mentioned: from 1620 until Osman
II's untimely death, a governess (*daye hatun*, lit. wet-nurse) was appointed
as a stand-in valide, and she could not counterbalance the contriving of
Mustafa I's mother in the Old Palace. Osman II did not have a haseki, only
a politically insignificant consort called Ayşe. The one relation he did have,
potentially a very promising one, Genç Osman was unable to cultivate,
and if he did, it did not yield consequential results. It seems that from the
time of Mahfiruz's expulsion from the Topkapı (probably in the mid 1610s),
Kösem Sultan and little Osman grew fond of each other. She used to let
him join her for carriage rides where he showed himself to the crowd, until this came to Ahmed I's attention and he forbade any conversation between them. When Osman ascended the throne, he manifested his special
fondness for Kösem by paying her a three-day visit at the Old Palace in
1619. The bottom line of all this is that Genç Osman was a teenager who
ruled without a valide; and although he did have a loyal chief black eunuch
at his side, this could not compensate for the absence of what in the politics
of that period was a winning combination, valide/chief black eunuch, especially in the case of a young and very ambitious ruler.[19]

Concerning the political aspect of his relations with women, while the
structural weakness from which Osman II suffered was for the most part
independent of his own actions, his marriage was not. It severely tested a
fundamental given of the Ottoman state and ruling dynasty that had prevailed from the fifteenth century on: the supremacy of people of extrinsic
origins—mostly but not exclusively slaves—in the management and reproduction of the *Osmanlı* household. This marriage is an outstanding
instance of Genç Osman's nonconformism. In 1622, just a few months before his death, he married Akile, daughter of the sheyhülislam Esad Efendi,
member of one of the most venerated ulema lineages in Ottoman history

(Hoca Sadüddin Efendi's). From the time when the Osmanlıs endeavored to transform themselves from an outstanding family of gazis, whose status vis-à-vis other prominent gazi families was that of primus inter pares, into a ruling dynasty from which sovereignty emanated, one of the most fundamental notions that guided this ruling house was the prerequisite of avoiding consequential ties with the free aristocracy within the society. The sight of Akile, a free-born Muslim of exceptional pedigree, passing through the Babüssaadet and into the harem must have seemed an inconceivable nightmare to an Ottoman. Little wonder that Osman II's marriage not only alienated Akile's father, Esad Efendi, but also gave rise to popular protest and opposition.[20]

What was the reason for this politically harmful marriage, which, to make things worse, took place after the unsuccessful Polish campaign and while Osman II was trying to carry out a most controversial venture (see below)? One possible reply might be related to the gazi image. Though the marriage certainly was unpopular, the union of a sultan named Osman and a woman of an exalted ulema lineage evoked an inevitable memory for Ottomans. Some three centuries earlier, the eponymous founder of the Ottoman dynasty, Osman Gazi, had reportedly married the daughter of a foremost Sufi *sheyh* (head of a religious order), Ede Bali.[21] This alleged marriage embodied what Kafadar aptly calls the gazi-dervish milieu as an energetic social alliance that carried the Ottoman venture through its frontier phase.[22] Kafadar observes that "this rancher-dervish [Ede Bali] may have been a fictive character, but the fictionalizing chroniclers of the early Ottoman gaza exploits had so much respect for the character that they made him the father-in-law of Osman Gazi."[23]

In addition to marrying Akile, three things Sultan Osman did might be interpreted as especially meaningful in conveying an image of a gazi-sultan; all three seem to have been unfavorably received by the Ottoman polity and Ottoman historians. One was that he led the army in the 1621 Polish campaign, which not only was unsuccessful but caused a further deterioration of the relations between the sultan and the *kapı kulları* (the sultan's servants, *kul* in the shorter version; in the context of the present study, the term refers to the backbone of the standing army: the janissary corps and the six regiments [*altı bölük*] of the imperial cavalry). Another was the sultan's initiative, in company with the *bostancı başı* (head of the palace's gardeners and at the same time an officer of the sultan's "praetorian guard"), to raid incognito the taverns and coffeehouses in Istanbul and severely punish the kul he had seized there. The third was his austere appearance, in plain clothing and on a horse whose trappings were unadorned. Naima captures the mood of his earlier colleagues when he notes that Sultan Osman's public appearance was "like that of a vagabond;" he also observes that for this reason the Istanbul folk rejoiced at Sultan Mustafa's outfit in his second accession ceremony.[24] The extent to which the mode of the sedentary sultan, that silent, remote, and withdrawn persona, had been absorbed in this age of transition is illustrated not only by the Ottoman historians but significantly also by a keen foreign observer, Sir Thomas Roe. He observed that the collapse of Osman's reign and his personal tragic end stemmed from the fact that he lacked majesty.[25]

If the marriage to Akile and the attempt to construct a gazi mode of sovereignty ran counter to lengthy processes of transition, the third thing Sultan Osman did—though related to the gazi image—threatened a very recent change: he resorted to fratricide and would have proceeded more thoroughly with it if he had been allowed to do so. Before leaving the capital for the Polish campaign in 1621, Osman ordered the execution of his brother Prince Mehmed; the special relations between Kösem and Osman alluded to above may account for the fact that other princes were spared. The Ottoman historians, from Tuği to Naima, are so deeply shocked by this event that one might be misled to assume that fratricide was unheard of in Ottoman history. Following Tuği, they all cite Prince Mehmed's *dua* (personal prayer) prior to his execution and see in Osman's fate a sign that God accepted the prayer. Tuği further identifies it as the reason for which, as we shall see below, Genç Osman was publicly humiliated after his deposition: "'Osman, I ask of God that your reign come to an end. However much I may not partake in life, may you not have a share in a long life too.' [Narrator's voice:] The personal prayer of the innocent prince was accepted, and within a short while Sultan Osman was also killed."[26]

This point warrants two brief comments. First, whereas Naima's astonishment may be explained by his perspective—that is, at the end of the seventeenth century it is plausible that fratricide seemed an outdated and unnecessary cruelty—Tuği's reaction is more puzzling. He was a contemporary and, as will be amply demonstrated in the following chapters, had a substantial axe to grind. That granted, a partisan bias alone does not satisfactorily account for this taken-for-granted disapproval of fratricide, for even a partisan view cloaked in moral garb must have some grounding in its context for the text to make sense. It might be that seniority, once introduced, promptly became accepted as customary. Second, there appears to be a correlation between fratricide and the image of gazi-sultans. It seems more than mere coincidence that all four cases of fratricide in the first half of the seventeenth century were perpetrated by sultans with gazi aspirations, Osman II and Murad IV, and that these cases occurred in conjunction with war campaigns that the two led: Osman II executed Prince Mehmed just before the 1621 Polish campaign; Murad IV used his successful campaign against the Safavids in 1635 to kill two of his brothers and the recapture of Baghdad in 1638 to get rid of the third.[27]

Significant as the above cluster of actions is in the interpretation of Genç Osman as a nonconformist and by and large unpopular ruler, it is dwarfed by the magnitude of the venture he and his confidants had conceived and were about to implement in 1621–22. In terms of *histoire événementielle*, it was this venture that eliminated the padishah and his regime. If the content and scope of this venture were really consonant with their historical representations, then its successful realization would have surely meant a drastic alteration of the course of Ottoman history.

This is a convenient point to resume the unfolding of the story of the Haile-i Osmaniye. Sultan Mustafa had been deposed and Genç Osman had been the padishah for three years. Having had his brother, Prince Mehmed, executed, the sultan was now ready and willing to lead the Victorious Army into Poland. Osman II and his advisers were perhaps trying to take advantage of Europe's politics and reinvigorate Ottoman expansion there. Skirmishes notwithstanding, strategically the European front had been dormant since 1606. It should be pointed out that the year in which Sultan Osman ascended the throne (1618) was also the year in which what came to be known as the Thirty Years' War erupted (1618). Through Bethlen Gabor, the prince of Transylvania and an Ottoman vassal, a sizable delegation of the Protestant Union arrived in Istanbul. It sought Ottoman support against the Catholic League.

The Polish campaign turned out to be a sorry affair in more ways than one. Despite a prolonged siege and six consecutive onslaughts, "the infidels" (a force that comprised Poles and Cossacks) did not surrender and the fortress of Hotin (in today's Ukraine) was not taken. The performance of the Ottoman troops is reported to have been questionable. The soldiers, or rather their spokesmen, ascribed it to the sultan's attitude toward them. In the opinion of Sultan Osman and his advisers, this was yet another illustration of the incompetence of his present kul. Tuği, whose text *is* the kul's voice, labors to justify their performance. He reports that at what seemed an arbitrary point on the way north the padishah decided that those who had reached a certain bridge he had ordered to erect would be paid while the rest would be denied similar payment. Later, those who had been denied payment said: "Let the kul who received *bahşiş* [bonus] do battle with the enemy." If that were not enough, Tuği continues,

> The bonus of the padishah to those who sacrifice their lives for him and bring heads of the foes of Religion and State being not more than the allowance a master gives his slave, they [the kul] turned war and combat into an infants' game. They were unable to conquer the camp of the dustlike infidels and came to conclude peace.[28]

Peçevi offers a different perspective. Like the other historians, he identifies the Hotin campaign as an occasion that worsened the already edgy relations between the sultan and the kul. But what Tuği presents as an arbitrary decision on payments, Peçevi exposes as an attempt by Sultan Osman to make the janissaries undergo a *yoklama* (administrative inspection) under the pretext of granting donative. This, Peçevi observes, annoyed them. It should be clarified that the yoklama in this context was an administrative device whose application might be a political risk, for in it the payrolls were checked against names to make sure that only active and serving soldiers, and veterans entitled to pensions, were paid rather than members of the janissaries' civilian networks. That the yoklama did not rank among the janissaries' best preferred leisure activities is not surprising. Peçevi adds another incident that contributed to these acrimonious relations. During the siege of Hotin, Karakaş Pasha, apparently a charismatic and bold commander, was "martyred;" this prompted the sultan's reproach of the *sipahis* (imperial cavalry), who were already in low spirits, and they were deeply distressed.[29]

Throughout the latter part of 1621 and early 1622 the mutual mistrust and animosity between the padishah and his kul were intensifying. As noted, Sultan Osman endeavored to impose discipline upon the troops, not infrequently supervising this incognito. From the point of view of the kul, the sultan was constantly tormenting them for no apparent reason apart from his aversion to them, instigated by his confidants; the chief black eunuch, Süleyman Ağa, was foremost among them and most vituperatively reviled and hated by the kul. In anticipation of an important theme in this study, namely the political and discursive conflict between the imperial standing army and the increasingly regular irregular troops in Anatolia and other regions, it might be interesting to quote Tuği. The Dresden manuscript of Tuği's text in particular details the alleged agitation of the chief black eunuch against the kul. He was relentless in his attempts to convince the sultan to conscript Turcoman horsemen and *sekban* (irregular Anatolians) instead of the existing body of kul. Süleyman Ağa repeatedly said to the sultan:

> The skills of the janissary corps in using the musket and of the imperial sipahis in horsemanship in days of battle are well known. These kul have come out of the kul institution [i.e., they are properly trained]. Had they been [proper] kul [however], they would have been [i.e., performed] like the Egyptian and Syrian horsemen, and like the Anatolian sekban in using the musket. Last year, at the Hotin campaign, they were unable to defeat a small infidel force. Incompetent and useless, is this lot of salary-drawers [really] kul?[30]

The rift between Osman II and the kul should be contextualized before the story unfolds further. As Murphey observes, "The relationship between the sovereign and his kul was never as simple and predefined as that between master and slave."[31] By the seventeenth century this relationship already had an established pattern and reciprocity that could not be easily violated. As this event amply demonstrates, the kul felt that they had the right—and power—to determine whether the ruler was adhering to the established pattern or straying from it. Instances of parsimoniousness and an arbitrary attitude as a major cause for the kul's resentment abound. The importance of performing certain rituals that demonstrated imperial largesse as well as acknowledgment of the kul's commitment and effort were central to keeping the relationship harmonious. Loyalty to a particular sultan, let alone to a commander in chief who was not the sultan, was both personal and contingent; remarkably, this was never construed—by the kul or the ruling house—as compromised dynastic loyalty.[32] Tuği's pro-kul predilection notwithstanding, this discursive and material context explains why the kul's contention in his text, that the behavior of Sultan Osman had justified their lackluster performance, not only was not considered a priori preposterous but could actually make sense.

All this resulted, sometime before May 1622, in a plan the padishah had conceived with Süleyman Ağa. This plan, due to its potential magnitude and boldness, was tantamount to a political earthquake: the present body of kul—lest we forget, the janissary and imperial sipahi corps—would be done away with, a new one would be recruited in Anatolia, Syria, and Egypt, and the throne would be transferred from Istanbul to either Bursa, Damascus, or Cairo. Sultan Osman himself would lead the way and "cross over to Anatolia with the pretext of performing the hajj." Illustrative of Ottoman politics, perhaps politics in general, was the way in which the plan gained another significant supporter, the sultan's *hoca* (royal tutor) Ömer Efendi. He had obtained the Mecca kadiship for his brother a year earlier but was refused by the Şerif of Mecca (a descendant of the Prophet and a particularly powerful person there), who nearly managed to kill this brother. Ömer Efendi was furious and joined forces with the chief black eunuch in the hope that the latter's plan would enable him to take vengeance on the Şerif and secure the office for his brother.

The seriousness of Osman II's intentions is evinced by the series of orders (emirler) he dispatched to some Anatolian ümera (provincial governors) whom he had deemed faithful. These orders, it is reported, contained instructions that would facilitate a successful realization of the plan. However, by setting the preparation in motion Sultan Osman divulged his intentions. There commenced a concerted effort, headed by the sheyhülislam Esad Efendi and the grand vezir Dilaver Pasha, to make the padishah abandon his venture. At one point, sometime in late April, it seemed to yield results when Osman indicated that he might withdraw. Then, however, one night in early May, the sultan had a dream. In it he was sitting on his throne reading the Kuran. Then the Prophet appeared, snatched the Noble Pages away from the sultan's hands, stripped him of his gown, and gave him a hard slap. The padishah fell from his throne, only to realize that his efforts to prostrate himself at the Prophet's feet were to no avail, at which point he woke up. Sultan Osman first ordered an interpretation from Ömer Efendi. He told the padishah that the dream's meaning had been to reproach him for having resolved to perform the hajj and then neglecting it. Therefore, and especially since he was already a gazi, the padishah must go to Mecca and become a *haji* too. This interpretation did not satisfy Sultan Osman, and he requested another opinion from the eminent *Sufi* sheyh Üsküdari Mahmud Efendi. Among his followers was Esad Efendi, and Mahmud Efendi acted as Genç Osman's proxy in his marriage to Akile.[33] According to Tuği, Üsküdari Mahmud Efendi wrote in response to the sultan's request: "The Kuran represents the authority of the Noble *Şeriat* [Islamic Law], and the gown represents the world of substance. The padishah ought to obtain divine companionship through repentance."[34] It might be possible to understand this interpretation as implying that the dream conveyed the message that Sultan Osman was divinely rejected as both a political leader (the gown) and the imam of the community (the Kuran).

Whatever the meaning of the dream and whatever the sultan made of it and of its interpretations, following this experience he became firmly resolved on proceeding with the plan that he had resolved on earlier. Even a *fetva* (legal opinion) in which the sheyhülislam forbade him to go on the hajj went unheeded. The Haile-i Osmaniye in its narrower definition (18–

20 May 1622) began on Wednesday, 18 May 1622, when the padishah ordered the transfer of his belongings and pavilion to Üsküdar on the Asian side of the capital. The timing too might be related to Osman II's awareness of the gazi-sultan image: early to mid-May was traditionally the beginning of the campaign season.[35]

Another pause is necessary before reaching the plot's dramatic climax. Murphey's study makes it possible roughly to estimate the size of the "political public" involved in the Haile-i Osmaniye. It seems plausible that in the 1620s, excluding times of actual campaigns, there were about thirty thousand janissaries in the Istanbul barracks (i.e., excluding those on garrison assignments in the provinces). With less plausibility, it might be assumed that the number of imperial sipahis in the capital was around twenty thousand.[36]

Sultan Osman's grand venture was consequential for all of them. How many of them actually took part in the increasingly violent activities of the kul throughout Istanbul is more difficult to assess. My impression is that the tumultuous and violent three days in mid-May Istanbul we are about to present witnessed the participation of at least thousands of kul, perhaps even more. Numbers could also vary according to particular activities: a gathering at the Hippodrome might be very large, whereas the submission of a petition to the sultan via the ulema was done by an elected delegation. Comments by the Ottoman historians that shops in the markets were closed and that the city halted its daily life suggest that the civilian people of Istanbul stayed away from the confrontational drama at least until the result was clear.

The restlessness of the sipahis and janissaries erupted. They assembled at the Süleymaniye mosque and, increasingly agitated, marched from there to the *At Meydanı* (Hippodrome) and to the janissaries' barracks *(Yeni Odalar)*. At the latter site they drew up a petition, demanding that the padishah relinquish "crossing over to Anatolia," and punish those who in the kul's view had led him astray. The latter demand was sanctioned by yet another fetva, a copy of which the kul obtained. The city came to a halt. Meanwhile the ulema were summoned to the sultan and submitted the petition of the kul. Osman gave his consent to abandoning the passage to Anatolia but would not hear of punishing, even removing, his hoca and the chief black eunuch. In the evening the kul had another heated gathering in which they decided to reassemble in the morning, only this time fully armed.

Sometime in the middle of the second day (Thursday, 19 May 1622), the kul realized that the ulema had failed successfully to convey their petition. They exploded. Initially with great hesitation but with gradually growing rage and momentum, the kul marched to the Topkapı. Pausing in front of each of the three gates, and for longer pauses as the gates were becoming less publicly accessible, they finally faced the imperial harem *(Harem-i Has* or *Harem-i Hümayun)*. The pause there was even more hesitant and further prolonged; some rank and file rushed to the imperial kitchens *(matbah-i amire)* to equip themselves with more weapons, just in case. Finally, after brief encounters with some pages and eunuchs, the kul found themselves, bewildered, within the harem. They began to echo a voice that called, "We want Sultan Mustafa." Eventually the kul located Sultan Mustafa's kafes, pierced their way through and pulled him out. At this point, Tuği, at least in some of the extant manuscripts, seems unable to restrain his emotions and inserts a narrator's call to the audience: "In truth, being fair, wouldn't you say 'well done' to the heroes who on that day hacked through the roof of such a big dome [that of the kafes], tied themselves with ropes, and descended toward Sultan Mustafa?"[37]

Sultan Osman, who was within the palace, began to feel the heat and surrendered the grand vezir and the chief black eunuch to the kul; they immediately tore both men limb from limb. The ulema tried, in vain, to talk the kul out of re-enthroning Sultan Mustafa, guaranteeing on Sultan Osman's behalf that any further demand would be accepted. But the kul were determined: with drawn daggers they forced the ulema to render the biat to Sultan Mustafa, declared him the new padishah, and by implication deposed Sultan Osman. They transferred Mustafa I to the Old Palace, but as a rumor spread that Sultan Osman might prepare an attack, they collected the valide sultan and her retinue from the Old Palace and decided to guard the whole group in the janissaries' mosque, Orta Cami.

In the evening of the second day (19 May), Sultan Osman sought advice from his newly reappointed grand vezir, Ohrili Hüseyin Pasha. It was decided that the sultan would take refuge at the official residence of the janissary chief *(Ağa Kapısı)*, and through the janissary chief Ali Ağa would attempt to regain the support of the kul by bribing them. Early in the next morning (Friday, 20 May) Ali Ağa tried to execute this stratagem, but he was tricked by the kul and slain. Ohrili Hüseyin Pasha was killed too. Genç Osman was now doomed. He was seized and detained at Orta Cami, where Sultan Mustafa had been guarded.

On the way to Orta Cami unprecedented public humiliation was inflicted upon Sultan Osman. The description of his *via dolorosa* conveys a sense of politics in the public sphere in Istanbul. He was brought out and, mounted "on a workhorse," was led to Orta Cami. His head was uncovered, he looked "wretched with disordered locks of hair," and "tears dropped from the eyes of that sinless deceased." A sipahi called Pazanoğlu felt sorry for him "and put his own turban on the padishah's head."[38]

Things got worse for Genç Osman. The historians stress the extent of public exposure, and along the streets he was constantly abused. "Had the nonsense and filthy abuse uttered on the road been told here, it would have brought grief to men," Tuği remarks. He continues nonetheless:

> Only this much can be told [from what was uttered]: "Is this the precious Osman Çelebi who raided the coffee shops and put the sipahis and janissaries on galleys?" When one vile, disrespectfully nasty [person] named Altuncuoğlu pinched the foot of the blessed padishah and uttered some nonsense, the oppressed deceased wept: "O [you] bad-mannered, am I not your padishah? Are you not through with youth?"[39]

Sultan Osman had wanted to replace the kul and recruit Anatolian sekban (irregulars to whom much attention is paid in Chapter 8), whether or not he was following the advice of the chief black eunuch. This was definitely one of the most controversial and significant features of his plan, and it was now sarcastically thrown in his face:

> Others further said: "Was it with sekban that your forefathers conquered provinces? Owing to the disobedience of the sekban brigandage in the Anatolian provinces, territories were lost. Kalenderoğlu, Canbulad [famous rebels who were *celali*—bandits in Anatolia and northern Syria; see Chapter 8] and the like thugs, who shared with your father Sultan Ahmed his *hutbe ve sikke* [sermon and coinage—the Islamic symbols of sovereignty], brought desolation to the world with hordes of sekban."[40]

Peirce is absolutely correct in highlighting this episode to illustrate her point that part of the political transition described in this chapter was that the loyalty of the subjects came to be given to the dynasty, whose sovereignty was never challenged, rather than to specific sultans, who could be treated as Osman II had been.[41]

Genç Osman's emotional expressions of regret and appeals for forgiveness went unheeded. He was placed in a corner within Orta Cami, heavily guarded. The valide sultan (Mustafa's) was about to deliver the final stroke. The ringleaders of the coup held a consultation in Orta Cami about whom to appoint as the next grand vezir. The historian who should be followed on this fascinating scene is Peçevi, of whose writing much will be said in the following chapters. He claims to have had an informant, mediated through yet another informant, *within* Orta Cami: Karamizak, a janissary officer. From his description of that moment it seems that the janissary leaders sensed the valide's wish that her damad, Kara Davud Pasha, be appointed; the janissary officers consented. Parts of Peçevi's allegedly verbatim reproduction of Karamizak's account are worthwhile following, for they illustrate the modus operandi of the valide sultan and render tangible the drama of the Haile-i Osmaniye:

> As soon as the late Sultan Osman entered the mosque [Orta Cami], there remained no doubt in [the mind of] Sultan Mustafa's mother in the sultanate of her son. . . . The valide sultan began to consult us [a group of seven or eight janissary officers] as to who should become the grand vezir. We surmised that she was inclined to her son-in-law Davud Pasha. [So] we also said, "This is reasonable." She asked whether there was anyone among us who could write [i.e., whether there was a scribe]. The officers pointed at this humble one [Karamizak, Peçevi's indirect informant]. They instantly produced a scribe's pencase. First of all I wrote an imperial decree for the grand vezirate. Then according to procedure eighteen positions were granted with our decree. I even wrote the imperial decree for my own position of *başçavuş* [a senior officer in the janissary corps].[42]

Appointing Kara Davud Pasha to the grand vezirate was tantamount to signing Genç Osman's death warrant. Here all the historians stress the bad blood between the two and the extent to which Sultan Osman had undermined Davud Pasha's career. Although it is nowhere explicitly said that this was the valide sultan's intention in bringing about Davud Pasha's appointment, it seems plausible. Sultan Osman must have been aware of what the appointment meant and more generally of how grave his predicament had become. His several appeals to the janissary officers within the Orta Cami did not go unnoticed: "However, the queen mother whispered to us surreptitiously: 'Oh officers, you don't know what a spiteful person he [Sultan Osman] is. If he comes out safe and sound from this, he will not leave a living soul from among [both] us and you.'"[43]

Having been prevented from assassinating Sultan Osman in the mosque, Davud Pasha had him removed to Yedikule where, that evening (20 May 1622), the deposed sultan was strangled. He was buried next to his father, Ahmed I. His uncle, Mustafa I, was reinstalled at the Topkapı palace. To remove lingering doubts, Genç Osman's ear was brought to the valide sultan.[44]

THE CONCLUSION OF THE HAILE-I OSMANIYE

The trauma of the Haile-i Osmaniye did not subside during Sultan Mustafa's second reign (May 1622–September 1623). The instability and unrest were particularly severe in the eastern and central provinces of Anatolia and in the capital itself. The most marked event in the east (it assumes center stage in Chapter 8) was the rebellion of the *beylerbeyi* (governor) of Erzurum, Abaza Mehmed Pasha. Recruiting a local army, he extended his rule to adjacent provinces and harassed the kul; it is alleged that his motivation was to revenge the killing of Sultan Osman, for which he held the kul responsible. Under pressure applied by the kul and reports on Abaza's growing power and audacity, it was decided in Istanbul to send a force against him. This force, however, failed to encounter Abaza and returned to Istanbul without making serious contact. The Abaza affair was to end only in the 1630s under Murad IV.

In the capital, the effort of the kul to distance themselves from Osman II's killing culminated in the dismissal of Kara Davud Pasha from the grand vezirate and later in his execution. Pressures by various groups and factions yielded a period of sixteen months that witnessed five different grand vezirs: Kara Davud Pasha, Mere Hüseyin Pasha (to whom we shall return in the following chapters), Lefkeli Mustafa Pasha (another son-in-law), Gürcü Mehmed Pasha, and Kemankeş Ali Pasha. Eventually the empire's high officials decided to dethrone Sultan Mustafa, whom they again deemed feebleminded, and in the accession that followed Prince Murad, Ahmed I's oldest living son, became Sultan Murad IV. In return for her consent to his deposition, the request of Sultan Mustafa's mother that he be spared execution was granted, and he lived until 1639.[45]

2. The Formation and Study of Ottoman Historiography

The present chapter surveys the formation and development of Ottoman historiography up to the seventeenth century, including an attempt at a sociological portrayal of Ottoman historians, and offers some observations on the pertinent scholarly literature. It does not presume to be an exhaustive survey. It is rather an instrumental presentation that is intended to make plausible certain characterizations of this historiography and the ways it has been studied; these are an essential background for the interpretive approach proposed in the next chapter and for the discussion on the state in Part III. Although the presentation of the study of Ottoman historiography in this chapter is not exhaustive, it does raise significant questions that emanate from the dialogue between modern scholars and the works of their Ottoman colleagues.[1]

The discussion is meant to demonstrate four related observations. The first is that from its traceable inception Ottoman historiography, and this is by no means uniquely Ottoman, was conflictual and deeply ingrained in the politics and ideological accents of its time. By *conflictual* I mean not only that the historiographical production of a certain period was part and parcel of its historical environment but also something more general. An appropriate narrative of Ottoman historiography should foreground the extent to which it was an incessant competition among different, at times antithetical, story lines and versions; a linear or developmental narrative of Ottoman historiography would inevitably oversimplify it and render it one-dimensional. The second observation pertains to a central theme of this study: the history of Ottoman historiography and that of the Ottoman state are intimately related; at certain junctures (the first half of the seventeenth century is a good example), they might be inextricably intertwined.

The third observation concerns the sociology of the Ottoman historians.

The nature of Ottoman historiography in the period circa 1550–1650, including that of the genre of *Tarih-i Al-i Osman* (lit., Annals of the House of Osman, contextually "History of the Ottoman State"), should be interpreted in conjunction with the rapidly growing and increasingly specialized bureaucracy, or scribal service, and with what Cornell Fleischer has aptly termed "bureaucratic consciousness."[2] It would be erroneous to interpret, both contextually and textually, the Tarih-i Al-i Osman genre of the early seventeenth century as a linear progression from its fifteenth-century putative predecessor or as merely an "improvement" of it. The fourth and final observation alludes to modern scholarship. Two main trends, which are not mutually exclusive and may be found within a single study, are concurrent in the scholarship on Ottoman historiography. One primarily attempts to establish the extent to which Ottoman historical texts are reliable sources of information for the reconstruction of extrinsic referents, chiefly military and political events; the other trend studies historiography and the historians who produced it as a topic in and of itself and makes the occasion of history writing itself a historical topic. Both trends have always existed, but whereas in earlier stages the former was emphasized by most scholars, in recent years the study of Ottoman historiography as a "legitimate" *historical* topic—of the same order as waging wars or levying taxes—has been gaining momentum.

BEGINNINGS

It is convenient to begin with the most recent scholarly contribution. The debate on the inception of Ottoman historiography, which, not incidentally, is inseparable from the debate on the emergence and formation of the Ottoman state, has culminated (thus far) in an insightful and eloquent study by Cemal Kafadar.[3] What Kafadar basically shows is the formative conflictuality of Ottoman historiography in the fifteenth century, with special emphasis on what he rightly considers the most important genre, the histories of the House of Osman. The historiographical conflict lay at the heart of the domestic political, social, and cultural battle of the fifteenth century. In a concise formulation, the two social worlds that confronted each other were what Kafadar calls the gazi-dervish circles and the constructors of the emerging centralized, bureaucratic, and dynastic state; the latter comprised the sultans, the orthodox ulema and the courtiers, and, increasingly, the kul.[4] According to Halil Inalcik, by the end of Mehmed II's reign (the Conqueror, *Fatih* in Ottoman, r. 1444–46, 1451–

81), the political battle had been decided and the gazi circles were irrevocably marginalized.[5]

By drawing historiographical and political battle lines that demarcate two clearly defined sociopolitical groups, I might create the wrong impression of too neat a world. I am aware of the complexities and nuances, as well as of the fact that although the placement of historians within social contexts is pertinent to the interpretation of their works, the social context does not exclusively dictate this interpretation; the latter, in any event, is not monocausal.

Kafadar's main point of contention, regarding the formation of both historiography and the state, is with Rudy Lindner's thesis that tribalism accounts for the extraordinary success of the early Ottomans.[6] He compares his view of early Ottoman historiography to Lindner's by using a lovely metaphorical contrast between onion and garlic. For Lindner, he says, early Ottoman historiography is like an onion. The onion's core, which truly reflects what happened but does not exist in a form of an orderly *written* historiography, testifies to the tribal nature of the enterprise of Osman Bey and his immediate successors. Then, layer upon layer of what Lindner calls "state ideology," led and articulated by orthodox ulema and centralizing bureaucrats, mask the genuine tribal core, with the effect that this enterprise is overwhelmingly described in terms of the *gaza* ideology of the state (i.e., an ideology stressing the constant need to fight for the faith on the frontiers of Islam). Since a perfect ideological sealing is unattainable, especially in the age of manuscripts that attempt to construct a tradition on the basis of oral tales, the deviations from the state-led gaza ideology that have crept in allow glances at the onion's core through its distorting layers. Thus fifteenth-century Ottoman historiography, deviations notwithstanding, may tell us much about state ideology in this century, but it gives a distorted representation of the century and a half that preceded the formation of that ideology.[7]

In Kafadar's view, garlic is a more appropriate metaphor for early Ottoman historiography up to the fifteenth century. Like a garlic bulb, Ottoman historiography, from its inception, consisted of clusters of contrasting representations and narratives that were part of the history in which they were written, as well as clusters of oral and written traditions squeezed against each other. Kafadar totally rejects the evolutionary view of Ottoman historiography that is inherent in the onion metaphor:

> [I]t should be clear that by the time the major chronicles were composed [i.e., during the fifteenth century], there were many different layers of oral and written historical traditions. To envision them only

as layers of a linear progression would be misleading, however, since they also included competing or at least mutually incompatible accounts representing different political-ideological positions.[8]

To render this line of argument, which is central to my own approach and method, more concrete, it is useful to dwell for a while on two prominent historians of the fifteenth century, Aşık Paşazade (I shall use the shorthand *Apz* henceforth)[9] and Neşri, especially the former. The keen insights of Victor L. Menage laid the foundations for a deeper interpretation of early Ottoman historiography.[10] Concerning Apz in particular, Menage's work has pointed to the possibility, fully developed by Kafadar, that Apz was a child of the gazi-dervish milieu and that his history, far from being another construction in the state narrative, articulated the historical consciousness and ethos of a social world with which Apz identified.

Apz was a dervish-gazi from the region of Amasya. In the period of Interregnum (1403–13)[11] he threw in his lot with Prince Mehmed, who was to emerge triumphant from this turbulent period as Sultan Mehmed I (r. 1413–21). However, between the adventure with Mehmed I in the early 1410s and another with a member of one of the most illustrious gazi families, Mihaloğlu Mehmed Bey, a decade later, Apz fell ill. He chose to recover and spend some time with an old man, Yahşi Fakih, the son of the imam of Orhan Gazi (r. 1324–62). It was at the home of Yahşi Fakih that Apz became acquainted with the *menakib* (gaza tales) that the old man had collected and written down. Kafadar rightly observes that, apart from Apz's illness, nothing was accidental:

> There is every reason to assume [that] Apz felt comfortable in the sociocultural milieu he was born into. He chose to include Yahşi Fakih's menakib in his chronicle not merely because he happened to have access to them . . . but also because they made sense to him. The menakib he inherited from the fakih were skillfully woven into Apz's later fifteenth-century compilation because he wished to do so.[12]

Here, in a nutshell, lies the contention between Lindner and Kafadar; this study follows the latter's view of Ottoman historiography. For Lindner, the passages that are unique to Apz constitute the onion's core, and the fact that we have access to this authentic core of the early Ottoman enterprise stems from Apz's oversight. Drafting his history for the court of Bayezid II (r. 1481–1512) in the 1480s, Apz, now an old man, chose to conform to the overwhelming domination of state ideology that shaped the rest of Ottoman historiography. According to Lindner, in other words, Apz did not mean to include remnants of the authentic narrative in his history. By contrast, Kafadar senses in Apz's history (as well as in what is known among specialists of this subject as the texts of "Uruc and the anonymous chroniclers") the scent of garlic. He rejects the assertion that, even though it might be commissioned by Bayezid II, Apz's was a typical court history. Apz himself, it should be pointed out, owned a considerable amount of property in Istanbul (in Unkapanı and Galata) and was therefore exposed to the fiscal policies of the Conqueror and his officials.[13] These policies spearheaded the drive of the imperial project, which to a considerable extent was identified with Mehmed II's reign and with his administrators. Kafadar insists that "Apz's criticisms consistently reflect the worldview of a certain milieu which, particularly after the conquest of Constantinople and the adoption of the imperial project, stood outside and in some opposition to the Ottoman court, or at least the dominant centralist position upheld by most sultans and statesmen of the classical age."[14]

The garlic metaphor and the conflictual conception of Ottoman historiography are further reinforced when Neşri is compared to Apz. Unlike Apz, Neşri came from among the ulema. His work was written not more than a decade after Apz's and was an attempt to amalgamate three clusters of historical sources: the first was a group of works of which Apz's text is a major representative; the second comprised what can be called court histories (most notably Ahmedi's and Şukrüllah's); and the third comprised annalistic calendars. Menage's analysis of Neşri's text and Kafadar's argument suggest that although these clusters had common features, they at the same time kept their distinct identity. Further, on the basis of Wittek's work, Kafadar stresses his point through a more minute comparison between Apz's and Neşri's representations of the conquest of Aydos Castle. As is the case with Ottoman historiography of later periods, here the accounts appear at first glance so similar that it may seem obvious that Neşri lifted Apz's account lock, stock, and barrel. God, however, is in the details, and a careful examination reveals a significant difference. Whereas Apz's account displays intimacy with and passion for the gaza ethos, something the author experienced as a young man, Neşri's is indifferent and unappreciative. "Although Apz was transmitting a tradition he had obtained from another source," Kafadar concludes, "he was able to capture the mentality of his source while Neşri was not. This difference occurred, not because he was closer in time to the events than Neşri, who wrote only a decade or so after Apz, but clearly because they were from two different social worlds."[15]

A process of a century and a half (ca. 1350–1500) resulted, as far as the present discussion is concerned, in two sorts of historical consciousness. One, typical of sociopolitical groups that "once were" but are now aware of their marginalization and consequently feel alienated, is the historical consciousness and tradition of the gazi-dervish milieu. This was a historiography suffused with bitterness, hostility, and nostalgia. The nostalgia was for the good old, simple, days of fraternity and idealism. The bitterness stemmed from deep feelings of betrayal among a group that had delivered the House of Osman to the world and had gotten in return the harsh policies of Mehmed II, which, precisely at a crucial point in the formation of Ottoman historical tradition, the closing decades of the fifteenth century, Bayezid II (r. 1481–1512) was trying to soften. And the hostility was expressed against everything and everyone who, from the gazi perspective, embodied this process: *Yıldırım* (the Thunderbolt) Sultan Bayezid (r. 1389–1402), whose deviation from the gaza ethos led to the disaster in Ankara (1402); the notion of a central treasury; the Çandarlı dynasty of high-ranking officials and grand vezirs (their fate under Fatih did not matter); the infamous *pencik* (a levy applied from the 1370s, according to which one-fifth of the gaza's human booty belonged to the sultan's household); and more.

The alternative historical consciousness, the one that won the day, was what Lindner calls state ideology. It constituted the new identity of the House of Osman as the sovereign of a dynastic, increasingly sedentary, bureaucratic state, a ruling house that no longer saw itself as a distinguished family of gazis that, in relation to other families, was primus inter pares. And it was supported and articulated by groups whose interests were invested in such a state: the orthodox ulema, the central bureaucracy, and the kul. The conflictual nature of Ottoman historiography between these two alternative worlds is most evident with regard to the interpretation of gaza and its significance in the narrative. The bureaucrats of the *medreses* (Islamic institutes for higher education) who produced the eventual narrative were not, and could not be, anti-gaza. Their interpretation, however, severely undermined, even ostracized, the narrative of the gazi milieu in two ways: first, their allusions to gaza and gazis were devoid of the enthusiasm and passion that abounded in Apz and in the anonymous chronicles; second and most significant, they constructed a teleological narrative in which gaza was a necessary phase that inevitably culminated in a dynastic, bureaucratic state.

This schism, as well as the rewriting of what gaza should mean after 1453, is also emphasized by Colin Imber, who observes that Apz "was writing as a *gazi* for *gazis*."[16] In the historical tradition of the marginalized gazis of the fifteenth century, the House of Osman led and was faithful to the frontier society for the first three generations; things started to go wrong with Bayezid I and continued to deteriorate. Menage's inimitable formulation of this historical consciousness could have earned him an honorific gazi title:

> [I]n the good old days honest ghazis were not pestered by the central government; there was no penjik . . . to tax private enterprise; there were no laws compelling the surrender of an earlier sound currency for a debased one; and there were no nasty iç-oğlans [palace pages] (everyone knows how *they* won favor) coming out of the Palace to lord it over free-born Turks.[17]

CONTINUATIONS

Two closely related features are notable in the way Ottoman historiography continued to evolve from the latter part of the fifteenth century till the closing decades of the sixteenth century. These are the emergence of Ottoman high culture and the formation of an expanding and increasingly differentiated Ottoman bureaucracy. The title (and content) of Fleischer's study on Mustafa Ali—*Bureaucrat and Intellectual*—neatly captures this process and its constituent features.

Like other things Ottoman, historiography was an amalgamation of the cultures and traditions bequeathed to the Ottomans. The imprint of the older and prestigious traditions, the Arabic and the Persian, as well as the Turco-Mongol, Turkish-Anatolian, and Greek-Byzantine, is evident in Ottoman history. Like other things Ottoman, what renders the historiography Ottoman is precisely the eclectic amalgamation rather than the originality of a particular feature in terms of *Ideengeschichte*. Fleischer rightly observes that "the compilation of the great Ottoman histories of the sixteenth century constituted a statement, and a hope, that the Ottomans had achieved cultural as well as political legitimacy."[18]

Although periodization is unavoidably somewhat arbitrary, it might be suggested that the reign of Bayezid II, especially the late 1480s, marked a turning point in the history of Ottoman historiography. Bayezid II had to contend with and appease the groups that had been at the receiving end of the harsh centralizing policies of his father Mehmed II. Having thwarted the challenge of his brother, Cem Sultan, he proceeded with proving himself as a gazi. When he returned to the capital in 1484, Bayezid II launched his historiographical project. "Most of the critical chronicles," Kafadar notes, "were published after that juncture, in a context that was ready to hear those voices, when Bayezid was searching for the right dose of appeasement . . . , and still hoping to tame cults that had not yet become fully anti-Ottoman by patronizing them (e.g., Haci Bektaş)."[19]

In addition to the histories of Apz and Neşri that were written in Bayezid II's reign, this sultan commissioned two works that, in retrospect, might indicate the shift from Persian to high Ottoman Turkish. Bayezid first asked Idris-i Bildisi, who had been chancellor at the court of the Akkoyunlu, to produce a history of the House of Osman in a learned fashion. The result was the famous *Eight Paradises (Hasht Bihisht)* in Persian. Slightly later the sultan decided that a history on a similar topic and of the same stylistic elegance and elaboration as Bildisi's, but in Ottoman Turkish prose rather than Persian, was necessary. The outcome of this decision was Kemal Paşazade's *Tevarih-i Al-i Osman*. Fleischer remarks that, contrary to current views, Kemal Paşazade's was not a translation of the *Eight Paradises* but an independent work and that although the author used earlier works bearing the same title, his *History of the House of Osman* was more scholarly in both form and content.[20]

The second half of the sixteenth century, with the latter years of Kanuni Sultan Süleyman as a marker (r. 1520–1566), can be seen as the next significant period in the history of Ottoman historiography. In a thoughtful essay Christine Woodhead follows the ways that rendered what might be termed Süleyman's grand exercise in collective memory and historical consciousness so effective and successful, in the sultan's own time, as well as in the centuries that followed his reign.[21] "Like his grandfather Bayezid II," she observes, "Süleyman was especially appreciative of the merits, both political and cultural, immediate and long-term, of historiography."[22] Linguistically and culturally too, the process that had begun under Bayezid II of constructing an Ottoman high culture in general and prose in particular matured under his grandson Süleyman, and to a considerable degree thanks to his patronage. In turning Ottoman into a principal literary language, even though Arabic and especially Persian did not disappear and retained their prestige, historiography played a major role and gained popularity.[23]

The developments during Kanuni's reign notwithstanding, in scope and content historiography was confined to enhancing the ruler's desired image. The most notable product was written by the sultan's loyal *nişancı* (chancellor), Celalzade, under the title *Tebakatü'l-memalik ve deracatü'l mesalik* (Levels of the dominions and grades of the professions). It was meant to be a comprehensive history, and it had significant impact on later historians; first and foremost, however, *Levels* was a portrayal of Süleyman as *zübde-i Al-i Osman*, "the quintessence of the House of Osman."[24]

If Celalzade's history was at least intended to be general, the more common and state-sponsored subgenres of this period were inherently narrower and ideologically purposeful. The first subgenre, which quickly gained popularity, was the *gazaname* (campaign book), and it enhanced Süleyman's gazi image. This was followed by the institutionalization of the *şehname* (book of kings). The model for this subgenre was, of course, the famous *Shahname* by the medieval Persian writer Firdausi. This does not mean that Süleyman was the first to introduce this kind of historiography to Ottoman culture, for it had been occasionally used from the middle of the fifteenth century on. Under Süleyman's patronage, however, the şehname was given a twofold twist. First, ideologically, it was part of the project of giving Kanuni's reign a universal claim. Second, institutionally, it was accompanied by the establishment of the salaried post of the *şehnameci* (şehname writer). This particular trend culminated in the fact that the şehname was soon transformed into a *Süleymanname* (book of Süleyman), completed in 1558 by the first şehnameci, Arif.[25]

The post of şehnameci died out irrevocably by the end of the sixteenth century. As discussed in Chapter 1, the decline of the *haseki* (the sultan's favorite) occurred roughly at the same time, perhaps a decade or two later. This correlation may support the argument in Chapter 1 that Kanuni's reign, rather than having been the zenith of Ottoman civilization, was actually strewn with anomalies when compared to the "regular" course of Ottoman history. Just as the haseki institution is best accounted for by the particular personalities of Hurrem and Süleyman (and their union), so is the şehnameci post best explained by Süleyman's extraordinary investment in the construction of his own image and his obsession with posterity. In this respect the establishment of the post of state historian *(vakanüvis)* at the end of the seventeenth century should not be seen as a continuation of the şehnameci post on a grander scale.[26]

The reign of Murad III (1574–95), Süleyman's grandson, witnessed what Fleischer calls a "historiographical explosion." Thus at the end of the sixteenth century we find an Ottoman historiography that was highly varied and differentiated along two main lines: one thematic (the scope and content of a given work) and the other stylistic and literary. Three types, or subgenres, emerged. The first comprised works confined to a single event or reign *(fethname, Süleymanname, gazaname, or Eğerliname)*. The second was the *Tarih-i Al-i Osman* in straightforward Ottoman Turkish. The third consisted of universal histories into which Ottoman history was woven; their language was high and suffused with Persian, and their authors were highly educated, usually in the more prestigious medreses.[27]

Mustafa Ali (d. 1600), one of the most outstanding Ottoman historians, who wrote precisely in this period, offers interesting—albeit highly personal—insights on the state of Ottoman historiography. In the introduction to his ambitious historical endeavor, *Künhü'l-ahbar* (Essence of histories), Ali surveys the main works he used. The purpose of this bibliographical essay was not only informative; here Ali attempted to construct a sort of canon of Ottoman historiography leading up to his own work. In the first category of his expose, which went according to authors, were the early chroniclers discussed above. The second category was doubtless the *silsila* (chain of cultural transmission) within which Ali wished to be placed. It included such scholars as Idris-i Bildisi, Kemal Paşazade, and Kanuni's chancellor Celalzade. They wrote comprehensive dynastic histories and distinguished themselves, in Ali's judgment, as both historians and litterateurs. The apex of this category was reached by the famous chief mufti of the early sixteenth century, Hoca Sadüddin Efendi, author of the *Taciittevarih* (Crown of histories). The third category, the şehnamecis of Ali's own time, incurred his wrath and contempt, especially Seyyid Lokman (all of whose works Ali used). He thought they all lacked independent judgment and literary prowess, and he highlighted the fact that they were professional scribes rather than scholars. To a significant degree, Ali's low opinion of the şehnamecis ought to be seen in the context of his constant complaints about the decline of cultural patronage and his desire that a post of a serious state historian be established.[28]

Since Ali's life and work bring us to the threshold of the seventeenth century,[29] three points concerning him adequately conclude this section. The first is concerned with his self-placement. The fact that he wished to be seen as a significant contributor (at least) to the silsila of imperial histories in high Ottoman Turkish and the fact that the right to join this club in earnest had to be won by literary virtuosity as much as by informational wealth and accuracy underscore the fruition of a high Ottoman culture, with emphasis on prose, and the role played by historical writing in this process. However much Ali might be subjective in taste and judgment does not matter in this respect. The second point, concerning the relationship between history and literature in the Ottoman historians' own discourse, is concisely articulated by Fleischer: "While Ali the litterateur might identify those works with which he wished his *Essence* to be compared, Ali the conscientious historian (the two personae are not, of course, dichotomous) made a point of knowing about, and where necessary comparing and citing, every source relevant to his Ottoman history."[30]

The third point presents a scholarly controversy whose focus is Ali's work, the *Essence* in particular. What has given rise to it is the fact that Ali was a most outspoken and critical historian and an eccentric person; these traits have made him at once popular and controversial with modern scholars. Beyond Ali as a historical topic, this controversy illustrates both the growing interest in Ottoman historiography and the questions that engage its students.

Following Fleischer's comprehensive study on Ali's life and work, Jan Schmidt dedicated a whole book to an analysis of the historiographical, literary, and Quellenkritik aspects of the *Essence*, entitled *Pure Waters for Thirsty Muslims*.[31] Schmidt's interpretation of the *Essence* explicitly challenges Fleischer's with regard to four central issues: the historiographical innovation of the text; the scientificity of Ali's historical scholarship; the originality of Ali as a sociopolitical critic; and the relationship between the literary nature of the *Essence* and the social reach Ali had intended it to have.

Schmidt insists that Ali's *Essence* was not a historiographical innovation and that it remained within "the limits posed by traditional Islamic historiography." Within these confines, Schmidt agrees that Ali was an intelligent and exceptional historian.[32] As regards the scientificity of Ali's historiography, Schmidt's contention with Fleischer is twofold and is concerned with Fleischer's association of the *Essence* with Ibn Khaldun's *Muqaddima*. First, drawing on Aziz al-Azmeh's interpretation of Ibn Khaldun, Schmidt argues that the *Muqaddima* itself, though of outstanding quality, was a traditional description rather than a proleptic precursor of the modern social sciences. Second, Schmidt doubts the prevalence in the *Essence* of ideas and concepts that have prompted scholars to deem the *Muqaddima* scientific; to the rather limited extent that these do appear in the *Essence*, they can hardly be identified as scientific.[33]

The disagreement about the originality of Ali's critical faculties has two facets. One, more strictly historiographical, prompts Schmidt to observe that although Ali might be a critical historian in his own time and place, he cannot be said to have been one according to the practice of modern, scientific historiography. As regards the other, more general facet, Schmidt is adamant that there is nothing in the *Essence* on the alleged ills that had plagued the Ottoman Empire that did not appear in other histories or the growing bureaucratic advice literature *(nasihat)*.[34]

The fourth and final bone of contention is focused on the literary aspect of the *Essence* and its social implications. Schmidt's overall conclusion is that much of the justified greatness of the *Essence* and its author lies in the literary achievement and that the literary aspect of this work is as important as the historical, not only to the modern interpreter but also, consciously, to Ali himself and his contemporaries. Schmidt's observation is at variance with Fleischer's (and others') with regard to the intended social reach of the *Essence*. He insists that despite Ali's pious statements to the contrary, the *Essence* was not, nor was it meant to be, a work written in simple Turkish intended solely to convey historical knowledge and to be read and understood by a wide audience. The style of the *Essence*, Schmidt maintains, is for the most part *inşa* (adorned prose), and, contrary to current scholarly views, it is not simplified toward the end of the *Essence*, which covers Ottoman history.[35]

Apart from its direct contribution to the present résumé of Ottoman historiography, the debate between Schmidt and Fleischer embodies the growing scholarly interest in Ottoman historians and their work as topic in itself and as a distinct historical phenomenon rather than solely as "sources" whose factual reliability has to be assessed. I would like to use this view of the debate to make a few comments.

First, regarding Ali's (or Ibn Khaldun's, for that matter) scientificity or lack thereof, I think that this particular debate is not only anachronistic and moot but also rather absurd. Of course, neither Ali nor Ibn Khaldun was a "scientific" scholar. With all the critical literature that has emerged over the past three or four decades on modernity, modernism, modern science, and so forth, it is so obvious that "the scientific historian" is a discursive—and therefore historical—category that investing great energy in showing whether Mustafa Ali was scientific seems bizarre. The belief, implicit in this debate, that a historian who wrote within an Islamic-Ottoman paradigm was "schemata-guided" (Schmidt's phrase), whereas one writing from within a modern Western context is "scientific," might have been shaken if, for instance, Thomas Kuhn's *The Structure of Scientific Revolutions* had been borne in mind.

Second, regarding Schmidt's judgment of Ali in general, I would venture that *Pure Waters* and its author may be subjected to the same judgment as that to which Schmidt subjects the *Essence* and Mustafa Ali. Schmidt's evaluation of his subject matter is no less "limited" by premises and conventions contingent upon time, place, and culture than Ali's *Essence* was by "traditional Islamic historiography," "the ideal Islamic state," and an "Islamic world picture." What underpins this judgment is a series of premises characteristic of empiricist historiography coupled with Orientalist overtones. Some of these become evident when, in his first chapter, Schmidt stresses that Ali's "source-criticism" does not even remotely resemble what modern historians find acceptable and that Ali's selection of sources was based on what had been regarded "sound" and "reliable" in his cultural tradition. Actually, the way in which modern historians select their sources is in principle similar to Ali's: in both cases, conventions contingent upon time and place determine which sources are considered "sound" and "reliable," and according to what criteria.

When Schmidt categorically asserts that Ali's historical horizon was limited by his adherence to the concept of the ideal Islamic state, he seems oblivious to the fact that what is commonly considered the birth of modern historiography, namely Leopold von Ranke's historical writing, obsessed as it was with the state, its institutions and archives, cannot be detached from the Hegelian "schema" that the state is the apex of history's dialectical progress. Further, the fact that in modern historiography an authoritative and truthful status has been accorded to documents emanating from official state archives stems not from a "scientific source criticism" but from the ideological reification of the modern nation-state and its teleological narrative.

HISTORIOGRAPHY AND BUREAUCRATIC CONSCIOUSNESS

If history is indeed a dialogue between the present and the past, then the reification of the Ottoman state (which is the pivotal concern of Part III) must be a prime illustration of this view. If one were to conduct a continuous reading of Ottoman historians from the sixteenth and seventeenth centuries and of their modern colleagues, one might infer that reification was the result of a collusion between past and present historians. The construction of the Ottoman state as an omnipotent "thing" that possesses intentions and dispositions and a life of its own is so strongly evident because the consolidation of historiography (and prose in general) and the expansion and professionalization of the bureaucracy were concomitant phenomena. The people, in other words, who inscribed the state in the bureaucratic domain were the same people who constructed it as an independent subject in the realm of writing: the bureaucrat-historians.

A note on terminology seems necessary. I consciously ignore the debate on whether we should call the nascent Ottoman institution discussed here "bureaucracy" or "scribal service" or something else. Any such deliberations are plagued, I think, by the all-too-familiar bias of the modernist/modernization theory narrative of early modern history, the implication being that bureaucracy (*à la* Weber implicitly) is modern whereas scribal service is traditional. It would seem more important simply to note that for the Ottomans the institution and the growing variety of career paths it offered were known as *kalemiye*, a term derived from the word *kalem* (pen).

In the formation of a sizable, differentiated, and professionalized bureaucracy two periods may discerned (in this case, Weberian terminology may be appropriate): the first, circa 1450–1550, was charismatic; the second, spanning the late sixteenth and early seventeenth centuries, was the period of the bureaucracy's institutionalization. Two such bureaucrat-intellectuals, Mustafa Ali and Okçuzade Mehmed Şah Bey (d. 1630), concisely convey the relationship between the two components of the process (bureaucracy and high culture articulated in prose). Ali ceremoniously declares that "in the cage of the imperial cipher *[tuğra]* is the peerless phoenix of the [chancellor's] dedication ever apparent, and the consolidation of the laws of [Ottoman] sovereignty is manifested in the prose composition which issues from them [the chancellors]."[36] Okçuzade, three times chancellor *(nişancı)* himself, elevates prose expression with the implicit assumption that it is obvious with whom this cultural responsibility rests: "Numerous skillful poets capable of originality in rare and beautiful expressions may always be found in every country, if not in every major city. But true prose stylists, those with natural talent, appear perhaps once in every generation. Hence there is a dearth of eloquent writers."[37]

An important phase in the institutionalization of Ottoman bureaucracy occurred in the period 1570–1630 (as much as a precise periodization of an institution is at all possible).[38] It had several noticeable features. First, at the top level, there emerged two main branches[39]—the finance directorship and the chancery—and within them four positions, with increasing differentiation among them: the chief financial officer of the empire *(baş defterdar)*, who was also the treasurer of Rumelia *(Rumeli defterdari)*; the chancellor, who was the chief of the imperial chancery *(nişancı)*; the secretary-in-chief of the imperial council *(reisülkuttab)*, who was formally under the authority of the chancellor and in charge of the imperial council's scribes *(Divan-i Hümayun katipleri)*; and the registrar *(defter emini)*, who headed the site where all imperial transactions were recorded *(defterhane-i amire)*. It should be clarified that there occurred both increasing differentiation (between the two main branches and the heads of each of them: i.e., the baş defterdar and nişancı), and the consolidation of hierarchies, career paths, and lines of promotion within each branch.

The second feature is the sociopolitical implications of this process, underpinned as it was by a substantial expansion in terms of both sheer numbers and functions and positions. In its more charismatic phase, the nascent bureaucracy, especially its high echelon, about which we know more, was for the most part based on ad hoc appointments of people who usually combined birth in distinguished families with education at a prestigious institution of learning, such as the *sahn-i seman* (a sort of Ottoman version of

Oxbridge). The same period witnessed a significant change in this respect. The growing number of graduates of the *ilmiye* system (system of religious institutions of higher learning), frustrated by insufficient supply of positions, bleak career prospects, and a rigid hierarchy, were attracted to the chancery in particular, where their social affiliation and education gave them an edge, at least initially. Further, unlike the position of *defterdar* (director of finances), which interestingly offered more money, the chancery offered both cultural prestige and an opportunity to exhibit one's cultural prowess. It was in and through the chancery that official, high Ottoman prose was formed in the inşa style. And even though, as Woodhead shows, the second phase in the development of inşa was more inward-looking, intimate, and private and less official, the foundations were nonetheless laid within what I have called the charismatic phase of the Ottoman chancery; moreover, the *münşeat* (collections of correspondence in inşa style) of the seventeenth century may well have assumed the nature they did because the style of writing of official documents had already been shaped, and writers who wished to experiment with the inşa style were pushed into other domains such as unofficial correspondence.

The expanding bureaucracy, however, recruited others besides the frustrated ilmiye graduates who eventually came to regard it a vocation, not just a forced necessity. While the enhanced prestige that became attached to a chancery career may well be due to its increasing popularity among these ilmiye graduates, two other sources of recruitment were of considerable importance: one might be termed, for want of more accurate information, "plain" reaya families; the other consisted of sons of middle- and low-ranking kul, who not infrequently rendered bureaucratic services to the units in which their fathers served or had served. Unlike the ilmiye graduates, many of those recruited from the other two groups had to begin as apprentices (sing. *şagird*, pl. *şagirdan*). It seems that the ilmiye graduates had the advantage in the initial stages of a given career path, but an aspiring şagird might catch up in later stages. This was true especially with regard to the treasury, which required concrete skills and which, because it offered higher income, was more attractive to recruits from humble families, for whom cultural prestige and prowess were presumably luxuries they could ill afford.

The third feature highlights the position of the nişanci (chancellor). Although his actual, as distinguished from formal, status was gradually overshadowed by that of the reisülkuttab (secretary-in-chief of the imperial council), the chancellor is historically significant for three reasons. First, his was the single most important role in the formation and elaboration of high prose in Ottoman Turkish. Second, several chancellors were not only prose stylists but also historians. Third, as Fleischer perceptively observes, in the second half of the sixteenth century the chancellor conceptually became "the mufti of *kanun*" (the interpretive authority of sultanic regulations), the equivalent of the head of the ilmiye hierarchy who was the mufti of the Şeriat. The model of this was the combination of the two pillars who were responsible for the portrayal of Kanuni's reign as an Ottoman ideal: the mufti Ebusuud and the chancellor Celalzade.

BRIEF BIOGRAPHICAL NOTES

The historians whose works are the chief concern of this study illustrate the process charted above. Although the study does not presume to offer comprehensive biographies, the present section provides a series of brief resumes that both illustrate the type of people who wrote history in the seventeenth century and constitute an important component of the interpretive process in the following chapters.[40]

Hüseyin bin Sefer/Tuği Çelebi (died sometime during the reign of Murad IV, 1623–40). At the time he composed his history of the Haile-i Osmaniye, Tuği was most probably a retired bodyguard of the sultan *(solak)*. A son of a Christian boy from the Balkans who was recruited to the janissary corps, Tuği was born in Belgrade and, in his father's footsteps, became a janissary too. He took part in several campaigns in Anatolia and Persia. Tuği's presumably fruitful *intisap* (social network of patron-client relationship) to the *ağa* (commanding officer) of the janissary corps earned him entry to the elite unit that escorted the sultan on his outings (campaigns and others). At the time he chose to retire, his years of service amounted to less than twenty. It is highly significant that as a janissary veteran he was entitled to a pension. As mentioned in Chapter 1 in conjunction with the yoklama of the kul, one of the steps taken by Sultan Osman against the central army is reported to have been the severance of the lucrative pensions of the janissary veterans. Tuği indeed mentions this step as one of the greatest evils in that sultan's reign.

Hasanbeyzade (died 1636–7?). Hasanbeyzade's career so neatly fits the processes charted above that is tempting to present it as a stereotypical case. He was the son of Küçük Hasanbey, a member of the emerging kalemiye who held the post of reisülkuttab. Küçük Hasanbey graduated through the palace system, so it is possible that, like Tuği's father, he was a Christian recruit. Hasanbeyzade began to acquire college education that would set him on an ilmiye career. His father's death in 1586, however, forced him to abandon it and seek a kalemiye career instead. Hasanbeyzade soon became one of the imperial council's scribes. He managed to hold the post of reisülkuttab for a short term, and then also held the post of *defterdar* of Anatolia. The office Hasanbeyzade held for most of his career, however, was that of *tezkereci* and *baş tezkereci* (secretary and head secretary respectively) to various campaign commanders *(serdars)*. Like Tuği, he too had an axe to grind. His career was apparently hindered under the post of *başdefterdar* of Baki Pasha. The latter's was one of the heads demanded in the kul's petition during the three turbulent days in May 1622.

Ibrahim Peçevi (1574–1650). He was born in Fünfkirchen (Pecs in Hungarian), whence his epithet Peçevi. On his paternal side were two generations of provincial commanders in the Bosnia region who had derived their income from the *timar* (prebendal land grant) system. Through his maternal side he was related to the famous Sokollu (Serbian Sokoloviş) lineage. Having become an orphan at a young age, Peçevi was first taken to the household of his uncle, Ferhad Pasha, and then to the household of another relative, Lala Mehmed Pasha, where he spent fifteen years. In 1593 he joined the army and participated in Sinan Pasha's Hungarian campaign. Much of Peçevi's career was spent in the provincial administration, in both Anatolia and Rumelia, within which he mostly held the office of defterdar of several provinces. He had forged close relations with several provincial governors (*ümera*). Crucially, as we shall see as the book unfolds, in 1622–3 he was the defterdar of Hafız Pasha, the beylerbeyi of Diyarbekir and one of Sultan Osman's staunchest supporters; Peçevi also knew quite well Abaza Mehmed Pasha, the beylerbeyi of Erzurum and a central figure in the politics of the 1620s. He retired in 1641 to Budapest and most probably wrote his Ottoman history between that year and his death in 1650.

Katip Çelebi (1609–57). Katip Çelebi was born in Istanbul. His original name was Mustafa bin Abdallah, and later he also became known as Haci Halife. He was one of the foremost intellectuals of the seventeenth century. In addition to history, he also wrote works in the fields of bibliography, biography, geography and nasihat. Katip Çelebi was most interested in European politics and culture. He initiated translations of texts from Greek and Latin and supplied information on the structure and institutions of European states. His thorough knowledge of Ottoman historiography and literature earned him the appreciation of contemporaries and later generations alike. As demonstrated in Part II, the fact that he was held in high esteem by Naima (see below) meant that Katip Çelebi's writing had considerable—if posthumous—impact on the historical representations of the seventeenth century that became the state narrative. Katip Çelebi was present in several campaigns, among them one against Abaza Mehemd Pasha in 1624. His working career started at the age of fourteen, when he became an apprentice in the Anatolia Accountancy Office *(Anadolu Muhasebesi)*, where he learned the *siyakat* (finance cipher). Katip Çelebi's career in the state's service was undistinguished, and much of it he spent as a low-ranking scribe at the Muhasebe department. An inheritance in 1645 enabled him to live comfortably in Istanbul and dedicate his time to scholarship. Many of his works were composed between 1648 and his untimely death in 1657.

Mustafa Naima (1665?–1714). Ehud Toledano suggests an interpretive framework whose gist is the Ottomanization of local elites in the Middle East and North Africa and the concomitant localization of the representatives of the imperial center in these regions. He observes that this dual process created an Ottoman space within which both types of elites moved confidently and with a sense of familiarity.[41] One could hardly find a better example than Naima's biography to add plausibility to Toledano's framework. Naima was born in Aleppo in 1665(?) into a family of localized janissaries *(yerliye)*. This fact alone meant two things that had incalculable impact on his career: he possessed substantial intisap in Istanbul even before he went there; and he was bilingual (Ottoman Turkish and Arabic), if not trilingual (he certainly acquired Persian, but it is difficult to ascertain whether this came "from home"). His grandfather, Küçük Ali Ağa, was a janissary officer in Aleppo, and his father, Mehmed Ağa, was the janissary commander of that city. Of significance to Naima's career at the capital was also his connection, from his childhood in Aleppo, with the Bektaşi order. Naima went to Istanbul in the mid 1680s, and launched his kalemiye career. He first underwent a formal palace apprenticeship, rendering scribal services to the *Teberdaran-i Saray-i Atık* (Halberdiers of the Old Palace). The key to the zenith of Naima's career lay with his patrons, two successive grand vezirs, Hüseyin Köprülü Pasha and Moralı Hasan Pasha. Owing to this intisap, he became the first vakanüvis of the empire, from 1697 (perhaps earlier) to 1704, and enjoyed a high income derived from the customs revenue. In this period he composed the history for which he became so well known. The downfall of his patrons brought about the end of his *vakanüvislik*. From then until his death in 1716 Naima returned to a more ordinary kalemiye career.

CONCLUSION

This chapter surveyed the history of Ottoman historiography up to the seventeenth century. It presented three main points: that the story of this historiography, from its observable inception, should be understood as conflictual rather than linear or developmental (which should not be taken to mean that there were no developments); that at least at certain, and significant, junctures the histories of Ottoman historiography and of the Ottoman state were closely related, if not inextricably intertwined; that the expansion of an increasingly specialized bureaucracy, with its own esprit de corps, gave birth to and shaped the bureaucrat-historian, the "typical" Ottoman historian of the seventeenth century.

The final observation is presented at this stage as a thought, in the hope that by the end of this study it will become convincing and plausible. Fleischer, for instance, when mentioning the historiographical varieties at the end of the sixteenth century, notes the continued existence of the Tarih-i Al-i Osman genre, and it may be implicitly understood that it more or less resembled what had existed at the formative stages of the Ottoman state.

Bearing in mind the arguments put forth in this chapter, I think that this could not be the case. To begin with the historians, it is evident that sociologically we have a significantly different sort of people: professional bureaucrats. Second, the site of historiographical activity ceased being the state versus the state's absence (i.e., the frontier); even when there were conflicting narratives, as there always were, the conflicts were over the depiction of the desired state. Third, it is not a coincidence that the chancellor was deemed, as Fleischer himself says, the mufti of kanun. What this meant, in the widest possible sense of *kanun*, was that the bureaucrat-intellectuals conceived of themselves as *the* group that was responsible for defining and preserving everything that was Ottoman about the state, its modus operandi and etiquette.

In the seventeenth century, the genre of Tarih-i Al-i Osman was, in this respect, one of the chief sites where the bureaucrat-historians, through the representation of concrete events and protagonists, waged the discursive battle over the definition of the state. Lest I be accused of resorting to obscurantist jargon, I should note that I use *discursive* advisedly. One of the main characteristics of Foucauldian discourse is that it has the power to determine and control the boundaries of knowledge, of what is considered legitimate or illegitimate knowledge. The Tarih-i Al-i Osman works of the seventeenth century constitute a discourse, or are part of the discursive battle over the state, precisely in this sense. As will be shown in Part III in particular, the essence of the conflicting narratives was the drawing of the sociopolitical boundaries of the state, the power to define who was Osmanlı and who was not, the power to determine who was entitled to be included "within" the state and who might be excluded from it.

3. An Interpretive Framework

> So . . . where is it "where we are now" in historical theory as an aspect of practice and consciousness? Don't ask me. I went to that session as if to the first day of school with an entire new pad of paper, the pen I made sure would write, and came away two and a half hours later with a few illegible doodles on the margin of one page I seem to have lost. I'm afraid that I've had to replace the high-concept "critical taxonomy" with something more like an autopsy report.
>
> NANCY PARTNER, "Hayden White (and the Content of the Form and Everyone Else) at the AHA"

This chapter was written with a certain trepidation. Its immediate purpose is to present the interpretive framework that guides the reading of the historical texts and the theoretical environment that informs it. There is, however, another, more ambitious purpose: to introduce to the study of Ottoman culture in general and Ottoman historiography in particular what has become known as the linguistic turn or the new cultural history.[1]

The heavy emphasis laid by Ottomanist scholarship on social, economic, and institutional history, its adherence to what Dominick LaCapra terms a "documentary model of knowledge,"[2] and its sanctification of archival documents have had mixed results. An impressive scholarly corpus that reflects these preferences has emerged; and the attentiveness of Ottomanists to pertinent fields and schools such as the *Annales*, the new social history, and world economy theories has been noteworthy and insightful. A price has been paid, however: the relative oblivion to which were doomed culture, intellectual life, "unsuitable" sources, and the engaged, nuanced reading of sources of any kind.

Recently, scholarly interest in the cultural and intellectual life of the Ottomans seems to have been rekindled. But the linguistic turn, which rocked the historical discipline—indeed the social sciences as a whole—to its foundations, has gone largely unnoticed. The larger purpose of the present discussion is therefore to suggest how this phenomenon might be brought to bear on the materials and concerns of Ottoman history. That the discussion occasionally extends beyond what is absolutely necessary to set forth my own interpretive approach stems from a conscious attempt to address that larger purpose.

One need not be a rigid postmodernist or zealous deconstructionist to benefit from the linguistic turn. The subversive reading of the modern social sciences was the endeavor that propelled the linguistic turn forward, but by now it has been done ad nauseam. Its promise and benefit, I contend, lie in the fresh and stimulating ways it leads one to read and reread one's source material. My aim is, consequently, not to address the tedious question of whether there is or isn't reality, but to argue that a measured application of the linguistic turn may add another dimension to the process of interpretation.

CORPUS AND DISCOURSE

In the previous chapter it was observed that in the study of Ottoman historiography two approaches might be noticed. One seeks to establish the informational reliability of historical texts as sources for the reconstruction of extrinsic referents. The other is concerned with the historians and their writings as historical phenomena in their own right. It was also said that although these two approaches might occasionally be found within a single study, in the early stage of the study of Ottoman historiography scholars tended to emphasize the former, whereas in recent years they have preferred the latter.

What renders this observation less neat than it would seem is the scholarly literature on the early centuries of Ottoman history. Because for that period archival documents hardly exist, its historians (especially Paul Wittek, Victor Menage, and Colin Imber[3]), even when their fundamental purpose was to ascertain informational reliability, were led to consider its pertinent sources in ways that amounted to a historiographical investigation. It is not incidental that the growing tendency to look at the writing of history from the sixteenth to the nineteenth centuries (a period for which research sources are predominantly archival) as itself a historical event has emerged relatively recently.[4]

Another way of classifying the study of Ottoman historiography is based on the subject matter—that is, the distinction between works that focus on a single outstanding historian and his writings (e.g., Fleischer on Mustafa Ali and Lewis V. Thomas on Naima) and those that examine a group of texts (e.g., Kafadar on early Ottoman historiography); the latter type naturally tends to be comparative and to offer less biographical elaboration. Although his Orientalist overtones are objectionable, I nonetheless find John R. Walsh's views on this issue stimulating.[5] Walsh had a concept of past historiography in general, and Persian and Ottoman historiography in particular, that was atypical of his generation. Consider, for instance, the following declaration:

> In its prejudices and its assumptions, in its omissions no less than in its contents, it [historiography] is the reflection of the inconstant human situation, and even where it is least informative it supplies us with data which no explicit statement could convincingly express, and which, perhaps, are as valuable to the understanding of the past as the dates and the deeds. . . . Every such [historical] work, therefore, however inadequate and inaccurate it may be in detail, *is itself a historical fact of singular importance* [Emphasis added], and is best understood when considered with its fellows in their mutual complementary relationship throughout a total situation rather than being merely confronted with them on the particulars.[6]

Within this general view, the approach suggested by Walsh has two essential aspects. One has already been mentioned, and it is literary: the central significance, for both the contemporary Ottomans and the modern interpreter, of the historical text as a literary artifact and as a domain in which a writer could and was expected to exhibit his literary prowess; and the centrality of historiography in the formation and development of Ottoman prose. The other is that "such historical works cannot be treated individually; as our reaction to them is conditioned by our awareness of the complex of which they form a part, this must also influence our judgement of their authenticity."[7] In addition to recommending an examination, in one way or another, of a body of works rather than of works "individually," Walsh raises the thorny question of authenticity. What he means by this is the extent to which certain historians were original and independent or derivative and "servile copyists." He mentions Mustafa Ali and Ibrahim Peçevi as examples of original historians and Katip Çelebi, whom he utterly dislikes, as a representative of the derivative type. Further, Walsh argues that the study of a group of texts, what I call a historiographical corpus, would bring to the fore both "a conventional pattern" and "a discernibly individual response to the affairs and activities of their [the Ottoman historians'] times"—this, of course, if we study the "authentic" historians rather than the "plagiarists."[8]

Like Walsh, I see the advantages of selecting a historiographical corpus. But Walsh's harsh castigation of those he calls "plagiarists" is unacceptable, and the distinction he draws between the "derivative" and "authentic" historian is excessively rigid. Let us consider what modern scholarship, which is the implicit—perhaps un-self-conscious—model against which Walsh judges Ottoman and Persian historiography, does with authoritative historical knowledge. The late Albert Hourani, for instance, doubtless an "authentic" historian rather than a "plagiarist" or "servile copyist," wrote two introductory chapters in his famous *Arabic Thought in the Liberal Age* (1963), one of which presented the Ottoman state. This chapter is basically a summary of what was then considered to be the standard, authoritative literature on the Ottoman Empire. He neither criticized his sources (chiefly the works of Gibb and Bowen and Bernard Lewis) nor sought to form an independently "authentic" interpretation of Ottoman history; and, of course, it was not his business to do so in this particular book.[9] The fact that Hourani, and all of us, for that matter, did not lift whole passages from Gibb and Bowen or Lewis but for the most part summarized, paraphrased, and gave references stems from the rules of the modern historical discourse, not from a qualitative gap between modern and Ottoman historians, even those who were less imaginative than others. Of course, some historians among the Ottomans were more original and imaginative and others were more ordinary, but this is a superfluous truism.

The fundamental choice of this study, then, is to interpret the ways in which a clearly defined series of events, contained in the title *Haile-i Osmaniye*, were represented in a corpus of seventeenth-century historical texts up to the point at which an official state narrative was conceived. This choice entails a constant comparison among the various texts that compose the corpus; because the history I seek is that of the conception of the state narrative, including the alternative representations that existed along the way, most of this comparison is done diachronically. The advantages and disadvantages of this approach are not absolute but relative to the concerns of a given study. In this case, the underlying argument that Ottoman historiography was neither transparent nor an unstructured mine of "facts" of varying degrees of accuracy and reliability almost necessitates the corpus and the constant comparison. Such an approach, if carried out meticulously, brings to the fore differences not only in narrative events but in the minutest interpretive nuances. It severely curtails erroneous statements such as Walsh's, whereby "that besetting evil of all Islamic historical literature, the mechanical repetition, verbatim or in paraphrase, of earlier works, is endemic in the Ottoman historians of this period."[10] Moreover, the approach charted here shows that even when verbatim repetition occurs, it is not merely "mechanical" but on many occasions a consciously interpretive preference of one representation over another.

To take the interpretive framework a step farther, I propose to examine the textual corpus as a narrative discourse. Although with the gradual collapse of rigid disciplinary boundaries the following exposition may be deemed redundant, I nonetheless think that I ought to clarify what is meant by *narrative discourse* in this study specifically and how this concept is employed. In general, the term *discourse* is used here in its Foucauldian sense. Foucault rejected the more conventional units of interpretation such as the text and the genre and was not interested in ultimately refuting or validating the frameworks constructed by modern science itself—that is, the theory and the paradigm. Presupposing that any knowledge is relative and contingent to begin with (tautologically presupposing, critics may charge), Foucault was concerned with exposing how certain knowledge was conceived and who the object of that knowledge was. Here is a useful definition:

> A discourse is best understood as a system of possibility for knowledge. . . . [I]t is what allows us to produce statements, which will be either true or false—it makes possible a field of knowledge. But the rules of a discourse are not rules which individuals consciously follow; a discourse is not a method or a canon of enquiry. Rather, these rules provide the necessary preconditions for the formation of statements, and as such they operate "behind the backs" of speakers of a discourse. Indeed, the place, function and character of the "knowers," authors and audiences of a discourse are also a function of these discursive rules.[11]

Envisaging discourse in this sense, I argue that what fundamentally took place in the historiographical story of the construction of the state narrative of the Haile-i Osmaniye was a battle over the boundaries of knowledge of the Ottoman state and of Ottoman identity in the seventeenth century. The authority of the discourse, shaped in this case by the narrative form, was supposed to make two determinations. One was whether the nature of the state was in congruity with its history and therefore whether its "Ottomanness" was preserved or strayed from. The other, correspondingly, was whether certain practices were legitimate ("true") or illegitimate ("false") within these discursive rules. A politically meaningful instance of this is the power struggle of inclusion/exclusion, or, put differently, the discursive drawing of the state's boundaries. Concretely, a pivotal issue here was whether some powerful Anatolian provincial governors of *celali* social origins had become legitimate *Osmanlıs*, and could therefore be *included* within the state, or had essentially remained rebels *(asılar)*, and consequently ought to have been *excluded* from the state.[12] As discussed thoroughly in Part III, all this should be seen in the context of the crisis of the seventeenth century in Eurasia and the attendant transformation and redefinition of several states, including the Ottoman, within that vast area.

HAYDEN WHITE'S THEORY OF THE HISTORICAL NARRATIVE

> Form is the essence of a thing or that which makes it to be what it is.
> ROBERT GROSSETESTE, Oxford's first chancellor, in *The Oxford Book of Oxford*

Hayden White's theory of historiography has evoked a healthy mixture of religiosity, adoration, contempt, and vehemence.[13] I do not intend to conduct here a thorough and orderly presentation of White's theory;[14] rather, I intend to discuss concrete aspects of it that stimulate my own reading of the Ottoman texts.[15] The basic trait of White's approach that I find appealing is that it lends itself to universal application. Although his main subject matter is European historiography in the nineteenth century, White recognizes that the historical narrative may be a universal, almost transhistorical, cognitive device by which human consciousness makes sense of time and "reality":

> [N]arrative might well be considered a solution to a problem of general human concern, namely, the problem of how to translate knowing into telling, the problem of fashioning human experiences into a form assimilable to structures of meaning that are generally human rather than culture-specific. We may not be able fully to comprehend specific thought patterns of another culture, but we have relatively less difficulty understanding a story from another culture, however exotic that culture may appear to us. . . . This suggests that far from being one code that a culture may utilize for endowing experience with meaning, narrative is a *meta-code*, a human universal on the basis of which transcultural messages about the nature of a shared reality can be transmitted.[16]

Rejection of the Content/Form Dichotomy

As Michael Oakeshott's work, to take one example,[17] clearly demonstrates, conventional positivist scholarship makes a twofold dichotomous distinction regarding the narrative: between the content and the form and between the historical and imaginary narrative. According to this distinction, the narrative as form is indifferent and adds nothing to the content of the representation. Historical reality is self-offered and self-structured (as, say, a tragedy or a farce). All the narrative as form does, if competently written, is mimic a certain segment of that reality as it offers itself. That this form of representing events is shared by fictional/imaginary forms, such as the epic and the historical novel, need not be a source of concern, for the historical discourse is distinguished by its content, by the fact that this content consists of events that really happened (i.e., found events) rather than ones that are imagined (i.e., invented or constructed events).[18]

On the basis of the premise that reality "in itself" is formless and meaningless, White rejects this view and insists that making narrative sense of a segment of that reality must be a construction expressed in certain forms of language. It follows that representing a past reality through historical narrative is not an indifferent form that is, at best, an adequate mimesis of how the content offers itself but a form that constitutes content and is indistinguishable from it. Like the dichotomy, White's attempt to subvert it is twofold: past reality innately possesses neither meaning nor form; form constitutes content. This contention is central to White's theory, and it manifests itself in many of his arguments in varied ways; his first major work, *Metahistory*, might be seen as the most comprehensive instance of it.[19]

How a Chronicle Becomes a Narrative

According to Roger Ray, a prefatory note made by Gervase, a monk at Christ Church, Canterbury, in his *Cronica* (composed at the end of the twelfth century) discerns between *cronici* (chroniclers) and *historici* (historians). The mode of presentation of the historian, Gervase asserted, ought to be "full and elegant" whereas that of the chronicler should be "brief and simple." In Ray's understanding, Gervase made his remark to designate himself a chronicler and to censure other writers, notably John of Salisbury with his *Historia Pontificalis*, who had declared themselves part of the great tradition of Christian "brief and simple" chronicles but ended up writing "full and elegant" histories.[20]

This medieval distinction encapsulates the distinction drawn by conventional modern scholarship between the chronicle and the proper historical narrative. The chronicle is perceived as an imperfect and inferior history, as a narrative that failed to materialize. In Ottoman scholarship, it is reminiscent of Mustafa Ali's distinction between the inferior—in both literary and historiographical terms—Tarih-i Al-i Osman and the superior imperial histories by such writers as Hoca Sadüddin and Ali himself. It is important to point out that the "fullness" Gervase attributed to proper history (in contrast to the brevity of the chronicle) is in fact analogous to the conventional assumption that the narrative is a more comprehensive historical explanation than the chronicle. In this view, no matter how accurately and judiciously the chronicle presents a series of events, the narrative is superior in that it reveals the coherent story structure that the sequence inherently possessed.[21]

In passing, I would venture that, like so many other things, the chronicle/narrative itself is the protagonist of a modernist metanarrative of linear progress from A (traditional, hence inferior, historiography) through B ("classical" narrative historiography of the nineteenth century) to C ("scientific" historiography).[22]

White accepts the notion that the chronicle and the historical narrative are different, but he seeks the difference elsewhere. Among his various arguments concerning this question, two are particularly pertinent to the interpretation of Ottoman historiography proposed here. One is the way in which a list of events, in itself a chronicle in White's view, is transformed into a historical narrative. This transformation is facilitated by what White calls encodation, a process in which "the events, agents, and agencies represented in the chronicle must be encoded as story elements of specific story types."[23] When he explains how the reader grasps the content of the chronicle transformed into narrative form, it becomes clear why content and form are inseparable:

> On this level of encodation, the historical discourse directs the reader's attention to a secondary referent, different in kind from the events that make up the primary referent, namely, the plot structures of the various story types cultivated in a given culture. When the reader recognizes the story being told in a historical narrative as a specific kind of story—for example as an epic, romance, tragedy, comedy or farce—he can be said to have comprehended the meaning produced by the discourse. This comprehension is nothing other than the recognition of the form of the narrative.[24]

Further, White's comprehension of the historical narrative and his rejection of the content/form dichotomy engender the emphasis laid on the narrative discourse "as an apparatus for the production of meaning." White is adamant "that to change the form of the discourse might not be to change the information about its explicit referent, but it would certainly change the meaning produced by it."[25]

The other pertinent argument that, according to White, characterizes the narrative discourse is the emergence of alternative representations of the same event or series of events:

> In order to qualify as historical, an event must be susceptible to at least two narrations of its occurrence. Unless at least two versions of the same set of events can be imagined, there is no reason for the historian to take upon himself the authority of giving the true account of what really happened. The authority of the historical narrative is the authority of reality itself; the historical account endows this reality with form and thereby makes it desirable by the imposition upon its process of the formal coherency that only stories possess.[26]

A Critique of White's Modernist Bias

While the following critique has gradually emerged from a simultaneous reading of White's work and the Ottoman texts, I have found LaCapra's comments on White's theory helpful and illuminating.[27] It might be proposed that, taken as a whole, White's approach is premised on the fundamentally Hegelian presupposition that historical reality as it is experienced is chaotic, formless, and meaningless. What gives it form, structure, and meaning—in other words, what shapes it—is the historian's consciousness that reveals itself through language (the poetic faculty of a prose discourse, narrative strategies, rhetorical tropes, and so forth). My contention with White is focused on *the way in which historical reality is rendered accessible to the historian,* for his premise lumps together both historical reality as it was experienced *and* "its" pertinent record; obvious though it may seem, the latter is what the historian actually sees, not the former.

Put differently, while it might be valid to observe that the world of real events does not present itself as coherent stories, it would be as significant to bear in mind that between the historian and past reality there stands another (other than the historian's) textual tier: the historical record. As thus envisaged, historical reality *as it is accessible to the historian* is not necessarily chaotic and formless but rather language-processed; it is a story already told, prior to historians' application of their forms of language to it. I do not mean to suggest, of course, that White fails to realize that experienced reality and the texts and documents seen by historians are not coterminous. However, the fact that he reads the works of modern historians within a framework that identifies poetic subtexts, and ultimately exposes power, authority, and prevailing moralities, but in effect denies the same framework to the record of the past is tantamount to the inclusion of that record in his premise of a chaotic reality. This has serious implications for his overall theory.

One is that it might be seen as another instance of the crude dichotomy between "modern" and "premodern" or "traditional" in modernization theory, with historiography as the subject matter rather than society, polity, and economy. It implies that conveying authority through narrative historiography is exclusively a modern phenomenon. To be consciously crude, it implies that the study of historiography is consonant with the view that "traditional" societies were less sophisticated than their modern successors; that they were more virginal and therefore more susceptible to being represented by others.

The other implication is, oddly enough, that White's ascription of the manipulation of the past as it occurred solely to *modern* historiography brings us back to the empiricist concept of history, away from which he himself seeks to draw historical scholarship. For although arrived at via completely different avenues, the final analysis as regards the tier of texts we call the historical record is similar: whether the historical record is deemed formless (White) or transparent (empiricist history), the underlying implication remains that it simply corresponds to or reflects reality as it occurred. The impression with which one is left is that somewhere "underneath" the layers of modern linguistic manipulation the *wie es eigentlich gewesen ist*—or the real Orient for that matter—may be found.

On the whole, I find White's critical theory of modern European historiography valuable and stimulating; most important, I find it—cautiously and with necessary adaptations—applicable. However, the combination of a White-inspired reading of the Ottoman texts and the concomitant critique has had a dialectical yield. Equipped with White's theory of historiography, my analysis of a portion of the historical record, a corpus of Ottoman histories, questions the validity of White's assumption that historical reality along with the historical record is chaotic and formless. What this analysis illustrates is precisely the extent to which that portion of the historical record is not formless but already language-processed—a variety of stories already told and of meanings already produced.

The dialectical approach to White's theory—that is, criticizing his exclusive focus on modern historical consciousness and at the same time using his theory to realize that the formless reality of the past has already been ordered by people from the past—may fulfill the promise of the linguistic turn that is mentioned in the introduction to this chapter. This is not meant to suggest that if we cannot attain an objective reconstruction of the past as it happened, we should be comforted by the prospect of reaching an ultimate and objective reconstruction of the texts that represent that past. It is rather suggested, especially in the context of Ottoman scholarship, that the linguistic turn may yield an interpretive process in which the texts of the past and their authors are approached more as interlocutors than as informants. The linguistic turn may result, to borrow Gadamer's term, in an engaged "fusion of horizons."

SPEECH, WRITING, AND THE PROBLEM OF THE AUTHOR'S INTENTIONS

In a reply to Rhoads Murphey's severely critical review article[28] on his otherwise acclaimed book, Cornell Fleischer marvels at what he read:

> It was a curious experience to read Rhoads Murphey's observations on [Fleischer's book]. It is sobering for a writer to recognize that his work, however carefully crafted, might yield an understanding completely at odds with his intention. I was frankly puzzled to find summarized . . . a reading of this particular work of history so variant that I could recognize neither the book nor its author.[29]

The dispute between Murphey and Fleischer is a striking illustration of the problem of the author's intention and how it is interpreted by the reader. Furthermore, it is hard to think of a greater contextual proximity than that shared by the two disputants in time, place, culture, and scholarly expertise. Yet the author is adamant that his intention was misinterpreted by one of his most qualified readers. The problem is of course compounded when the text in question is one that came down to us from the past, when there exists a contextual distance between the text's author and the reader, when that author is safely dead and alas unable to publish a comment on a reader's (mis)interpretation.

The debate over authorial intentions may be found in—among other sites—an intense exchange that appeared a decade ago in the "Forum" section of the *American Historical Review*. Its participants, David Harlan and David Hollinger, may be seen as representatives of two contesting approaches to intellectual history and the interpretation of texts: one is contextualist (Hollinger) and the other poststructuralist (Harlan).[30] This debate ought to be understood in conjunction with the reinstatement of the text to a central position in historical scholarship and the resurgence of intellectual history. This field, which once seemed doomed to oblivion by the domination of social history, was redeemed by the influential works of

J. G. A. Pocock and Quentin Skinner, two of the most prominent exponents of what came to be known as the Cambridge Group[31]. Across the Channel another form of writing the history of intellectuals and culture was developed by a generation of *Annales* historians best represented by Roger Chartier.[32] To focus the discussion concretely on authorial intentions, I confine it to Skinner and his poststructuralist critics.

The "new orthodoxy" Skinner introduced to intellectual history and political theory emanated from his devastating criticism of the "old history of ideas." Skinner denounced that school as ahistorical because of its concept of ideas as independent entities, floating "in the air" from Rousseau to Stalin and from Herder to Hitler, detached from the historical contexts in which they were expressed. He offered invaluable insights on the flaws of the ways that tradition read texts, and he fundamentally doubted whether ideas were at all adequate units of interpretation.[33] His alternative, amply exemplified in his work, insists that intellectual history should be studied *in context* and that the most important task of the intellectual historian is the recovery of primary authorial intentions: "In order to recover such intentions, it is essential to surround the given text with an appropriate *context* of assumptions and conventions from which the author's exact intended meaning can then be decoded."[34]

It ought to be clarified that by *context* Skinner means neither the social, economic, and political circumstances that surrounded the site of the text's production—though these are not immaterial—nor a monocausal relationship between the social and ideational or intellectual. Rather, by context as a central ingredient of the interpretive process, Skinner has in mind the cultural, literary, and semiotic conventions—what others might call the discursive boundaries—within which a text was uttered.

Before long Skinner's approach was challenged, for, as Harlan, a vehement critic of it, charged, "Orthodoxies generate heretics." Emanating from the poststructuralists, the challenge has been fundamental. First, if the unity of the sign is broken and language is a closed system that bears no relation to extrinsic referents—that is, it is intertextual rather than intersubjective—then by extension there is no context, only texts pointing to other texts ad infinitum (or, according to personal inclination, ad nauseam). Second, this intertextuality rewriting the original author's intentions and thereby rendering them unrecoverable means, to use Roland Barthes's dictum, "the death of the author." With this "death," primary authorial intentions and the original contextual meaning vanish too.[35]

The poststructuralists also direct their criticism of Skinner to his own language paradigm: speech act theory.[36] Skinner espouses speech act theory for good reasons from his vantage point. First, speech act theory is a comprehensive paradigm of language use: that is, it conceives of both spoken and (by extension) written utterances as speech acts. Second, it assumes that a speech act is a concrete and intended social situation in which the speaker/writer seeks to convey meaning to an audience. As thus envisaged, language regains its referential quality, thereby rendering recoverable and relevant both the context and the author's intended meaning. To use Harlan's sarcastic comment, we can read "a historical text and peer through its language as if staring through a window, discovering all sorts of things about the author and the world in which the author lived, almost as if we had become one of God's spies."[37]

The poststructuralists reject this solution. They concede that speech acts are intended social situations that occur in a discernible context, but only as far as spoken utterances are concerned. In other words, they draw a dichotomy between the contextual speaker-hearers relationship and the textual writer-readers relationship. This, Harlan contends, acutely undermines Skinner's implicit concept of writing as "a sort of frozen speech."[38]

One of the clearest and most stimulating attempts to establish the relationship between speech and writing, and its bearing on authorial intentions, was made by Paul Ricoeur, a hermeneutic philosopher.[39] Following his definition of the written text, Ricoeur proceeds with a statement that brings to the fore the problem of authorial intentions:

> It does not suffice to say that reading is a dialogue with the author through his work, for the relation of the reader to the book is of a completely different nature. . . . The writer does not respond to the reader. Rather, the book divides the act of writing and the act of reading into two sides, between which there is no communication. The reader is absent from the act of writing; the writer is absent from the act of reading. The text thus produces a double eclipse of the reader and the writer. It thereby replaces the relation of dialogue, which directly connects the voice of one to the hearing of the other. . . . This emancipation of writing. . . is the birth of the text.[40]

Following this line of argument, the referential quality of language, hence also authorial intentions, is lost when writing comes *instead* of speech. In speech, Ricoeur maintains, language compensates for "the separation of sign from things" and retains its referential disposition thanks to the fact that "the interlocutors are present . . . to one another" and that they and "the instance of discourse itself" are surrounded by the same context. Aided in addition by such tools as "demonstratives, adverbs of time and place, personal pronouns, [and] verbal tenses, ... the movement of reference towards the act of showing" is facilitated. The result is that "the *ideal* sense of what is said turns towards the *real* reference, towards that 'about which' we speak."[41]

The referential process that enables the speakers unequivocally to convey their intentions is abruptly altered "when the text takes the place of speech. The movement of reference towards the act of showing is intercepted, at the same time as dialogue is interrupted by the text" (I shall shortly consider the significance Ricoeur himself ascribes to *intercepted* rather than *suppressed*). Because of this temporary deferral, the text is left "outside or without a world" and "is free to enter into relation with all the other texts which come to take the place of the circumstantial reality referred to by living speech." This engenders what Ricoeur terms "the quasi-world of texts or *literature*."[42]

At this juncture Ricoeur's postulates appear to be quite congruent with Harlan's poststructuralist pronouncements: writing is purely intertextual, the author is dead, and meaning is endlessly deferred, to use the more common catchphrases. But it is precisely here that his aforementioned emphasis, that meaning is "intercepted" rather than "suppressed," becomes acute. Following this emphasis Ricoeur anticipates his position very clearly:

> [I]t is in this respect that I shall distance myself from what may be called henceforth the ideology of the absolute text. On the basis of the sound remarks which we have just made, this ideology proceeds ... through a course that is ultimately superstitious. As we shall see, the text is not without reference; the task of reading, *qua* interpretation, will be precisely to fulfill the reference.[43]

The climax of Ricoeur's essay is the way he restores the meaning and reference of the text promised above. He sees the reading of a text as a continuum, what he calls a "hermeneutic arc," that comprises two steps. The first, explanation, is in fact a structuralist analysis in which the meaning and reference of a text remain in suspense (Ricoeur has interesting things to say on the nature of the structuralist analysis, but they do not concern the present discussion). That the suspense is lifted and meaning and reference are restored is owed to the second, and in Ricoeur's view ultimate, step of reading: interpretation. Interpretation achieves "the recovery of meaning" because it is essentially the investment of the readers and their world in the text.[44]

It might be appropriate to conclude with Ricoeur's final and refined definition of what reading a text is:

> [T]o explain is to bring out the structure, that is, the internal relations of dependence which constitute the statics of the text; to interpret is to follow the path of thought opened up by the text, to place oneself *en route* towards the *orient* of the text. We are invited by this remark to correct our initial concept of interpretation and to search—beyond a subjective process of interpretation *on* the text—for an objective process of interpretation which would be the act *of* the text.[45]

CONCLUSION
The Use of White's Theory

At a general level, the proposition to interpret the corpus of historical representations of the Haile-i Osmaniye, up to the point where it was sealed as the state narrative in Naima's history,[46] as a narrative discourse follows both Foucault and, more closely, White. The conclusion from my critique of what I think is in effect White's modernist bias is that his theory may be applied to yield fresh interpretations of the historical record. The dialectical state of mind of being inspired by and critical of White's theory might extricate it from a rather stultifying predicament, whereby all it ends up suggesting is that modern historians tell stories rather than "do science." This theory might thus become more pertinent to historians who actually "do history" and use source material, rather than mainly to those who "do" methodological pontification.

Also significant for the general approach of this study is White's attempt to undermine Karl Popper's dichotomy between "proper" history and "historicism," or between history and the philosophy of history.[47] This manifests itself in two ways. One is the mere choice of the Tarih-i Al-i Osman works, so much abused as unstructured sites of information of varying degrees of accuracy, and the view that they contain no less "preconceived ideas" (to use Popper's term) than "philosophies of history" and other, more elevated, relatives. The other is the belief that a historiographical study should reflect not only thoughts about history but also—perhaps mainly—the ways in which it was actually written. This belief seems to be shared by scholars of medieval and early modern European historiography.[48] In this respect the systematic philosophical treatises on history are in a way misleading, for what such writers as Ibn Khaldun, Mustafa Ali, and Naima had to say about history and how it ought to be written often did not coincide with how they themselves practiced it.

The fundamental limitation that determines the use of White's theory is the near-absence of systematic studies on Ottoman theory and practice

An Interpretive Framework / 65

of poetics and rhetoric, especially in prose writing. There is a substantive infrastructure of literary theory and tradition that makes it possible for White's analysis to be precise and even mechanical (see especially the structural grid in *Metahistory*). Although a tentative and preliminary attempt suggesting a few themes for future research on the poetics of Ottoman historiography is offered in the Epilogue, the absence of an equivalent infrastructure for Ottoman literature imposes an application of White's theory that is more loose and less committed to precise literary forms.

More specifically and even technically, White's theory of the narrative guides my reading in the following ways.

First, I adopt the notion of the content/form unity, and the fact that form becomes a sort of secondary referent, but I deploy it differently. For the reason stated above, I omit White's emphasis on story types and by *form* refer rather loosely to any way of arranging a group of facts that is meaningful because the facts are arranged in this particular way instead of another, and because this particular way is constituted by the text rather than being innately found in the facts themselves.

Second, White's argument that chronology is a code shared by the chronicle and the narrative but that the latter employs other codes that are important for the ways meaning is produced has drawn my attention to such codes in the Ottoman texts. Among these, emphasis is laid upon two codes: digressions from the chronological account and the presentation of events in an order that does not adhere to their chronology.

Third, the notion that the very formation of narrative discourse means that at least two ways of representing the same event emerge is highly pronounced in my reading, as is the view that the narrative discourse is a pivotal site for the production of meaning. Moreover, whereas for White it suffices if the alternative representation opened up by the narrative discourse can be imagined, in my constant, mostly diachronic, comparative reading the alternatives actually exist within the discourse.

Finally, to elaborate the previous point, I specifically look for the production of meaning temporally and spatially. Regarding time, a typical series of guiding questions might be the following: If fact X occurred *before* fact Y (according to the chronology proposed by the text in question), why is X presented in the narrative *after* Y? Is there within the discourse another text that conforms to the same chronology but presents X and Y in a different order? Does this difference yield an alternative meaning, and, at the same time, does it highlight the meaning produced by the first presentation? As for the production of meaning through space, I seek the actual eyes perspective and location from which an event, or episode within it, is seen by the narrator. This can be better clarified by borrowing vocabulary from the domain of filmmaking. Many of the scenes represented in the historical corpus offer more than one location where the director's seat and lead camera may be poised and the "take" may be shot. Once the precise location of a given narrator's seat and camera is identified with regard to a specific scene, the guiding questions that follow are in principle similar to those of the time dimension. Does this location serve to convey meaning? Is there in the discourse another narrator the location of whose seat and camera is different? Does this convey an alternative meaning, and, at the same time, does it highlight the meaning conveyed by the location of the first narrator's seat?

The Problem of the Author's Intentions: A Proposal

Together with the adaptation and critique of White's theory presented above, the proposal set forth below constitutes my interpretive framework. Like my engagement with White's theory, my attitude to the debate on authorial intentions is dialectical: I am both inspired by and critical of certain facets of this debate, and I focus my remarks on Ricoeur's views.

It is evident that Harlan's rejection of the Skinnerian attempt to interpret the text as a contextual phenomenon draws heavily on Ricoeur's dichotomous separation between speech and writing. I think that while this separation is theoretically sound, it might be found severely wanting in terms of historicity. The combined content-and-form of Ricoeur's argument, in which he presents "the double eclipse" in the relations between writing and reading, which then underpins his speech/writing dichotomy, looks so impregnable because it is sustained only theoretically. However, a dose of Skinnerian historicity, which would be concerned with spatially and temporally concrete texts and audiences, would inevitably problematize Ricoeur's convenient dichotomy, in the way that a historically minded investigation always dilutes the clarity of theoretical purity.

The proposal I wish to submit assumes that a neatly linear narrative that leads from anterior speech to posterior writing may not exist and that there may exist texts that are both written and said, both heard and read. This proposal is focused on what might be termed the urtext of Ottoman historiography of the Haile-i Osmaniye: the representation of this series of events by Tuği Çelebi. Tuği's text, *Tarih-i Tuği*, was exclusively dedicated to the Haile-i Osmaniye and was the first comprehensive and detailed account of it. As is thoroughly shown in Part II, the whole historiographical discourse diachronically evolved out of and in reference to Tuği's account. The state narrative of the Haile-i Osmaniye may be seen as the final stage of the cumulative—though clearly not linear—rereading and rewriting of Tuği's representation.

What I propose is to read Tuği's text twice. But my own "hermeneutic arc," unlike Ricoeur's, is not a structural explanation of the text (first reading) and its referential interpretation (second reading). Rather, I wish to read Tuği's text, first, literally as a speech situation (i.e., as an oral address) and, second, as a writing situation. I shall explain what makes this reading possible and how it is carried out and then examine how it faces the theoretical literature that informs it.

It is well known that in "the age of manuscripts" and when the prevalence of literacy was limited—perhaps in other circumstances too—the act of reading aloud was a major sociocultural feature. Ottoman scholars have been aware of this important phenomenon. Halil Inalcik notes that such histories as Aşık Paşazade's (discussed in Chapter 2) in the second half of the fifteenth century "were designed to be read and listened to by groups during the military campaigns, in *boza*-houses [anachronistically, pubs and bars] or in other meeting places."[49] In his insightful study on the Arabic historiography of Ottoman Egypt in the seventeenth and eighteenth centuries, P. M. Holt identifies a similar characteristic and highlights a certain type of texts in particular, what he calls "popular chronicles." He argues that they were composed to attain the effectiveness of the oral address.[50]

In a similar vein, my first reading of Tuği's work interprets it as an address to gatherings of kul, who in this context were the sipahis and janissaries at the capital and their comrades throughout the Anatolian provinces.[51] Envisaged as a contextual and intended instance of discourse, I seek the meaning Tuği's address endeavored to convey to its audience. I contend that the purpose of Tuği's text as speech was not only to entertain but also to establish a narrative of the Haile-i Osmaniye that would depict the kul favorably, justify the role they had played in the event, and render intolerable what was consequently inflicted upon them in Anatolia, especially in Erzurum and its vicinity.

My second reading of Tuği's text interprets it as an instance of writing. This reading is fascinating because of, and is facilitated by, the fact that his work, having been the first comprehensive representation of this traumatic sequence of events, was abundantly and comprehensively employed by some of the most important historians of the seventeenth century. What these historians did with Tuği's text—as readers and writers rather than hearers—is the chief concern of the second reading. From a theoretical perspective we have here readers who did not participate in the meaningful speech situation in the context of which Tuği's account had initially been disseminated; at the same time, since these historians were not only readers but also writers, we may look at their own texts as recordings of their reading experience of Tuği's work, now seen as a written artifact.

The main source of tension between my proposal, which owing to its insistence on context and authorial intentions is consciously Skinnerian, and part of the theory that informs it (Ricoeur) lies in the substantial remoteness between myself and Tuği's text as speech. Tuği's text may be an oral address, it may be charged, but it came down to me as a purely written text. The response below, it should be stated, does not completely harmonize this tension, and in any event a perfect harmony is not necessarily sought.

Like the texts that Inalcik and Holt read, Tuği's is not the sort of text Ricoeur has in mind. In fact, herein may lie the crucial difference between one argument that is driven by theoretical purity and another that is guided by historicity. The texts whose explanation and interpretation Ricoeur seeks are without history; they constitute hypothetical hermeneutic relationships that are imposed on a heuristic narrative, namely the passage from a relation of speaking-hearing to a writing-reading one. Ricoeur refers to something that could have been said but was fixed in writing precisely because it was not said. By contrast, since my concern is with the history of the production and dissemination of an actual text, that text could be both said *and* written, and the precise chronology of which came first—the speaking or the writing—matters little.

For the charge that Tuği's text still came down to me as a written artifact I have no theoretical solution. But if I am correct that the history of Tuği's text contains a meaningful speech component, then while not wishing to embark on a futile, rather Romantic attempt at re-experiencing the speech situation, I see no harm in evoking, in a tempered and measured way, Vico's fantasia. At this juncture, it would seem, both readers and writer could do with allegedly real events and how they are told.

PART II

Historiography

4. Tuği's Representation of the Haile-i Osmaniye

The Perspective of the Imperial Army

This chapter interprets Tuği's representation of the Haile-i Osmaniye as an instance of speech and thereby carries out the first part of the double reading of this text proposed in Chapter 3. In conjunction with the problem of authorial intentions and the speech/writing debate, I suggested interpreting Tuği's text first in its own context as an oral address to the imperial troops in the capital and then as a written artifact that was read and reworked by several Ottoman historians. It should be clarified that I am not concerned with the precise order in which Tuği's text was conceived. Whether it was orally delivered first and then written, written first and then orally delivered, or written and orally delivered more or less simultaneously, I am just convinced that the text was orally delivered and that this is a pertinent context for its interpretation. Tuği's history is significant on two accounts. First, as an independent text, it was the first known attempt of an Ottoman to deal with this traumatic episode in the empire's history. Second, through its various reappearances in later seventeenth-century Tarih-i Al-i Osman works, and eventually in Naima's history, Tuği's work became a pivotal component of the official Ottoman narrative of the Haile-i Osmaniye. It must be registered at this initial stage that however much later Ottoman historians might reinterpret Tuği's text and however tortuous its path to Naima's history was, it nonetheless remained the foundational text of the state narrative.

Tuği's work, unlike the other works studied here, should not be classified as a Tarih-i Al-i Osman work, for that sort of historiography was spatially and temporally a more comprehensive account of the state and dynasty. For want of a better term, the proper category to which Tuği's work belonged was "special event" histories. These were historical works that were confined to an event such as a campaign and/or conquest, or a single reign (the *gazaname* (book of gaza), *fethname* (book of conquest), and *Selimname* or *Süleymanname* (book of Selim or Süleyman; see Chapter 2). The richness of illustrative material (e.g., the digressions from the chronological account, which will be discussed in detail in this chapter) is another characteristic Tuği's work has in common with the "special event" histories. This can be gauged from an impressionistic comparison between the examination of Tuği's work presented here and Christine Woodhead's study of Ta'likizade's history of the Ottoman campaign into Hungary (1593–94).[1]

Since scanty attention has been paid to Tuği's text, I first briefly lay the Quellenkritik foundations, then explain the choice of the particular manuscript I mainly work with, and finally proceed with the interpretation.

EXCURSUS ON A SOURCE

Two scholars have thus far edited and published extant manuscripts of Tuği's text:[2] Midhat Sertoğlu and Fahir İz.[3] Before them, Tuği's account had attracted the interest of several French writers in the seventeenth and eighteenth centuries, and it was later also noticed by German and English Orientalists of the nineteenth-century tradition. From this accumulation of research it is impossible conclusively to identify the original manuscript. İz, who probably looked at more manuscripts of Tuği's work than any other scholar, reiterates this.[4] But however important it might be to identify the original manuscript, one may ask whether and with what purpose in mind originality ought to take precedence over other criteria. To relate this to the proposed double reading of Tugi's text, I am suggesting that when this text is read in itself and as an instance of speech, it is crucial to try to identify the manuscript that represents the version that was orally delivered, assuming that this version might be the original one. However, when the purpose is to interpret a whole discourse that evolved diachronically, then what becomes crucial is to identify the manuscript that was most pertinent to the discourse of which it was part—that is, the version that the later Ottoman historians employed.

On the basis of the available evidence I tried to show elsewhere that MS Flügel 1044, at the Austrian National Library in Vienna, best meets both criteria.[5] Though arguments concerning the identification of this manuscript (or an identical rendition) as the one that was orally delivered are circumstantial, it is more directly certain that when Hasanbeyzade, Peçevi, Katip Çelebi, and Naima referred to and employed Tuği's work, the copy they saw was MS Flügel 1044 or an identical rendition.⁶ At the basic textual level, the usefulness of the latter criterion can be illustrated by two notable examples. One is that several scholars (Sertoğlu and İz among them) observe that Katip Çelebi was the first historian who noticed Tuği's text and made use of it. The use of MS Flügel 1044 as part of the discourse reveals that, in fact, Hasanbeyzade rather than Katip Çelebi was the first historian who used Tuği's work. That he did so without any reference or acknowledgment is precisely what renders the criterion adopted here so advantageous. The other example of the use of MS Flügel 1044 as part of the discourse reveals a basic mistake made by Flügel himself in his catalogue of the Turkish manuscripts at the Austrian National Library.⁷ Flügel relates, with regard to the first version of Hasanbeyzade's history, that the author, by his own testimony, carried out the writing of this work between 18 May 1622 and 21 March 1623 (7 Receb 1031 and 19 Cemazi'levvel 1031). Flügel is wrong on two counts. First, the above dates originally appeared in the epilogue of Tuği's MS Flügel 1044, and Hasanbeyzade simply copied them. Second, Flügel misreads the text, for what Tuği says is that *the events that had begun to unfold from 18 May 1622 were written down by 21 March 1623.*⁸

TUĞI'S ACCOUNT AS AN ORAL ADDRESS

My interpretation of Tuği's representation of the Haile-i Osmaniye is as follows:

1. It can also be seen as the performance of an actual speech act, regardless of whether it was inscribed before or after having been orally delivered.

2. Even when envisaged as an oral address, Tuği's text is not a "chronicle," as conventional Middle Eastern scholarship would have it, but a historical narrative that, generally, falls within the concept of narrative charted in Chapter 3 and, specifically, was a contextual site that conveyed meaningful political and cultural messages. The gist of this meaning was the reassertion of the identity and interests of the kul.

3. The audience to whom the meaning of Tuği's address was directed were the kul. To clarify possible confusion, within Tuği's text the term *kul* is interchangeable with the janissaries and imperial cavalry *(sipahis)* in the capital.

4. The text as speech can be characterized as kul-centric not only because the kul were the target audience but even more because the actual perspective from which almost everything was narrated was the perspective of the kul.

5. The contextual purpose of the meaning conveyed by Tuği's text as speech was to equip the kul with a reassuring version of the role they had played in the Haile-i Osmaniye. The crux of this version was, first, that the kul were not the perpetrators of Sultan Osman's killing and should not bear its consequences, and, second, that their actions, which eventually led to the deposition of Osman II and the re-enthronement of Mustafa I, were at least justifiable, if not praiseworthy. This was so not only because the implementation of Sultan Osman's plan meant that the existing body of kul would perish but also, more important, because the future of the Ottoman state "as we know it" was at stake.

6. Two pertinent contexts surrounded both speaker and hearers. First, they shared the a priori assumption that the view that Sultan Osman's venture was disastrous and had to be prevented, and that Sultan Osman himself was a bad ruler whose reign had been rejected by both God and subjects, was the objectively true state of affairs and not the result of perspectival logic. Second, the sense of urgency that might prompt both Tuği and the kul to present a favorable representation of their part in the Haile-i Osmaniye, such as would convince other groups in the Ottoman polity, was the persecution of the kul in central and eastern Anatolia as part of the alleged rebellion of the governor of Erzurum, Abaza Mehmed Pasha.

THE TRACES OF ORALITY IN A WRITTEN TEXT

Tuği's text employed, within its prose, at least one code in addition to the chronological account, and it contained sufficient indications to suggest that it was also an oral address. There are two basic types of material in Tuği's history: prose and poetry. I concentrate on the prose, but it should be stressed that the poetry is by no means negligible, and some of it will be treated at a later stage. It is convenient to begin with a similar impression by other scholars. İz, who read another extant manuscript of Tuği's work (the one at Dresden), bases his conclusion that this text was read in gatherings on notes on the margins of the manuscript he studied and on a comparison to other, nonhistorical texts.⁹ P. M. Holt, in his masterful study of Arabic historiography in Ottoman Egypt in the seventeenth and eighteenth centuries, explains and amply exemplifies the notion of oral address with respect to what he calls the "popular chronicles" (as distinguished from the "literary chronicles").¹⁰

Tuği's account conforms to Holt's description of the popular historical texts. His style is not too high and rather simple. One wonders, however, whether this stylistic choice stemmed from his scant literary education, or from the fact that he had a specific audience in mind. In fact, the poetry scattered throughout Tuği's work and several occasions on which a narrator's voice appears indicate that he was also capable of displaying higher and more literary styles and that he was knowledgeable in pre-Islamic and early Islamic history.¹¹ It therefore seems that Tuği might have received more literary education than the colloquial style, which dominates most of his work, would suggest.

Another aspect that Tuği's history has in common with Holt's "popular chronicles" is the excessive fondness of presenting the "authentic voice" of the actors, whether in monologues or dialogues. Wherever Tuği could, he let his actors "speak for themselves." The source of my assumption about the "allegedness" of these voices—that is, their source being an oral "received wisdom"—and about their use as a narrator's device resembles Holt's. In both cases the same voice may appear in different histories, conveying the same content but phrased differently. Since the seventeenth-century Tarih-i Al-i Osman works will be discussed at a later stage, suffice it to point out here that their authors adopted the spirit of the voices Tuği had presented. However, they phrased them differently.

There is a striking example of this aspect of orality in the extant manuscripts of Tuği's work. Formulations of what is reportedly one and the same voice vary from one extant manuscript to another. Moreover, what may vary are not only speeches of actors but also written documents. The wordings of a fetva issued by the sheyhülislam that tried to dissuade Sultan Osman from carrying out his plan by preventing his declared pilgrimage to Mecca are quite remarkable. In the Dresden manuscript of Tuği's work that İz published, the fetva reads: "It is not permitted for monarchs to go to the Ka'be [i.e., to perform the hajj]. It is better for them to attend justly to the affairs of [their] subjects."¹² The wording of the same fetva in MS Flügel 1044 is not only different but also perplexingly categorical: "The padishah's going to the Ka'be is not obligatory *(Padişahın Ka'beye gitmesi caiz değildir)*."¹³ Clearly, although Tuği usually tells that the kul obtained a copy of this or that fetva, what we have is circulating oral knowledge of, first, the alleged issuance of fetvas and, second, their putative content.

Finally, as is the case with the texts Holt examined, it seems that Tuği's text was meant to be read aloud to gatherings of troops. In Tuği's case, however, the purpose was not only to entertain but, perhaps more important, to supply them with a reassuring version of events for which, according to this version, they unjustly suffered the consequences in the Anatolian provinces. In addition to the style and the abundant use of the alleged voices of the actors, there are two more direct indications for this impression. One is that Tuği constantly inserts passages that seem intended to address a listening audience and stimulate its immediate reaction. An illustration of this is Tuği's insertion after the kul find Sultan Mustafa's place of confinement in the palace and break their way in through the dome of the chamber in which *Osmanlı* males were detained *(kafes)*. The narrator says to the audience: "Truly, being fair, wouldn't you say 'well done' to the heroes who on that day hacked through the roof of such a big dome, tied themselves with ropes, and descended toward Sultan Mustafa?"[14]

The other indication is the regularity with which Tuği uses two particular phrases, thereby effectively creating a formula. The constant and laborious repetition of this formula strongly suggests that the text was an oral address.[15] Within the prose part of Tuği's history there are, again, two main types of codes: one, the main theme, is Tuği's presentation of what happened chronologically; the other is digressions, mostly in time, from the main theme (the chronological account). I shall elaborate shortly on the important role of the digressions in producing the meaning of Tuği's work, but concerning the communication between the speaker and his audience the point is that Tuği often alerts his addressees that he is about to digress from the main theme, sometimes explaining why, and almost invariably notifies them that he is about to resume the chronological account. He does this by employing one phrase before a digression and another at its end; and by repeating these two phrases, particularly the latter, he produces a pattern, or a formula, for his audience that marks the boundaries of each digression.

Tuği precedes many of his digressions with the phrase "Let [the matter in question] be briefly explained" *(ala sebilülicmal beyan olunsun)*.[16] And he inserts "Let us return to our talk" *(biz yine sözümüze gelelim)* between almost every ending of a digression and the return to the chronological presentation.[17] This clear marking of the digressions' boundaries seems particularly important when the addressees are hearers rather than readers, for if the former "lose" the narrator, they do not possess a text to "find" him again.

IN THE EYES OF THE BEHOLDER

Having assessed the type of communication between Tuği and his audience and shown that chronology is but one code in his work, I shall now dwell on what I believe to be the location of the essential meaning produced by Tuği's text: its latent level.[18] The most fundamental latent characteristic, taken misleadingly for granted on the manifest level, of Tuği's representation of the Haile-i Osmaniye was the actual viewpoint from which this event was narrated. This was the viewpoint of those whom Tuği interchangeably alludes to as the kul, the janissaries and sipahis, the Army of Islam, and simply the troops. This point can be better clarified if we borrow a metaphor from the domain of filmmaking. Many of the scenes in the Haile-i Osmaniye offer more than one spot where the director's seat and lead camera could be placed and from which the "take" could be shot. Yet under Tuği's direction, almost the entire event is "filmed" with the lead camera and director's seat behind or among the kul. Two examples may illustrate the significance of this choice (a third and highly significant example will be discussed in the Chapter 8).

The first example is the description of the kul's surge into the Topkapı Palace. Initially they go there to see that their demands are satisfied, but, by a coincidence, they find Sultan Mustafa there, so they pull him out of the kafes and reinstall him as the new padishah.[19] The Topkapı was structured as a series of courts separated from each other by gates: the nearer to the outside a court was, the more public—and hence more accessible—the function it had. By this logic, the most inner and intimate court was precisely that where the kafes was located—the Harem-i Has or Harem-i Hümayun (the private or imperial harem).[20] This structure offered two alternatives: either to accompany the kul's centripetal movement from the outer wall of the palace toward the harem, where they eventually found Sultan Mustafa, or to describe this movement as it was seen and felt by those located deep within the palace, such as Sultan Osman or the chief black eunuch.

Tuği consistently opts for the first alternative. His camera—except for one short pause to depict Sultan Osman's reaction[21]—constantly follows the kul from their assembly at the janissaries' barracks, their march to the palace, and their hesitant halts before they pass through each of the three gates, up to the point when they find the dome of the kafes and pierce a hole through it. At that point Tuği has an even more obvious choice, for as soon as the hole is pierced there emerges yet another option—to describe the kul as they are seen from below, by Sultan Mustafa. But Tuği remains loyal to the kul's angle and portrays Sultan Mustafa as *they* see him from above, reading the Kuran while two harem maids were at his feet.[22]

The second example, even more suggestive, is one of the scenes in the third day of the event's dramatic eruption (Friday, 20 May 1622), when both sultans—Mustafa I and Osman II—find themselves at Orta Cami (the janissaries' mosque at their barracks), guarded by a few officers, together with Mustafa's mother (the *valide sultan*) and the new Grand Vezir Davud Pasha, while the kul assemble outside the mosque awaiting further developments. Sultan Mustafa, it may be recalled, was brought to the mosque on the previous evening, when the kul suspected that if they placed him at the Old Palace Sultan Osman would seize him. As for Sultan Osman himself, he is carried off to Orta Cami that morning by the kul, who find him at the residence of the janissary chief *(Ağa Kapısı)*, after they spoil his last-resort plan to win them over and kill his remaining confidants.[23]

The reason why the scene at Orta Cami is so suggestive of the latent meaning produced by perspective from which things are narrated is that we have another account—Ibrahim Peçevi's—whose lead camera is positioned elsewhere. Whereas in the first example the alternative representation is something that can be imagined, here the alternative representation actually exists. The uniqueness of Peçevi's account of the Haile-i Osmaniye is his remoteness from the chain of transmission of seventeenth-century Tarih-i Al-i Osman works. Peçevi culls his information from a different source, so he takes the "shot" from a different angle. Peçevi's source, as he himself discloses, is Sıdkı Çelebi, the secretary of Ohrili Hüseyin Pasha, whom Sultan Osman reappointed as grand vezir once the kul found Sultan Mustafa, and whom the kul later killed. Sıdkı Çelebi, whose account is reportedly reproduced verbatim by Peçevi, followed his master in company with Sultan Osman when the latter went to the residence of the janissary chief. When the kul seized Sultan Osman and took him to Orta Cami, Sıdkı Çelebi sought refuge in that residence. Later, he heard what had happened when the two padishahs were at Orta Cami from a janissary officer whom he had known and who was present there—Kara Mizak.[24]

We come to the moment when the kul ask to get a glimpse of Sultan Mustafa, who responds and is enthusiastically cheered. In Tuği's text, consistent with its angle, the camera is poised behind or among the kul: "The blessed padishah accepted the requests of his kul and showed his graceful face through the window of the mosque. The Army of Islam called out the *tekbir* [i.e., "God is Greatest"] and cheered Sultan Mustafa."[25] Peçevi's camera, from Kara Mizak's perspective, is poised at the opposite end— within the mosque. It yields a diametrically opposed meaning:

> At this point [after the kul had requested to see Sultan Mustafa] his mother seated Sultan Mustafa by the *mihrab* [a niche indicating the direction of Mecca]; she made his [Sultan Mustafa's] attendant [lit. *daye*—a wet nurse] sit alongside him, and hold his hands. From time to time, when the noise of the people outside grew, Sultan Mustafa slipped out of his attendant's hand, grabbed the grille of the window of the mosque and tried to look outside. Every time he did this, his mother came alongside him, calling "my lion, my panther;" with great care and with his attendant's aid, she pulled his fingers away from the grille of the window, brought him again to the *mihrab* and seated him there. This incident recurred many times.[26]

The contradictory meaning produced by each of the narration angles is obvious. Through Tuği's camera we see a sovereign who responds to the request of his loyal troops, who correspondingly acknowledge his gesture. Through Peçevi's we see a feeble and pathetic person. His picture is colored with sarcasm when the queen mother, while imposing her will upon him as if he were an infant, calls him "my lion, my panther" *(arslanım, kaplanım)*. Finally, whereas in Tuği's account Sultan Mustafa has two harem maids *(cariyeler)* with him, quite normal for a sultan, according to Peçevi's he is held by a *daye*, or wet nurse.

DEFENSIVE ESPRIT DE CORPS

The first stage of Tuği's defense of the kul—showing that they did not kill Sultan Osman—is, in comparison to the next stage, straightforward, possibly because the accusation was concrete. The basic layer of this defense is deployed through the chronological part of the narrative: that is, telling "things as they happened." Two "facts" in Tuği's chronology constitute the foundation for his claim on the kul's behalf. One emphasizes their concern for Sultan Osman's safety; the other asserts that they simply were not present at Yedikule when the killing took place. Immediately after the scene described above where the kul cheer Sultan Mustafa's appearance through the window of Orta Cami, Tuği reports a rumor that has spread among the troops, according to which Sultan Osman has been assassinated inside the mosque. They become agitated and assert firmly that while Sultan Mustafa is their favored padishah, no harm should come upon his predecessor and he should be put in confinement. They quiet down, Tuği stresses, only after Davud Pasha shows them Genç Osman through the same window of the mosque.²⁷ Later that day (20 May 1622), according to Tuği, Davud Pasha transfers Sultan Osman to Yedikule, where the sultan is later strangled, *only* "when the army had been dispersed."²⁸

Tuği's manifest case for the defense of the kul is further supported latently. This brings us for the first time to what in my view is the main function of the second code in the prose component of the text—the digressions. The function that these fulfill, together with the perspective from which the whole event is represented, is the production of the text's latent meaning. The principle on which many of the digressions operate in Tuği's text varies: in some cases the manifest reason for making them masks their latent purpose and meaning; in other cases the latent meaning reiterates and makes plausible what is manifestly said.

With respect to clearing the kul of the accusation that they killed Sultan Osman, two latently significant digressions are presented. The first is a relatively detailed report of Davud Pasha's career, the manifest reason for submitting it being that at that point (Friday morning, 20 May 1622) Mustafa I conferred upon him the grand vezirate.²⁹ The latent purpose, however, is not merely informational. First, because the period covered by Tuği witnessed, apart from Davud Pasha, five grand vezirs (Dilaver, Ohrili Hüseyin, Mere Hüseyin, Lefkeli Mustafa, and Gürcü Mehmed); all of them appear in Tuği's history, but the career of none is presented. Moreover, the only other person whose career is specified at similar length is the chief adversary of the kul, the governor of Erzurum, Abaza Mehmed Pasha.³⁰ Not by coincidence, the feature shared by Davud and Abaza Mehmed is the unequaled bearing of both on the kul's fate. Second, Tuği's text, arbitrarily but again not coincidentally, presents Davud's résumé not from its starting point but from the day Sultan Osman ascended the throne and Davud was a fourth vezir. From that point all Tuği relates are the undeserved dismissals Davud suffered under Osman II, only "because of Davud Pasha's relation *(intisap)* to Sultan Mustafa Han" [he was married to Mustafa's sister and thereby acquired the status of damad].³¹

As thus envisaged, this digression endows the chronology that follows—the actual killing of Sultan Osman in Yedikule—with meaningful background. After stating that the new grand vezir assassinated Genç Osman, a remark made plausible by the digression that precedes it is inserted: "For Davud Pasha underwent excessive suffering, for no reason, in the reign of Sultan Osman Han. Having been ill-treated, he did not grant protection and security *(aman)* to Sultan Osman Han and killed him."³² All this is related to Tuği's defense of the kul in that it not only points at the "real" killer but also ascribes a perfect motive to him and shows that he betrayed the aman that the kul had guaranteed to Sultan Osman.

The second digression that is latently related to the actual killing of Genç Osman appears in a later part of the chronology, within Sultan Mustafa's second reign. On Saturday, 9 July 1622, Tuği reports, the kul raised an official allegation *(dava)* against Mere Hüseyin Pasha, who had been dismissed from the grand vezirate the day before. Mere, the kul are reported to have said, had slain the dismissed Janissary Chief Derviş Ağa. Tuği expresses ostensible astonishment at this allegation for, as he relates, Mere did not kill Derviş Ağa but sent him away on a boat.³³ Manifestly to stress the absurdity of the kul's allegation, Tuği gives two instances from the past that, in his view, contrary to the present case, ought to have yielded davas but had not done so. For his first illustration Tuği returns to Friday, 20 May 1622, the day Genç Osman was put to death.³⁴

In this digression, the only place where Tuği openly finds something deplorable in the kul's conduct, he asserts that the event of Sultan Osman's killing was for a long time the focus of much strife and discord. Yet the kul, whom he says were "fed" (i.e., supported in a patron-client relationship) by Osman's forefathers, did not raise an allegation in this matter. It was especially grave, Tuği continues, because the kul, when they brought Sultan Osman to Orta Cami, had warned Davud Pasha not to harm the deposed padishah. After Genç Osman had been murdered, they were silenced with gifts and promotions.³⁵ The latent logic employed here resembles that of a plea bargain between the defense and prosecution in a trial, because by conceding the kul's fault in not having reacted once they realized that the aman they had guaranteed was violated, Tuği's digression clears them from the more severe accusation and pins the blame on Davud Pasha.

But Tuği's address does not stop with proving that the kul did not kill Sultan Osman. It endeavors further to show that their rising in sedition against the young ruler was justifiable for two reasons. First, the padishah, incited by unworthy confidants, tyrannized and hurt the kul to the extent that he completely estranged them and they had every right to feel injured, both physically and emotionally. Second, their undertaking to hinder Sultan Osman's venture was essential not only for their well-being but, more important, for that of the state, and the kul were successful where others had failed. As was the case with the previous part of Tuği's defense, here too the meaning is conveyed mainly—not exclusively—at the latent level, and its chief carriers are the digressions.

Up to the point in the chronology where Sultan Osman is "martyred," Tuği makes seven digressions that pertain to the present discussion (there are altogether fifteen throughout the text). These can be classified into three groups. One group, which comprises three digressions, conveys the extent to which Sultan Osman has hurt the kul and correspondingly, the degree of their estrangement. Another group, again consisting of three digressions, shows that the kul, who during the event demanded—at times successfully—the execution of several officials, did so not arbitrarily but for substantial reasons. The remaining digression stands apart and is highly significant, chiefly because it underpins the premise that Sultan Osman's venture was something that had to be prevented.

The first digression of the first group is inserted at the outset of the text and is the author's explicit and formal explanation of the causes for the Haile-i Osmaniye. Immediately after the first paragraph of his chronological account, the initial gathering of the kul where they demand that the padishah relinquish his plan and punish his confidants (the morning of 18 May 1622), Tuği uses the formula alluded to earlier: that is, he alerts his audience that he is about to digress from the chronological account and gives a reason:

> Let it be briefly explained what the causes were for the enmity between the padishah and the kul corps, and for his [Osman II's] wanting to go in the direction of Anatolia. *[Padişahı kul taifesiyle düşman edip Anadol(u) semtine gitmek istediğine sebeb olanlar ala sebilülicmal beyan olunsun].*[36]

The introductory statement encapsulates not only the meaning conveyed by the digression it introduces but also much of the meaning conveyed by the work as a whole. By tying together in one sentence what could conceivably have been two independent statements, Tuği's work establishes, as early as this stage in the narrative, a latently meaningful connection between them. Accordingly, the cause for the wedge driven between Sultan Osman and the kul and the cause for his intention to replace them were one and the same: his being led astray by unworthy advisers, notably the chief black eunuch and the royal hoca. The meaningfulness of the mere fact that the two utterances are tied together in one sentence can be further illustrated if, again, we imagine an alternative construction of the introductory statement. If there had been one full sentence stating the need to present the causes for the enmity between the sultan and the kul, and another stating the need to present the causes for the conception of the sultan's plan, the meaning produced might have been that there was one set of causes that explained the enmity and another that explained the plan. In Chapter 6 I will show that what is presented here as an imagined alternative grammar is precisely what Katip Çelebi did with Tuği's explicit explanation, and I will show how what Katip Çelebi did was meaningful.

The meaning encapsulated in the introductory statement is reiterated by what the digression manifestly says and is latently made plausible through the ordering of the digression itself. In this present digression, the text's explicit explanation of the event registers the causes.

1. The first is the fact that the chief black eunuch, continuously and over a long period, slandered the sipahis and janissaries to the padishah, particularly stressing their poor performance in the Hotin campaign. Saying "On becoming kul, they should be like the Anatolian soldiers and the Arab horsemen," and asserting that the kul had become a useless body of salary drawers, Süleyman Ağa advised Sultan Osman to do away with them and recruit new kul in Anatolia, Syria, and Egypt. Tuği further emphasizes that it was "that black-faced [one]" (both literally and figuratively) who turned the sultan away from his kul.[37]

2. The second cause in Tuği's explanation is that Genç Osman's mentor, Hoca Ömer Efendi, had obtained a year earlier the office of the Mecca *kadi* (judge) for his brother but was refused by the şerif of Mecca, who nearly killed this brother. Ömer Efendi was furious and joined forces with the chief black eunuch, hoping that the latter's plan would enable him to take vengeance on his foe and secure his brother's office.

3. The third cause was that Osman II, accompanied by the *bostancıs* (lit. "gardeners," one of the units that composed the sultan's retinue) and incited by their commander, used to raid incognito the coffee shops and taverns and severely punish the kul he seized there.

4. The fourth cause was the poor performance of the kul in the Hotin campaign in 1621.[38]

5. What Tuği actually does in the fifth "cause" is to demonstrate the extent to which the kul were tormented by the padishah and to justify their poor performance (he does not deny that they indeed performed poorly). As reported in detail in Chapter 1, Tuği's argument is that the sultan arbitrarily paid some of the troops and denied similar payments to the rest. The latter then sarcastically remarked that those who had been paid should do battle.[39]

The causal explanation fulfills the anticipation created by the introductory formula through the ordering of these causes, for the five causes listed above are presented in an order *opposite* to the chronological order of their occurrence according to Tuği's text itself. From the brief exposition of these five causes it is clear that according to the text's own chronology the first two causes to be presented, related to the chief black eunuch and the royal mentor, took place after the three whose presentation follows, which deal with the evolving enmity between the sultan and the kul before and during the Hotin campaign (1620–21). This ordering, precisely because it is opposite to the text's own chronology, masks the fact that the antagonistic relations between Osman II and the kul might emerge independently of the sultan's advisers, on whom Tuği's address seeks to pin the entire blame. It can be reasonably assumed that the kul, the audience of Tuği's address, were receptive to this ordering of time not only because it enhanced the drama of the speech situation but also because from their perspective the "villainy" of the sultan's confidants was a fresher irritation and therefore emotionally more meaningful.

The message latently conveyed through the textual ordering of the causes is repeated, for the only time in the text in the narrator's voice, in the second digression of the first group. It is inserted in the point of the chronology when Sultan Osman learns that Ohrili Hüseyin Pasha has been killed. He then bursts into tears and delivers a repentant speech, saying that if he had not heeded the advice of the chief black eunuch and the royal hoca, he would not have suffered this calamitous fate. The narrator notes with ostensible surprise that nobody, despite his emotional confession, has either mercy or compassion for the deposed padishah. To explain this lack of sympathy, Tuği makes a digression in which he briefly surveys the actions of the sultan that brought trouble on him, chiefly his poor judgment in selecting companions and his hurting the kul, to the extent that their "hearts were drawn away from the padishah."[40]

The third and last digression in this group demonstrates again the interplay between the manifest and latent levels and suggests that Tuği might have some literary education. After the rhetoric and poetry following Sultan Osman's death, Tuği delays resuming the chronology. He remarks that people who perceive only the outward appearance of things *(erbab-i zahir;* the poetic significance of this term is discussed in the Epilogue) hold that this affair ought never to have taken place. Unwilling to dismiss lightly the essence of the event he has presented, and categorically asserting that no ruler since the time of Adam underwent the magnitude of pain inflicted upon Sultan Osman, Tuği wonders what the reason for this immense pain was. Before replying, he submits a list of "padishahs" who either committed grave religious offenses or tyrannized their subjects or both and notes that despite this, none of them, unlike Genç Osman, "experienced harm from his subjects." [41]

The reason, according to Tuği, for the unprecedented pain inflicted upon Genç Osman was a personal supplication (*dua*), made by Osman's brother, Prince Mehmed, when the former had ordered his execution before leaving the capital to the Polish campaign: "'Osman, I ask of God that your reign come to an end. However much I may not partake in life, may you not have a share in a long life too.' [Narrator's voice:] The personal prayer of the innocent prince was accepted; and within a short while Sultan Osman was also killed."[42] Manifestly then, Tuği's explanation for Osman's fate is his unjustified execution of his brother, Prince Mehmed.

The manifest judgment of Genç Osman's painful fate is not only supported latently but rendered harsher. What the digression latently does is to transform the specific act of tyranny mentioned manifestly—the execution of Prince Mehmed—into the ruler's fundamental nature. The latent depiction of Sultan Osman as a tyrant is achieved merely by his being compared to a list of oppressive rulers. For the fact that a comparison is suggested, regardless of its outcome, means that it has been deemed conceivable at the outset. Admittedly, the manifest logic of this list is to illustrate that the "padishahs" included in it were far worse than Osman and still did not suffer a similar fate. But at the same time, it means that, albeit to a lesser degree, Osman was a tyrant too.

The second group of digressions is simple and straightforward. In three cases where the kul submit petitions to either sultan (Osman II and later Mustafa I) whose content is the demand to execute a number of high-ranking officials, the chronology pauses, and the reasons for the inclusion of each individual in a given petition are elaborated thoroughly.[43] This is done to stress that the kul acted not arbitrarily but on what is presented as a well-founded cause. Tuği's accounting for execution petitions is of two sorts. One, which is ascribed to most of the persons named in these petitions, is that a certain official wronged the kul in an unforgivable manner. The other, exclusive to the chief black eunuch and the royal mentor, is justified by an alleged offense committed against the state. This justification is sanctioned, according to Tuği, by a fetva issued by the sheyhülislam Esad Efendi. The question put forward by the kul is: "What should be done under the Şeriat to the individuals who led astray the padishah of the world, caused the destruction of the Treasury of the Muslims, and were the cause for this much turmoil?" And the reply is: "They should be put to death."[44]

We come now to the digression that stands apart and is very telling of the underlying view Tuği must have shared with his audience, perhaps with other Ottomans too. What makes this digression unique in underscoring the text's latent meaning is the ordering of events in the narrative vis-à-vis their chronological occurrence. The "ordering of time" was emphasized earlier with regard to the first digression of the text, which is also its explicit explanation. But whereas in that case the significance stemmed from the arrangement of time *within* the digression itself (in opposite order to the chronology), in this case the digression is so meaningful first and foremost because of the time of the occurrence with which it deals and the place where this occurrence is inserted in the narrative; this digression is so meaningful, in other words, because of its position in the text.

Following the end of the chronological account of the first day of the Haile-i Osmaniye "proper" (18 May 1622), when the kul decided to disperse and reassemble the next morning fully armed, Tuği goes back in time to the beginning of May 1622 and presents a dream Sultan Osman is said to have had one night. In the dream the sultan is sitting on his throne reading the Kuran. Then the Prophet appears, takes the Noble Pages from the padishah's hands, strips off his gown, and slaps him hard. The padishah falls off his throne, only to realize that his efforts to prostrate himself at the Prophet's feet are to no avail, at which point he wakes up.[45]

Sultan Osman was duly perturbed and ordered an interpretation from Hoca Ömer Efendi. He told the padishah that he had been reproached, through the dream, for having made a *niyet* (formal resolve to perform a religious act) to perform the hajj, and then having neglected to fulfill it. Therefore, Ömer Efendi concluded, the padishah must go to Mecca.[46] This interpretation did not satisfy Sultan Osman, and he ordered a second opinion from the eminent Sufi sheyh, Üsküdari Mahmud Efendi. The latter wrote in response: "The Kuran represents the authority of the Noble şeriat, and the gown represents the world of substance. The padishah ought to obtain divine companionship through repentance."[47]

Following these interpretations, "The blessed padishah was determined to cross over to Anatolia on the pretext of going to the Ka'be," and he stepped up the pace of preparations. All the efforts of the ulema, vezirs, and sheyhs to hinder this bore no fruit. Even the fetva mentioned earlier, which in whatever wording tried to discourage him from proceeding, had the same result: the furious sultan tore it to pieces.[48]

The notion conveyed through the digression proper—the dream and its interpretations—is obvious. First, it illustrates once more Sultan Osman's poor choice of advisers, Ömer Efendi in this case. Second, it implies that his reign had failed both spiritually and materially (Sheyh Mahmud's interpretation). Third, it shows that Genç Osman's venture was rejected by all the state's grandees, except the chief black eunuch and the royal mentor, both of whom, in Tuği's judgment, had instigated it.

As in other digressions, here the introductory formula is as meaningful as the digression it introduces and justifies. Tuği intimates that he is about to insert this digression to explain "the cause for which the sipahi and janissary corps ventured this much and took action."[49] Then he relates that at that point (early May 1622) the padishah, momentarily convinced by his high officials, indicated that he might go back on his religiously flavored resolution. However, "while in the process of changing his mind,"[50] he dreamed one night the dream described above. From that moment, as we have seen, his determination became irreversible, and Tuği stresses at the end of the digression once more: "For that reason the kul corps took action."[51]

Through this digression, then, Tuği's address announces, first, that not only the kul but the most preeminent state officials were opposed to Sultan Osman's venture, and, second, that the kul were striving to prevent its implementation only when all other measures had proved futile. What is so significant in all this is the latent premise Tuği's text seems to have shared with its audience: that the padishah's venture had to be spoiled for considerations that went far beyond the kul's interest and concerned the wellbeing of the state as a whole. At the same time it means that whether Sultan Osman's venture was a useful idea needed no discussion: its disastrous potential, were it implemented, was presupposed and taken for granted, and uttering this was redundant.

The latent existence of this premise is evident because Tuği's address seems to assume that the mere fact that the kul acted only when the sultan had become determined beyond persuasion justified their initiative and its consequences and even made them praiseworthy. Unuttered but prevalent premises are often more significant than those which are explicitly expressed; the former are often more significant not because there is a conspiracy to conceal them but precisely because such premises are so deeply ingrained that there is no need to utter them. The question of whether Sultan Osman's venture was disastrous and had to be stopped by whatever means and agency, then, was never a matter for discussion because Tuği's speech and its kul audience shared its a priori rejection at such a fundamental level that it literally went without saying. It is this fundamental premise that underpins the whole work as speech and manifests itself in different ways; and most important, it is this fundamental premise, shared by both speakers and hearers, that makes Tuği's text as speech not only judgmental but also a contextual situation.

Finally, coming back to the ordering of time, this premise may account for the location of the digression within the narrative. For if, unlike the other digressions, what is presented in here took place sometime in early May 1622, why not begin the chronology there, rather than insert it as a digression between the first and second days of the turmoil in Istanbul (18 and 19 May)? Bearing in mind that this digression supplies a solid justification (again, within the judgmental logic of Tuği's work rather than in absolute terms) for the kul's initiative, its location within the narrative deploys this justification most effectively by placing it immediately before the most drastic, and at the same time most controversial, actions the kul are said to have taken: their forced entry into the imperial palace and then into the imperial harem, and their deposition of Sultan Osman that led to his assassination.

CONCLUSION

This chapter interpreted Tuği's text as an oral address and demonstrated the extent to which it was contextual and fundamentally kul-centric. The next two chapters will unfold the story of historiography of the Haile-i Osmaniye and will emphasize the use of Tuği's text by the later Ottoman historians as a written artifact. They will highlight not only the points on which these historians agreed or disagreed with Tuği but also how the mere fact that they were not part of the contextual oral situation may explain the reworking of Tuği's text by these historians in meaningful ways. At the same time, the following two chapters will establish that however much reinterpreted, Tuği's work nonetheless remained the urtext of the historical narrative of the Haile-i Osmaniye.

Before this historiographical story proceeds, an interesting and general theme in Tuği's work might be noted and briefly discussed: the theme of preordained and divinely guided inevitability. The theme of an inevitable grand scheme can be found, in one or another garb, in both religious and secular paradigms. The philosophical and moral dilemma in this respect is usually whether human beings, individuals or collectives, had any freedom of choice when acting as they did or whether they were merely agencies in human guise, fulfilling a course of events the essence and purpose of which were beyond their grasp and control. This in turn prompts the question of whether there is a point in elaborating and judging the actions, motives, and personalities of particular protagonists if they did not have much choice in the matter of how they acted in a given circumstance.

The theme of preordained destiny of individuals and events clearly exists in the Ottoman historical texts and will recur when Katip Çelebi's and Naima's accounts of the Haile-i Osmaniye are examined. Its basic characteristic in Tuği's text (and in Katip Çelebi's) is that the earthly, human factor and that which is divinely designed simply coexist. The impression the reader gets is that they supplement each other, but there is no indication whatever that their appearance side by side is problematic, let alone contradictory, or that the latter may render the former nonsensical. Specifically, the theme of preordained fate is manifested in Tuği's text on two occasions. Within its context these manifestations supplement and lend further credence to the assertion, at the earthly-human level, that the kul acted to secure the well-being of the Ottoman state rather than out of self-interest and that they succeeded where others had failed. Similarly, at the level of a divinely designed scheme, the kul again acted as agents of a larger cause, only this one was larger than the state.

The first instance where the theme appears is the digression, discussed earlier, in which the narrator submits a list of infamous tyrants, none of whom had had pain inflicted upon him in the magnitude suffered by Sultan Osman. This is then explained by the execution of Prince Mehmed and his prayer that Sultan Osman should suffer a similar fate. In addition to suggesting that God sanctioned Genç Osman's death, this digression also illustrates the complementary coexistence of the human and divine explanations. For, as was mentioned earlier, the narrator remarks in this context that those who think that the whole affair, especially Osman II's death, should never have taken place are erbab-i zahir, people who observe only the outward appearance of things.[52] This implies that the human and immediate aspect of things is their *zahir* aspect, which is complemented by the esoteric inner essence, the *batın*. It should be clarified that this does not exhaust the implication of the zahir/batın distinction for the interpretation of Tuği's address. The fuller meaning of the distinction is developed in the Epilogue.

The second instance is the digression where the sultan's dream is inserted.[53] Here the divinely preordained theme is manifested in several ways. First, the dream itself is a recurring device for indicating extrahuman designs in all sorts of historiographies, a notable example being the Ottoman historical works of the fifteenth century, which deal with the foundation of the Ottoman state. Second, the sultan's state of mind consequent upon his dream, whereby his resolve to carry out his plan cannot be altered, is also hinted to have been part of the divine scheme; it should be remembered that in Tuği's text, not by coincidence, I think, this resolve is termed niyet. Third and last, the dream's content, which is patently "religious," and Üsküdari Mahmud Efendi's interpretation of it, which, unlike Hoca Ömer Efendi's, is implied to have been truthful, strongly suggest that Sultan Osman was rejected by God as both the spiritual imam of the community and its political leader.

If the punishment inflicted upon Genç Osman during his life were not enough, things did not get better for him in the realm of Ottoman memory and posterity.

5. The Formation of Alternative Narratives
Hasanbeyzade and Peçevi

In the hermeneutic framework charted in Chapter 3, I proposed to interpret the historiography of the Haile-i Osmaniye through reading the foundational text, Tuği's, twice. The first reading has interpreted Tuği's text as a speech situation, an oral address to the kul. The second reading will look at the same text as an instance of writing and reading rather than speaking and hearing, by following the ways in which it was employed by some of the most important Ottoman historians of the seventeenth century. The previous chapter was chiefly concerned with the first reading. What the later Ottoman historians did with Tuği's text—as readers and writers rather than hearers—is the underlying purpose of this chapter and the next.

The basic historiographical chain of transmission is a necessary guide for these two chapters. It can be summarized as follows.

1. Hasanbeyzade, the first author of a Tarih-i Al-i Osman work in the seventeenth century, adopted, in the first instance, the prose part of Tuği's account lock, stock, and barrel.

2. Peçevi was most probably aware of the content of Tuği's work, if not directly then through its reproduction in Hasanbeyzade's history. Yet he produced a totally different, at times contradictory representation of the Haile-i Osmaniye.

3. In consequence, when Katip Çelebi composed his *Fezleke-i Tarih* there were before him two alternative representations: Tuği's/Hasanbeyzade's and Peçevi's; he opted for the former. The *Fezleke*'s account is thus Katip Çelebi's reading of Tuği and Hasanbeyzade, and his implicit—but, as will be shown, clearly conscious—rejection of Peçevi. Interestingly, although Katip Çelebi rejected Peçevi's overall

interpretation, he did not refrain from occasionally using Peçevi's history without acknowledging it.

4. Naima, in his turn, adopted the version offered by the *Fezleke* with few, albeit not insignificant, alterations. Thus the official Ottoman version of the Haile-i Osmaniye is, in fact, a cumulative reading of Tuği by three historians and the implicit rejection of Peçevi by two of them.

5. With regard to the Haile-i Osmaniye as an illustration of the modus operandi of the Tarih-i Al-i Osman historiography in the seventeenth century, it reaffirms two characteristics that recur in the accounts of other events. One is the position of Katip Çelebi's judgment as a sort of historiographical junction that was most influential on the state narrative that eventually appeared in Naima's history. The other is the relative remoteness of Peçevi from the main line of transmission in this historiography (from Hasanbeyzade to Katip Celeb to Naima), and the independence of his judgment, sources, and line of presentation.

A NOTE ON THE MANUSCRIPTS
OF HASANBEYZADE'S HISTORY

Before proceeding with the interpretation of the historiographical discourse, a brief remark on the extant manuscripts of Hasanbeyzade's text is essential. This historical text, as yet unpublished, was the earliest Tarih-i Al-i Osman work in the seventeenth century, and it served as a major source of reference for many of the later works, which in turn found their way to Naima's history at the end of the century. Hasanbeyzade's history consists of two main parts. The first, from the early period of the frontier Ottoman principality down to the reign of Selim I (the Grim, *Yavuz*, r. 1512–20), is an abridgement of the famous *Crown of Histories (Taciüttevarih)* by Hoca Sadüddin Efendi. The second part, which covers the period 1520–1623 (later extended to 1636), was apparently Hasanbeyzade's own composition with possible variations and additions by later copyists.[1]

The extant manuscripts of Hasanbeyzade's history vary not only in time span but also in content. This is evident and acute with regard to the Haile-i Osmaniye. I dwell on these variations and suggest a working hypothesis on the extant manuscripts elsewhere.[2] Briefly, I suggest that Hasanbeyzade's manuscripts be classified into three versions: the narrative of the first version ends in 1623, that of the second ends in 1629, and the third extends up to 1636. In this study, each of these versions is represented by one extant manuscript: the first version by MS Flügel 1046 (Austrian National Library, Vienna), the second by MS Nuruosmaniye 3106 (Nuruosmaniye Library, Istanbul), and the third by MS Flügel 1049 (Austrian National Library, Vienna). Concerning specific representations, the choice of version/manuscript is guided by two criteria that are not mutually exclusive. The first is the actual content of one or another version, while the second takes into account the version that other Ottoman historians seem to have used. This method makes sure that Hasanbeyzade's text is considered as both a composition in itself and part of an unfolding discourse.

THE CHIEF BLACK EUNUCH MUSTAFA AĞA: VILLAIN OR LOYAL SERVANT?

In the previous chapter, Tuği's virulent disapproval of another chief black eunuch *(darüssaade ağası* or *kızlar ağasi)*, Süleyman Ağa, was a central feature. His predecessor, Mustafa Ağa, was also the focus of attention of the Ottoman historians who grappled with the account of the first accession of Mustafa I, his temporary removal after three months, and the enthronement of Osman II (22 November 1617 to 26 February 1618).[3] Tuği does not allude to this episode, and I therefore primarily focus on Hasanbeyzade's text as the underlying representation, and—via Peçevi and Katip Çelebi—unfold the historiography up till Naima.[4]

Naima's presentation of the first and brief reign of Sultan Mustafa begins with two lengthy and explicit citations. The first is from Hasanbeyzade's account and the second from Katip Çelebi's. Separating the two accounts is Naima's own "however," which implies that he might prefer Katip Çelebi's view to Hasanbeyzade's.[5] The matter on which Hasanbeyzade on the one hand and Katip Çelebi and Peçevi on the other had opposing views was the role that the chief black eunuch, Mustafa Ağa, had played in the deposition of Mustafa I and the ensuing accession to the throne of Osman II.

Hasanbeyzade condemned Mustafa Ağa for various actions. First was the fact that the chief black eunuch made publicly known what should be concealed, namely Sultan Mustafa's behavior and wanderings, and "that he caused the people to be averse to the padishah."[6] Second, the chief black eunuch engaged in trickery and fraud, which misled the high officials of the state, and "had the audacity to fabricate statements of many sorts."[7]

Katip Çelebi's defense of Mustafa Ağa's actions expresses his disagreement with Hasanbeyzade's judgment. As Naima sensed, Katip Çelebi "stripped the accusation of stratagem away from the chief black eunuch."[8] Katip Çelebi did this by asserting: "When the sick nature of the padishah became known due to his unstable mind, within a short while it acquired fame among the people. . . . All the people witnessed with their own eyes his senseless state of mind and realized the lack of judgment."[9] To infer from this assertion that Mustafa Ağa did not have to divulge the sultan's insanity is to state the obvious.

The controversy also includes the chief black eunuch's modus operandi, and specifically the messages he sent to high officials in order to dethrone Sultan Mustafa. Hasanbeyzade reports two such messages. The first predicted that the result of keeping Sultan Mustafa on the throne for much longer would be the destruction of the Imperial Treasury *(Hazine-i Hümayun* or *Hazine-i Amire)*. The second intimated that the sultan had intended to destroy the House of Osman by executing all the princes and that if the officials did not foil this it would also result in "conferring your distinguished offices on some riff-raff."[10] The author is adamant that the content of the second message was false. It might be implicitly deduced that the prediction made in the first message was reportedly valid.

In Katip Çelebi's account the second message does not appear, and it might be reasonable to assume that it was consciously ignored. Interestingly, although Hasanbeyzade was most probably Katip Çelebi's source for this episode, he formulates the message on the destruction of the treasury in a meaningfully different way. According to Katip Çelebi, the chief black eunuch opened his "fiscal" warning to the high officials with a statement not to be found in Hasanbeyzade's text: "The state of the padishah has become widely known to the people and well established among them. There is nothing in [Sultan] Mustafa's situation that can be veiled with concealing and covering up."[11] This statement, whether or not made by Mustafa Ağa, clearly shows that Katip Çelebi was reacting to Hasanbeyzade's accusation, for it was supposed to show that the sultan's madness was such that it hardly needed divulging; it was already public knowledge.

The attitude of Peçevi toward the actions of the chief black eunuch is similar to Katip Çelebi's. He begins by stressing that Mustafa Ağa, who had been a loyal servant under Ahmed I (r. 1603–1617), "this time too did not fail to speak the truth." Like Katip Çelebi and contrary to Hasanbeyzade, Peçevi implies that making the insanity of Sultan Mustafa publicly known was not necessary, for from the day the sultan had paid the customary visit to his ancestors' tombs, "the people disapproved of his behavior and inferred his lightness of mind." Furthermore, after illustrating the ruler's bizarre wanderings, Peçevi remarks, "Not [only] the grandees but also the common artisans became aware of his behavior."[12]

Hasanbeyzade was not content with strongly censuring what Mustafa Aǧa had done. He proceeded to expose lust for power, and frustration by the loss of power once enjoyed, as the motive behind the action:

> The Chief Black Eunuch Mustafa Aǧa was accustomed to gift and patronage, and to acting with complete power at the time of Sultan Ahmed Han. And while all the grandees of the state and pillars of the sultanate were submissive to him, obedient to his word and docile, the new padishah [Mustafa I], being of introverted and humble disposition, could not get along with [Mustafa Aǧa]. Since [Mustafa Aǧa] grew distanced in that respect and frustrated with [his loss of influence on] appointment and conduct, he made the little intelligence and lack of ability of the aforementioned sultan publicly known, and divulged and spread to everyone his wanderings, which should be concealed.[13]

Katip Çelebi, again reacting to Hasanbeyzade, attributes to the chief black eunuch not only judicious actions but also good intentions. According to Katip Çelebi, "Mustafa Aǧa, having been a conductor and planner of affairs in Sultan Ahmed's time, intended well, as required by an earnest rendering of service. He claimed to be protecting religion and state from confusion and turmoil."[14] Peçevi shares this view: "Mustafa Aǧa, to whose judgment the charge of state affairs had been totally entrusted at the time of Sultan Ahmed's reign, this time too did not fail to speak the truth."[15]

The views expressed by the historians *manifestly*, on the surface of the text, are enhanced *latently* by the figurative use of language.[16] This aspect of the discourse illustrates with special clarity how texts can convey precisely the same information but produce completely different—indeed antithetical—meanings. The figurative language employed Hasanbeyzade's text not only underscores the representation of Mustafa Aǧa as the story's villain but also underlies a narrative of inevitability, in which the evil force was too strong and that which could have counterbalanced it too weak. A significant feature is the way in which the power of the chief black eunuch is figuratively augmented in the presentation of his second "stratagem"— the summoning of the troops to the Imperial Council under the pretext of distributing salaries. In this presentation Mustafa Aǧa "*made* the followers of Sultan Mustafa *conclude [kiyas ettirdi]* that the people who had come to collect their salaries were assembled to depose him from the sultanate."[17]

While most other verbs in Hasanbeyzade's account are in the "normal" active or passive voice, the causative form *(kiyas ettirmek*—to make someone conclude) is not coincidentally reserved for the actions of the chief black eunuch, for only he possessed the power to manipulate others. The weakness of the force that could and should have curbed Mustafa Ağa's power is figuratively conveyed by the adjectives. The sultan's nature was "introverted" and "humble," and the pillars of the state were "submissive," "docile," and "obedient." Is it not obvious who would gain the upper hand in this event?

The opposite intentions ascribed to the chief black eunuch by Hasanbeyzade on the one hand, and Katip Çelebi and Peçevi on the other, are also made plausible latently by the figurative use of language. It is remarkable that the information supplied by all texts, the fact that Mustafa Ağa enjoyed power and influence during Ahmed I's reign, is perfectly identical, yet the meanings that the texts they convey are diametrically opposed. According to Hasanbeyzade, the sort of power he had was corrupt and made him accustomed to "gifts and patronage," and the way he wielded it made all state officials "submissive to him." By contrast, according to Katip Çelebi, Mustafa Ağa was "the planner and conductor of affairs" under Ahmed I, and Peçevi reckons that his judgment was so sound that the management of the realm was entrusted to him.[18] The figurative language underlies Hasanbeyzade's manifest argument that what motivated the chief black eunuch to plot the deposition of Sultan Mustafa was his lust for the corrupt power he had previously possessed; similarly but yielding the opposite meaning, it underlies Katip Çelebi's and Peçevi's view that Mustafa Ağa was driven by the considerations of a responsible and trustworthy servant of the state.

How might this controversy be explained and related to the context of seventeenth-century Ottoman history? The Ottoman historians shared a preoccupation with the fate of the Imperial Treasury in view of the expenses incurred by the frequent coronations. The trauma caused by the amount of bonuses and alms scattered in a sultan's accession to the throne is something they all mention. The only difference is that while Hasanbeyzade thought that stopping the chief black eunuch might have spared the treasury yet another coronation (Osman II's), Katip Çelebi and Peçevi argued that the danger to the treasury was rather Sultan Mustafa's madness and hence that the deposition was a responsible and necessary step.[19]

The general context within which this should be understood is the crisis of the seventeenth century throughout Eurasia (discussed thoroughly in Part III). Concretely related to the present discussion is the monetary and fiscal crisis skillfully charted by Şevket Pamuk. He lays emphasis on the period of the Haile-i Osmaniye as particularly unstable, and on the opposition of the janissaries, guild members, and the inhabitants of Istanbul in general to the fiscal and monetary policies of the government, especially to the debasements.[20] To follow Pamuk, within this context the historiographical controversy might be crudely put as a disagreement over what was more perilous to the Imperial Treasury: yet another accession ceremony or a mad sultan?

Another aspect of the phenomenon of mentally problematic rulers might pertain to the disagreement between Hasanbeyzade, on the one hand, and Katip Çelebi and Peçevi, on the other. The former did not deny the fact that Sultan Mustafa was feebleminded but strongly denounced his deposition. This might stem from a certain contextual difference. Hasanbeyzade did not experience, as did his two later colleagues, the much longer reign of another mad sultan, Ibrahim I (the Mad, *Deli*, r. 1640–48), who was assassinated and whose reign was replete with strife within the dynastic household. It is possible that Peçevi and Katip Çelebi, who wrote during and after the reign of Ibrahim I, were more reproachful of the mere phenomenon of mad rulers because they had just witnessed the eight-year-long term of one.

The greater proximity in time of Hasanbeyzade to the events on which he and his later colleagues wrote might explain his different view in other ways. That temporal perspective might carry explanatory force is suggested even by the differences between the first version of Hasanbeyzade's work and the second and the third versions. Most notable is his view of Mustafa I and the need to depose him. In the first version Hasanbeyzade was adamant that if an end had been put to the conniving of the chief black eunuch, Sultan Mustafa's reign would have been extended and he might have become a firm padishah.[21] This favorable statement disappears in the second and third versions, and we find instead a significant remark: "However, his [Mustafa I's] insanity grew severe and the span of lack of functioning was prolonged. Since he was the cause for the waste of money, wrong deeds, and the manifestation of much corruption, he was promptly deposed."[22]

Perspective was also personal, and Hasanbeyzade, as a contemporary, might have had an axe to grind. He translated a famous treatise by Hasan al-Kafi *(Usul al-Hikam fi Nizam al-'Alam)* from Arabic to Turkish, and dedicated it to the Grand Vezir Istanköylü Ali Pasha (1619–21).[23] This suggests that Hasanbeyzade might have been a client of that grand vezir. Since it was Ali Pasha who had become so close to Osman II that he was able to cause Mustafa Ağa's banishment to Egypt,[24] it is conceivable that Hasanbeyzade's resentment of the chief black eunuch was partly determined by the fact that the two belonged to rival sociopolitical networks *(intisap)* within the imperial establishment.

A less personal way in which perspective might account for Hasanbeyzade's judgment of this event highlights the changes in the dynastic household, which are analyzed in Leslie Peirce's pathbreaking study (see again Chapter 1).²⁵ As may be recalled, one of the outstanding features of this process was the ascendancy, especially in the first half of the seventeenth century, of the chief black eunuch and the queen mother *(valide sultan)*. Hasanbeyzade seems to have found it difficult to adjust to these changes, whereas Peçevi and Katip Çelebi, writing two and three decades later respectively, might deem it a given state of affairs. Repeating Tuği's phrase, Hasanbeyzade refers to Osman II's trusted chief black eunuch, Süleyman Ağa, as "that black faced [one]," literally and figuratively. On another occasion, when the ulema appealed to no avail to the queen mother (Mustafa I's) to banish Mustafa Ağa, Hasanbeyzade remarks that "she was deceived by his [the chief black eunuch's] sweet tongue and tearful eye."²⁶

This is a striking combination of racial and gender prejudices. Mustafa Ağa not only is "black faced" but also has a perceived feminine countenance ("sweet tongue and tearful eye"), both of which are deployed by Hasanbeyzade with derogatory connotations. It is, moreover, significant that in this presentation the chief black eunuch's "sweet tongue and tearful eye" could deceive a woman (the queen mother) but not men (the ulema). This combined prejudice might be a cultural signifier, the signified of which was an objection to the political and institutional changes at the heart of the empire.

HASANBEYZADE'S USE OF TUĞI'S TEXT

In his study of Naima, Lewis V. Thomas suggests with regard to the ultimate *literary* source for seventeenth-century historiography (i.e., historical texts as distinct from archival documents) that "most Ottoman historical works treating the eleventh century of the hegira are versions of, or at least incorporate, one basic account; that this account is the History of the Year 1000" *(Tarih-i sene-i elf)*; and that the general foundation of this account is a series of extracts from Ottoman official records . . . to which the individual 'authors' added opinions, anecdotes, personal experiences, and extracts from other versions of the same basic chronicle. . . . Apparently this version is what is meant by Hasanbeyzade's history although that version extends beyond the supposed day of Hasanbeyzade's death."²⁷ This literary source *(Tarih-i sene-i elf/*Hasanbeyzade's history), he continues, is in turn based on the ultimate source. The ultimate source comprised a series of condensed reports *(telhisler,* sing. *telhis)* drawn up by the scribal service for submission to the sultan. The official documents that were thus condensed were probably extracts from the more detailed output of the central imperial administration *(arz* and *mühimme defters).*[28]

My investigation of the use of Tuği by Hasanbeyzade (and others) shows that concerning the historiography of an explosive period Thomas's sketch is not entirely accurate. The comparison of the first version of Hasanbeyzade's history and Tuği's work reveals that the former's concluding section—the deposition of Osman II and most of Mustafa I's second reign—is, in fact, a near-verbatim and in toto transmission of Tuği's text.[29] This has two related bearings on Thomas's insistence that seventeenth-century historiography emanated, in one way or another, exclusively from Ottoman official records.[30] First, though it is possible that many Ottoman historical works of this period draw on Hasanbeyzade, it does not necessarily follow that the latter is exclusively founded upon "a series of extracts from Ottoman official records," for Tuği's work, fully incorporated into Hasanbeyzade's, is hardly an official record. Second, Thomas's conclusion that Hasanbeyzade's *Tarih* is the ultimate literary source underneath which lie only official documents is also questionable, for it is patently evident that for the Haile-i Osmaniye Tuği's text, rather than Hasanbeyzade's, is the ultimate literary source.

The manner in which Tuği's work was integrated into Hasanbeyzade's history seems to have been shrewdly devised. And although one ought to resist an anachronistic application of the modern notion of plagiarism to the seventeenth century, it is hardly possible not to speculate that Hasanbeyzade was guided by a resolute intention to avoid disclosing the source he had employed so profusely. What Hasanbeyzade did in practice was to transmit verbatim the prose of Tuği's text, but he carefully omitted all the poetry except for one case.[31] As for the prose, Hasanbeyzade's account of the Haile-i Osmaniye begins right from the point where Tuği's prose begins; it ends, thus the whole work is concluded, halfway through Tuği's formal epilogue *(hatime).*

This is suggestive because Hasanbeyzade's omissions are precisely the places where Tuği revealed either his pseudonym *(mahlas,* i.e., Tuği) or his real name (Hüseyin bin Sefer). The former is given almost invariably in each piece of poetry, and it seems more than coincidental that the one poem that Hasanbeyzade does include lacks any sort of name in the original.[32] While with the poetry it may be argued that Hasanbeyzade was reluctant to use it as generously as Tuği had, what he did with the epilogue leaves less room for doubt. Here Hasanbeyzade departs from Tuği's text, and in fact ends his own, after Tuği's reminder of the time span of his work but prudently before Tuği divulges for the first and only time his real name and the fact that he wrote the text.[33]

Thus far I have focused on the general pattern of the incorporation of Tuği's text into the first version of Hasanbeyzade's history, a hitherto unnoticed fact in the study of Ottoman historiography. The deviations of Hasanbeyzade's text from Tuği's—apart from the poetry—are few and far between. Two of them seem to me to be particularly interesting because they offer a glance at Hasanbeyzade's view of the Haile-i Osmaniye, both independently of and with implicit reference to Tuği. One very brief but telling deviation concerns the favorable view Tuği takes of the Grand Vezir Mere Hüseyin Pasha. Mere was appointed for the first time early in Sultan Mustafa's second reign, following Davud Pasha's dismissal. He was removed after a short while when the janissaries, on the basis of a rumor, suspected that he had killed the then janissary chief, Derviş Ağa. Mere was succeeded by Lefkeli Mustafa Pasha, who in turn was followed by Gürcü Mehmed Pasha. We focus on the point when Gürcü was removed at the behest of the kul, their claim being that owing to Abaza Pasha's sociopolitical relation *(intisap)* to him Gürcü was reluctant to suppress Abaza's rebellion. Asked for their preferred incumbent, the kul concertedly chose Mere, who was consequently given the seal for the second time.[34]

At this point Tuği inserts a narrator's remark whose purpose is to explain why the kul chose Mere. The narrator intimates that it was because the kul regretted his earlier removal and also "because after [Mere] Hüseyin Pasha there were two vezirs. Neither possessed Hüseyin Pasha's ability to govern."[35] Hasanbeyzade follows Tuği two-thirds of the way. He includes the remark on the kul's regret as well as the fact that Mere was followed by two grand vezirs before he was reappointed. However, he replaces the sentence on Mere's superior ability: "Because after Hüseyin Pasha there were two vezirs. In what manner they treated [the kul] has been noted in [the proper place] of the narrative."[36]

The discrepancy between the two texts, though merely the length of a sentence, should not be dismissed offhandedly. Hasanbeyzade's text follows Tuği's so meticulously that when a deviation does occur it is reasonable to seek its meaning. Tuği's remark conforms to his generally favorable attitude toward Mere. Overtly the remark attributes Mere's reelection by the kul to their regrets and recognition of his outstanding ability and authority. By presenting it as a general narrator's statement rather than the kul's, who were partisans, the text endows this argument with narrative objectivity: that Mere was an able and authoritative vezir was simply common knowledge, a matter of fact.

Hasanbeyzade's text alters precisely, and only, this last sentence. It thus tempers the pro-Mere attitude in Tuği's address in two ways. First, any traces of Mere's merits are erased. Second, by suggesting that the readers remind themselves of the manner in which Mere's "colleagues" had treated the kul, Hasanbeyzade subtly implies that Mere was chosen not because of his widely acclaimed qualities but because he knew better than the other two vezirs how to win the kul's support. The second deviation of Hasanbeyzade from Tuği is a substantial insertion after the execution of the ex-Grand Vezir Davud Pasha is described. Following a period of power struggles at the capital, it was agreed that upon becoming grand vezir, after the deposition of Sultan Osman and the reinstatement of Sultan Mustafa, Davud Pasha killed the former without the latter's authorization. His execution was sanctioned by a fetva, issued by the sheyhülislam at the kul's request, which was followed by the sultan's decree *(hatt-i şerif)*.[37]

At this juncture, Hasanbeyzade's text substantially diverges from Tuği's for the only time. This divergence is a relatively long digression in the shape of an apocryphal story on the foundation of the Sassanian dynasty by its first ruler, Ardaşir, son of Papak (d. 242 A.D.). The background of the story is the successful struggle of a minor vassal from Persis (today the province of Fars) against his Parthian overlords. On 28 April 224 (A.D.), in the decisive battle of Homizdagan, Ardaşir defeated the last Parthian ruler Ardavan IV, who died in this battle. Ardaşir immediately assumed the title of *shahanshah* (king of kings) and later came to be known as Ardaşir I.[38]

The apocryphal story in Hasanbeyzade's presentation is briefly the following.[39] After Ardaşir killed Ardavan to become the first padishah of the Sassanian dynasty, Ardavan's four sons and daughter remained. Two sons were captured by Ardaşir and imprisoned, whereas the other two fled to India. King Ardaşir's loyal vezir, "a possessor of wisdom and sagacity," advised his master that if he took Ardavan's daughter in marriage she would show him her late father's treasures; the king heeded the advice. Sometime later Ardavan's oldest son Bahman, who had fled to India, devised a plan to overthrow Ardaşir and restore Parthian rule. He sent a secret envoy to his sister with a letter and lethal poison. Her role was to make her husband, King Ardaşir, take the poison; as soon as he was dead, "Bahman b. Ardavan would emerge and become the shah over the land."

The opportune moment came when one day Ardaşir returned thirsty from hunting and asked Ardavan's daughter for refreshments. She mixed the poison with a drink, but approaching the king she began to tremble; drawing nearer, she dropped the cup, and the expression on her face betrayed her guilt. Ardaşir confirmed his suspicion by ordering a servant to mix the poured-out drink with dough and feed some chickens with it; they died instantly. He then summoned the aforementioned vezir and ordered him to execute Ardavan's daughter. The vezir took her away, and while he was preparing the bowstring with which to strangle her she told him that she was carrying Ardaşir's son in her womb and sought that her life be spared for the sake of her guiltless son.

The vezir went back to his king and told him what he had heard from Ardavan's daughter. But the furious Ardaşir firmly ordered him to show no mercy and execute her. The vezir returned to his home. First, he assigned a few women to serve Ardavan's daughter and arranged provisions for her. Then he retired to a solitary room and rendered himself a eunuch. He recorded what he had done and when, and he put the document together with the cut-off organs in a special box. He went back to Ardaşir and reported that his order had been carried out; then he requested that the box be deposited in the treasury, intimating that it contained jewels.

After several months Ardavan's daughter gave birth to a boy whom the vezir named Şapur. Şapur was brought up by the vezir until he was seven years old; the vezir also continued to spare Ardavan's daughter and kept her in hiding. At that point, when the vezir was in his master's presence, he learnt that the king was distressed and saddened at not having a son. He requested that the box be retrieved from the treasury, asked King Ardaşir to look at its contents, and unfolded the entire affair. The king devised a test in the shape of a polo game whose participants were one hundred children of similar physiognomy; Şapur was among them. The long and short of it was that Şapur's *farr* (divine majesty) stood out and he was taken together with his forgiven mother back to the palace. The vezir became Şapur's tutor and Ardaşir's fully trusted right-hand man in the affairs of his kingdom.

I shall first examine what Hasanbeyzade does with this story in relation to the source from which it is extracted and then how it functions within the text as a whole. The source from which Hasanbeyzade extracted the apocryphal story is unmistakable: the *Shahname* (Book of Kings) by the medieval Persian poet Firdausi (died between 1020 and 1025). Written in New Persian, the *Shahname* is a collection of mythical episodes that creates a continuous story of the various Iranian dynasties from the Creation to the Muslim conquest. It draws on oral traditions and written records in Middle Persian and Arabic.[40] Partial versions of the same story can be found in two earlier sources on which I shall not dwell in this study: the *Kar-Namak-i Artakhshir Papakan*, written in Middle Persian (Pahlavi), and Tabari's history, written in Arabic. Each of these contains two partial versions of the same story, which the *Shahname* seems to amalgamate into one plot. The story Hasanbeyzade presents clearly resembles this amalgamation rather than any of the partial versions.[41] Also, whereas it is very likely that Hasanbeyzade, having had a scribal career *(kalemiye)*, read New Persian, it is less likely that he commanded a knowledge of Pahlavi. It should be further noted that although there can be little doubt that the source for the story in Hasanbeyzade's text was the *Shahname*, I have not been able to ascertain whether he read it in the *Shahname* itself or in an Ottoman rendering.

What Hasanbeyzade does is to subvert the purpose of the story. In the *Shahname* the story is there, as others of its kind, to legitimize the Sassanian dynasty by showing that its members possessed the divine majesty *(farr)* and that the transference of this quality in an initial and acute phase was secured. Hasanbeyzade overtly ignores this purpose and reworks the story to make a point within the context of his own work. His stated purpose is to stress the extent to which Davud Pasha's treatment of Sultan Osman should not be tolerated. The basis of Hasanbeyzade's manipulation of the Sassanian story is the shifting of its focal point. Whereas in the original story the focal point is the fact that at the acute stage of the foundation of the Sassanian dynasty the transference of farr from father to son was secured, in Hasanbeyzade's reworked version the focal point is the vezir, and more generally, the extent to which having a trustworthy and wise adviser is vital to a ruler.

Following the account of Davud Pasha's execution (transmitted verbatim from Tuği) and before proceeding with the Sassanian story, Hasanbeyzade remarks that some of Davud's followers were pain-stricken by his death, for they had experienced his kindness. However, in the narrator's view, "as admonition to the world," Davud Pasha's body should have been "set on fire and its ashes scattered to the wind." He then adds that what Davud Pasha inflicted upon his padishah was unprecedented in the annals of the grand vezirate and that in ancient times the dynasty of a padishah was highly esteemed. A fate such as the late Sultan Osman's "would probably not have befallen even a person of no nobility at all." Then he presents the Sassanian story, stressing that it is related to the last point.[42] The same message is reiterated in Hasanbeyzade's conclusion at the end of the Sassanian story that emphasizes the harmonious relationship of Ardaşir and his loyal vezir:

"In ancient times vezirs much esteemed and venerated their padishahs.... In truth, what Davud Pasha did a vezir had not done to his padishah in the cycles of time."[43]

This modification, to the same effect, continues in the presentation of the story itself. Here Hasanbeyzade adheres to the basic plot but introduces changes that render it more pertinent to and effective for the point he wishes to make. He achieves this, first, by altering the position of the wise adviser: whereas in the Shahname he is a priest, in Hasanbeyzade's version he is an influential and trusted vezir. To this basic alteration Hasanbeyzade adds other means through which the focus is shifted from the transference of farr to the wisdom and loyalty of the vezir. Thus, while in the *Shahname* Ardaşir's marriage to Ardavan's daughter is something the king has done on his own, in Hasanbeyzade's story he is following the vezir's advice.[44] Further, while in the *Shahname* the priest appears in the story only when Ardaşir has discovered the poisoned drink and sought advice, in Hasanbeyzade's text the fifth sentence reads that "Ardaşir had a high-ranking vezir who was a possessor of wisdom and sagacity."[45] Finally, in the *Shahname* the priest's reward is the abundance of jewels and gold King Ardaşir bestows upon him; the priest then disappears from the scene, and it is related that "learned men" were brought to teach and educate young Şapur. In Hasanbeyzade's text not only do the loyalty and aid of the vezir become indispensable for the rest of Ardaşir's reign, but the vezir is also assigned as Prince Şapur's tutor and teaches him the craft of ruling.[46]

Manifestly, then, Hasanbeyzade's intention in this digression is, by reworking the Sassanian story so as to highlight the wisdom and loyalty of the vezir, to enhance the fault of his negative opposite—Davud Pasha. The latent level offers a multiplicity of meanings that neither contradict nor sustain the consciously intentional meaning conveyed at the manifest level. By *latent level*, in this case, I mean a potential of associations embedded within the text that relate to other episodes and views in Tuği's/Hasanbeyzade's representations of the Haile-i Osmaniye. This net of potential relatedness exists latently in the text because it is impossible to argue decisively that Hasanbeyzade wove it consciously, that he was even aware of it or that he expected his Ottoman readers to be aware of it. To some extent, it is the product of what I think the Ottoman readers might sense in the text.

Four notable points can be seen as instances of such latent relatedness. First, the narrative makes it possible to go one step beyond the loyal vezir— *the* protagonist in Hasanbeyzade's version—and give credit for the "happy end" of the story to King Ardaşir's wisdom. That the wisdom and loyalty of the vezir could manifest themselves in the first place, to the extent that they saved the shahanshah from his own wrong judgment, was the result of Ardaşir's perceptiveness in making that vezir his adviser. It is significant that one of the changes Hasanbeyzade introduces is that the vezir was rewarded not only materially, as the priest in the *Shahname*, but also by becoming the ruler's closest confidant and being entrusted with the affairs of the kingdom. This latent point relates to Sultan Osman's dubious choice of advisers in Tuği's and Hasanbeyzade's view. In the previous chapter it was pointed out that Tuği's chief criticism of Sultan Osman was that his failure as ruler stemmed from his inability to discern bad confidants from good ones. For this inability he eventually paid with his throne and life. We thus have within the same text two diametrically opposed figures and a latent relatedness in which one (Ardaşir) highlights the other (Osman II) negatively.

The second point of latent relatedness, though it does not present as perfectly diametrical an opposition as the first, is the prevention in the Sassanian story of the execution of Ardavan's daughter and hence also the loss of Şapur. This, again in a negative light, might be associable with Sultan Osman's execution of his brother, Prince Mehmed, out of fear for his throne before leaving the capital on his Polish campaign. Both Tuği and Hasanbeyzade strongly deplore this act as tyrannical and use the extent to which it was reprehensible to explain why Sultan Osman suffered more pain from his subjects than other infamous tyrants and how this was a major factor in dooming his reign.[47]

The third focus of associations lies in the supreme act of loyalty by the vezir—his self-castration—and in the fact that he remained a faithful and worthy adviser after he had rendered himself a eunuch. This point, again by negative contrast, is in conformity with Hasanbeyzade's consistent and vehement inveighing against the chief black eunuch, regardless, it seems, of who the incumbent of the office was. Although in principle this focus may be seen as a private case of the first point, it is significant precisely because it has such a strong association not to the function of adviser or confidant in general but to the eunuchship in particular, and because two eunuchs played important roles in the historiography of the period examined in this study.[48]

The fourth and last possible focus of latent meaning has to do with the appointment of the vezir as Prince Şapur's tutor, an addition by Hasanbeyzade to the *Shahname* version. This too is related to what I think was Hasanbeyzade's unwillingness, or inability, to accept the changes in the dynastic household. Before 1600 the tutor of the Ottoman princes *(lala)* was an important figure who might end up shaping the next sultan. When a prince was sent to a province to set up his own household and learn how to rule the empire, he was taught and guided by his mother and tutor. The latter was usually a high-ranking officer. When and if—this was the era of fratricide—that prince became sultan, his lala not infrequently became grand vezir. Mehmed III (r. 1595–1603) is said to have been the last Ottoman sultan who had been sent to the provinces as a prince. With or without conscious authorial intentions, Hasanbeyzade's text might be saying that in the days when princes were educated by vezirs in the provinces, rather than by eunuchs and women in the imperial harem, the sultans who ruled the empire were of higher quality than Osman II.

To conclude, the most significant feature of Hasanbeyzade's representation of the Haile-i Osmaniye is that the *first version* of this historical text incorporates Tuği's nearly verbatim. The only reservation that Hasanbeyzade introduces concerns Tuği's favorable view of Mere Hüseyin Pasha. The meaning conveyed through the Sassanian story, at the manifest level, conforms to Tuği's condemnation of Davud Pasha. At the latent level the potential foci of related meanings support and even enhance views and judgments made by both Tuği and Hasanbeyzade himself in other parts of his work. Hasanbeyzade's abundant use of Tuği is therefore not surprising: he must have found in Tuği's account not only useful information but also a representation of the Haile-i Osmaniye with which he agreed.

IBRAHIM PEÇEVI

Peçevi's account of the Haile-i Osmaniye is comprehensively different from those by Tuği and Hasanbeyzade. This is all the more noteworthy when we register that Peçevi was familiar with Hasanbeyzade's history. In his short introduction Peçevi lists the sources he consulted, and Hasanbeyzade's *Tarih-i Al-i Osman* is one of them. This appears in both the published edition and an unpublished manuscript that is not identical with the one used for the published version.[49] Although it is difficult to assess in the case of lengthy compositions such as Peçevi's when each section was written, it can be inferred that the Haile-i Osmaniye section was written not earlier (most probably later) than 1625, since in mentioning the sheyhülislam at that time, Esad Efendi, Peçevi refers to him as deceased.[50] By then, in all probability, the *first version* of Hasanbeyzade's history was ready and available. It can be therefore argued with reasonable certainty that Peçevi was aware not only of Hasanbeyzade's work in general but also of the Haile-i Osmaniye section in it in particular. It is, however, difficult even to speculate whether Peçevi knew anything about Tuği, for Hasanbeyzade does not mention him.

Regardless of the extent to which Peçevi was conscious of Tuği/Hasanbeyzade when he composed his account of the Haile-i Osmaniye, this account is significantly different from theirs. The fundamentally antithetic nature of Peçevi's representation lies in its favorable view of Sultan Osman and, more clearly, his strong disapproval of the kul, their role in the Haile-i Osmaniye, and the power they wielded. An interesting indication of how effectively Peçevi conveyed this view is the fact that Bekir Sıtkı-Baykal, the most recent "translator" of *Tarih-i Peçevi* from Ottoman to Modern Turkish, on many occasions refers to the kul as "rebels" *(asılar)*. Significantly, he does this even though Peçevi himself, in the Ottoman text, calls them kul or janissaries and sipahis, as Tuği and Hasanbeyzade do.[51] This suggests that the strong disapproval of the kul's behavior in Peçevi's text is so effectively conveyed that a modern reader (Baykal) took the liberty of using a derogatory term that the author himself (Peçevi) had never used, presumably because he sensed that the term was congruent with the spirit of the text.

Three main elements differentiate Peçevi's representation from those of Tuği and Hasanbeyzade. Two of these are expressed at the manifest level of the text: Peçevi's explicit explanation of the event and his views of the various grand vezirs who served during Mustafa I's second reign. Latently, there is one highly significant element: the perspective and location from which central episodes in the Haile-i Osmaniye are narrated, or what was earlier termed the representation of space. These episodes are the three dramatic days in Istanbul during which Sultan Osman was deposed and assassinated and Sultan Mustafa reinstated (18–20 May 1622) and the rebellion of the governor general of Erzurum, Abaza Mehmed Pasha (May–June 1622 on).

Introducing the Haile-i Osmaniye, Peçevi presents three factors, all of which are said to have precipitated the eventual state of "sedition and disorder." All three are bound together by Sultan Osman's failure to defeat the Polish king at Hotin and his blaming the kul's indifferent performance for this failure. The first reason is that under the pretext of performing the hajj the sultan decided to transfer the capital from Istanbul to Cairo, "with the approbation of the chief black eunuch" *(darüssaade ağası sevab-did ile)*. The second and third reasons are incidents occurring during the Hotin campaign that according to Peçevi stirred the enmity between the sultan and the kul. One is that with the pretext of granting incentives and bonuses Sultan Osman made the janissaries undergo an administrative inspection *(yoklama)*. This, Peçevi observes, annoyed them. The other is that after the "martyrdom" of Karakaş Pasha, apparently a charismatic and bold commander, the sultan reproached the sipahis, who were already in low spirits, and deeply distressed them.[52]

The comparison between the formal explanations of Tuği and Peçevi is revealing. To begin with the incidents in the Polish campaign, none of those that are explanatory according to Tuği are mentioned by Peçevi, and vice versa. More important, Peçevi accounts for why the kul were upset, but he does not as much as imply that being upset justified their poor performance and lack of zeal. What Peçevi does deem understandable is the sultan's consequent rage and frustration.[53] The purpose of the incidents Tuği recounted was to establish that the kul rightly felt hurt by the whimsical and ungenerous attitude of the sultan toward them and that the way they performed was only to be expected in view of this attitude.[54] Even more significant is the comparison of the main explanatory statements given by Tuği and Peçevi concerning Sultan Osman's dramatic venture. As was elaborated in the previous chapter, Tuği binds together several issues to produce the impression that those who devised the plan "to cross over to Anatolia" and those who led the sultan astray and estranged him from the kul were the same persons: unworthy confidants led by the chief black eunuch Süleyman Ağa and Hoca Ömer Efendi. Also, in Tuği's presentation the trouble emanated from the mere fact that such a plan could be conceived, for it was inherently evil.[55]

Peçevi's presentation of the same matter is substantially different. For one thing, the inception of the plan does not emanate from the chief black eunuch: as quoted above, he merely gives his "approbation." Osman II himself conceives the plan, and no adviser has incited the ruler against his servants, as Tuği tirelessly repeats.[56] The last important point in the explicit explanations is the attitude toward the chief black eunuch. Tuği's hostility toward and condemnation of Süleyman Ağa and their enhancement by Hasanbeyzade have already been discussed. Peçevi presents a more neutral view, innocent of vituperative terminology. In his account Süleyman Ağa does not incite the sultan against the kul or lead him astray; the sultan's venture is not his initiative, he just approves of it.[57]

As in the case of Hasanbeyzade, but to the contrary effect, Peçevi's balanced portrayal of the chief black eunuchship is consistent. Earlier, Hasanbeyzade's and Peçevi's opposite views of Mustafa Ağa, the chief black eunuch who masterminded Sultan Mustafa's first deposition, were pointed out. In another instance, concluding his account of the Hotin campaign,

Peçevi inserts an explicit remark on Süleyman Ağa. He intimates that his late friend Diyyak Mehmed Pasha, who had taken part in the campaign, told him about a conversation he had had with Süleyman Ağa about the failure to defeat the Polish "infidels." Relating this conversation, Peçevi describes Süleyman Ağa as "a clever and bountiful Abyssinian" who "on the whole had knowledge in some public domains" but not in warfare.[58] Peçevi, then, takes a fairly balanced view of the chief black eunuch. It is not as favorable as that of the previous incumbent, Mustafa Ağa, but compared with the vehement defamation of Süleyman Ağa by Tuği and Hasanbeyzade, it looks vindicatory.

Peçevi's account is also antithetical to Tuği's in the evaluation of two of the five grand vezirs who served during Sultan Mustafa's second reign (May 1622–September 1623): Mere Hüseyin Pasha and Gürcü Mehmed Pasha. It is not surprising that the contradiction is concerned with these two vezirs, for they were involved in two controversial affairs: the rebellion of Abaza Mehmed Pasha (Gürcü) and the factional strife in the capital (Mere). It should also be noted that all three writers—Tuği, Hasanbeyzade, and Peçevi—strongly deplore Davud Pasha as the slayer of Sultan Osman.[59] Faithful to his pro-kul stance, Tuği identifies with their disapproval of Gürcü Mehmed Pasha. In the complicated politics of sociopolitical networks *(intisap)*, he stresses several times that Abaza Pasha, the kul's arch-adversary, was married to the daughter of Gürcü's brother and that he was the favorite protégé of the admiral of the navy *(kapudan paşa)* and ex-grand vezir, Halil Pasha. Owing to these networks, Tuği contends, no firm action was taken to suppress Abaza's sedition. It was for this reason that the kul demanded the removal of Gürcü and indeed caused his dismissal. Tuği then explicitly states that in these circumstances—Abaza's growing audacity and Gürcü's reluctance firmly to deal with it—the kul's action was justified.[60]

Peçevi's account of the chain of grand vezirs who followed Sultan Mustafa's reinstatement is brief. Significantly, he does not mention Abaza's intisaps to either Gürcü Mehmed Pasha or Halil Pasha. Even more meaningful is his version of Gürcü's removal. According to Peçevi, it was not related in any way to the situation in the eastern provinces or to Gürcü's unwillingness to confront Abaza Pasha; nor was Gürcü in Peçevi's report removed by the kul en bloc. Rather, his removal was due to a concerted pressure that Mere Hüseyin Pasha and those whom Peçevi identifies as janissary *zorba*s (thugs) exerted. Under Mere's instructions they appeared one day at the imperial divan and told Gürcü: "A pasha who is against us will not be vezir." He surrendered the seal, and Mere was reappointed. Peçevi further comments that having been twice the grand vezir's deputy *(kaymakam)*, Gürcü was an able and experienced person.⁶¹ Tuği, it should be emphasized, does not utter the term *zorba* in this instance or any other throughout his work.

The contradictory nature of Tuği's and Peçevi's attitudes toward Mere Hüseyin Pasha is even sharper. Regarding Mere's appointments, Tuği reports that they resulted from requests by the kul as a whole to which Sultan Mustafa granted consent. According to Peçevi, Mere's appointments stemmed from the blunt and aggressive ultimata of the zorbas.⁶² The juxtaposition of Tuği and Peçevi on this matter also helps to pinpoint the group that constituted Mere's power base and gained Tuği's partisanship most specifically. Tuği says that the group, which represented the kul in their demand to remove Gürcü, comprised "thirty or forty experienced individuals from the sipahi corps and many from among the janissary ward officers (sing. *odabaşı*)."⁶³ As has already been mentioned, Peçevi argues that these were the janissary zorbas. It is therefore possible to speculate that this group of zorbas consisted chiefly of low- to middle-ranking janissary officers, the odabaşıs, and presumably the rank and file whom they commanded (they were officers of wards in the janissary barracks). It should be made clear that *zorba* denoted a social type, a thuggish behavior and countenance, and that Peçevi did not imply that all janissaries were zorbas or vice versa.

Mere Hüseyin Pasha's power base thus identified seems to be related to a similar phenomenon that Jane Hathaway observes in her illuminating study on the elite households in Ottoman Egypt. Among the various types of households she identifies, one of the most prevalent (and most difficult to notice in the sources) was what she calls the barracks households. These begun as loose patronage connections between middle- and low-ranking officers and the rank and file under their command within the barracks. The more successful among the officers left the barracks and took residence in the neighborhoods of Cairo in which the Ottoman Egyptian elite dwelt. Thus they founded "ordinary" elite households that emulated, as in other Ottoman provinces, the households in the imperial center.⁶⁴

It seems that what we have here is a similar phenomenon in the janissary barracks in Istanbul (Yeni Odalar) that was connected to the grand vezir at the top. It is further possible that Tuği's commitment was not only to the kul in general (this much is certain) but also to a particular janissary–grand vezir household. This possibility is supported by Tuği's account of Mere's first grand vezirate in one of the extant manuscripts of his work. In his first term as grand vezir, Tuği reports in the Dresden manuscript, Mere favored the sipahis and leaned on their support. He was duly dismissed. The formulation clearly conveys the narrator's disapproval of Mere's proximity to the sipahis during his brief first stint as grand vezir (thirty-five days): "Whatever kinds of positions and exalted appointments existed in the Ottoman state, he [Mere] gave to the sipahis."[65]

Back in the Vienna manuscript, Tuği finds several occasions to promote the qualities of Mere. The first occurs in the report on Mere's first removal (July 1622), which was the result of pressure applied by the janissaries, because of a false rumor that Mere had killed their chief, Derviş Ağa. For this Tuği scolds the kul (as a whole) and stresses the absurdity of their official charge *(dava)* against a successful vezir such as Mere. With a pinch of sarcasm he reminds the kul that although they had warned Davud Pasha not to harm Sultan Osman, they did not raise a dava when the former killed the latter; they were quieted with gifts and promotions. This is a rare occasion on which Tuği deems something the kul did deplorable, and it seems hardly coincidental that it concerns Mere.[66]

In the presentation of Mere's second appointment (sometime in late November or early December 1622), Tuği's sympathy becomes patently evident and markedly expressed. It was pointed out earlier that with regard to the second appointment Tuği asserts not only that Mere was the unanimous preference of the kul (with which Peçevi disagrees) but also that this preference stemmed from their recognition of his superior merits (from which Hasanbeyzade deviates).[67] But the most robust praising of Mere by Tuği is expressed poetically. Amidst the account of Mere's second grand vezirate Tuği inserts a long poem, one of the longest in the text, which is a passionate and unreserved eulogy of Mere's personality, governing qualities, and performance. Its spirit is best illustrated by a recurring couplet that emphasizes the theme of the poem:

> Hüseyin Pasha is Mustafa Han's just vezir
> The seal on his beneficence.
> *[Hüseyin Paşa vezir-i adilîdir*
> *Mustafa Hanın sahada hatemîdir].*[68]

The antagonistic judgment of Mere by Peçevi is poignantly conveyed through the term *adalet* (justice). Whereas Tuği essentially depicts Mere as a "just vezir," Peçevi implies that his first term in office was bad enough but, he charges, "This time [the second] he [Mere] abolished justice and law *(adalet ü şre')*, and there was no end to his strange conduct."[69] Peçevi then describes an incident in which Mere subjected a governor and a judge to violent beating, thereby prompting the ulema to demand his dismissal at a meeting in the Sultan Mehmed Mosque.[70] This ill-fated meeting will be recounted in the next chapter.

Peçevi's view that Mere leaned on factional power rather than general consent is further substantiated in the way he explains Mere's eventual downfall (early in 1623). Significantly, while Tuği does not mention this downfall, it is fully developed in Hasanbeyzade's *third version*.[71] Peçevi remarks that by favoring so clearly the janissary zorbas Mere alienated the imperial sipahis. Consequently, when a rumor spread that he had conspired with the former to destroy the latter, the sipahis were agitated and uncompromisingly declared: "This vezir is a vindictive person; we do not want him to stay in power." Mere, according to Peçevi, resorted to his janissary zorbas, who retorted to the sipahis: "You may not want [Mere] [but] we do. . . . What is this bullying of yours? What is your business with the padishah's vezirs?"[72]

Heeding Bayram Pasha's advice, the sipahis decided: "We have no business with the [janissary] odabaşıs." They approached the janissary rank and file, "those who are privates like ourselves," and together brought about the dismissal of Mere and the appointment of Kemankeş Ali Pasha. Peçevi concludes that the lesson of Mere's vezirate was well taken by grandees and commoners alike. According to him, they all said: "How long will offices [go on] being granted in this manner under the onslaught of the zorbas, and the poor and flock in the provinces [go on] burning in the heat of the zorbas' fire?"[73]

The third element in Peçevi's account of the Haile-i Osmaniye that renders it contradictory to those of Tuği and Hasanbeyzade is the meaning latently produced through the representation of space, or the perspective and location from which events were narrated. Earlier in this chapter it was stated that there are two central episodes concerning which the meaning produced by the representation of space is noteworthy: the three dramatic days of the Haile-i Osmaniye (18–20 May 1622) and the rebellion of Abaza Pasha. The first episode was thoroughly discussed in the previous chapter. Focusing on the scene at Orta Cami (Friday, 20 May 1622), I showed that whereas Tuği's perspective is kul-centric, Peçevi's text offers a different perspective that yields different meanings from the perspective and reports of Sıdkı Çelebi and the janissary officer Kara Mizak. The alleged rebellion of Abaza Pasha is of central significance. It is interpreted in Part III, in conjunction with the attempt to explicate the Ottoman state in the seventeenth century as a conflictual site.

CONCLUSION

This chapter has brought the historiographical story of the Haile-i Osmaniye to the point where two alternative representations emerged: Tuği's/Hasanbeyzade's and Peçevi's. The next chapter will establish that Katip Çelebi was aware of both alternatives and all three works and will show what his choice was. An examination of the official narrative of the event in Naima's history will then conclude the historiographical story of the Haile-i Osmaniye.

The historiographical controversy over the alleged rebellion of Abaza Mehmed Pasha, as part of the Haile-i Osmaniye writ large, is of tremendous significance. Suspending its interpretation, however, until the discussion on the conceptualizations and historicity of the Ottoman state (Part III) is warranted. In anticipation of that discussion, the controversy may be highlighted as the ultimate contextualization of the historical discourse interpreted in this part of the study. What is contrasted at this stage as Tuği's/Hasanbeyzade's representation versus Peçevi's will be transformed later, through the rebellion of Abaza Pasha, into the kul narrative versus that of the Anatolian provincial governors *(ümera)* and irregulars *(sekban)*. This in turn will sustain the view that the Ottoman state was, among other things, a discursively contested field of exclusion and inclusion.

6. The Conception of the State Narrative

Thus far the existence of two essentially different representations of the Haile-i Osmaniye has been established: the combination of Tuği's and Hasanbeyzade's accounts and *Tarih-i Peçevi*. These two interpretations were before Katip Çelebi when he composed his version in the *Fezleke-i Tarih*, which with few exceptions became Naima's version and thus the official Ottoman narrative of the Haile-i Osmaniye. This chapter is concerned with how Katip Çelebi's account was formed and its integration into Naima's history. It thereby constitutes a significant illustration of how the *Fezleke* operated as a decisive interpretive junction in seventeenth-century Ottoman historiography.[1]

The discussion comprises three stages. First I show that the presentation of the *Fezleke* suggests, implicitly and explicitly, that Katip Çelebi was familiar with both alternative representations and all three works (Tuği, Hasanbeyzade, and Peçevi) and that he consciously opted for Tuği and rejected Peçevi, though he did not refrain from using Peçevi's work without acknowledging it. The second stage examines Katip Çelebi's reading of Tuği and Hasanbeyzade and draws into the discussion the third version of Hasanbeyzade's history, which was referred to earlier. The third stage establishes that it was indeed the *Fezleke*'s account and Katip Çelebi's judgment that Naima decided to present as the official version and describes how this was done.

KATIP ÇELEBI'S ADOPTION OF TUĞI AND REJECTION OF PEÇEVI

Opening his account of the event to which he gave the name it came to bear (Haile-i Osmaniye), Katip Çelebi intimates that "at the distressful thought of mentioning its content, some historians refrained from elaborating this sort of story."[2] He adds that however painful an undertaking, this event must be presented lest the ethical code of historiography be violated. By abridging such an important work on this matter as *Tarih-i Tuği* and other sources, Katip Çelebi assures his readers, "we have given the writing of truth its full due and attained all the information on this event."[3] The explicit acknowledgment in the *Fezleke* is of course not the only evidence that Tuği is Katip Çelebi's main source for this event. Even a prefatory comparison of these two works up to the point where Mere Hüseyin Pasha is reappointed as grand vezir (end of 1622) validates Katip Çelebi's introductory remark.[4]

Two general points on Katip Çelebi's use of Tuği should be noted. One is that although this use is patently clear, in no way does it resemble Hasanbeyzade's verbatim transmission of Tuği's account discussed in the previous chapter. The other point concerns Katip Çelebi's introductory remark quoted above: Tuği's is the only text that Katip Çelebi identifies as one of his sources; for the rest, he seems content with the term *others (gayri)*.[5]

The fact that all Katip Çelebi explicitly says is that he made use of Tuği and other sources, which he does not specify, means that the following points require substantiation:

1. Since it is established beyond this event that Katip Çelebi was well acquainted with Hasanbeyzade's *Tarih-i Al-i Osman*,[6] and since it was shown in the previous chapter that Hasanbeyzade's early account of our event is a near-verbatim transmission of Tuği (in the first version), it is necessary to ascertain that the work Katip Çelebi actually employed was indeed Tuği's and not its reproduction in Hasanbeyzade's first version.

2. If Katip Çelebi indeed employed Tuği's text, as I shall immediately show, it is necessary to show that he also used Hasanbeyzade's account of the same event and, further, that he used Hasanbeyzade's *third* rather than *first* version.

3. It is necessary to show that Katip Çelebi read the account of the Haile-i Osmaniye in *Tarih-i Peçevi*, consciously rejected the interpretation it offered, but still used it on several occasions without acknowledging Peçevi himself.

There are two chief indications that Katip Çelebi indeed used Tuği's work and not its near-verbatim reproduction in Hasanbeyzade's first version. One, which is weaker, is that the Sassanian story does not appear in the

Fezleke. As was shown in the previous chapter, this story is exclusive to Hasanbeyzade's first version and does not appear in Tuği's history.[7] The other indication, more suggestive, is a poem that laments the killing of Sultan Osman. Following the strangling of the young ruler at Yedikule, Tuği inserts a poem whose message is best conveyed by its recurring line: "They slaughtered the ruler of the world" (*Şah-i cihana kıydılar*). Like the bulk of Tuği's poetry, this poem too does not appear in Hasanbeyzade's history in any version. The poem is presented in toto in the *Fezleke* and at the same point: that is, after the killing of Osman II.[8] In all probability, Katip Çelebi could not have seen this poem elsewhere, which strongly suggests that he employed Tuği's text itself rather than any of its reproductions.

To illustrate further the complicated tangle of interdependency prevalent in Ottoman historiography and to try to sort it out, I turn now to show that although Katip Çelebi seems not to have used the first version of Hasanbeyzade's account of the Haile-i Osmaniye, he did employ the third version. Relying on Tuği, Katip Çelebi must have faced a serious difficulty: Tuği's text ends abruptly on 21 March 1623, during Mere Hüseyin Pasha's second grand vezirate. Yet Katip Çelebi seems to have sensed what the modern reader senses: that the end, so to speak, of the Haile-i Osmaniye was "appropriately" marked by the second deposition of Mustafa I and the accession of Murad IV (September 1623). At that point, Katip Çelebi resorts to Hasanbeyzade's third version as his chief source of reference. This fact can be deduced from a comparison of the *Fezleke* and Hasanbeyzade's third version. For both texts, the comparison starts from the heading that reports on the dismissal of Gürcü Mehmed Pasha and the reappointment of Mere Hüseyin Pasha.[9]

Two remarks should be made here. First, as is the case with Katip Çelebi's use of Tuği, with Hasanbeyzade he does not incorporate the text verbatim but in a manner that I shall explore later; at this point I merely wish to clarify the pattern of interdependency. Second, it is significant that Katip Çelebi does not bear with Tuği until the very end of his account, which continues into Mere's second grand vezirate and is then brought to conclusion. Instead, Katip Çelebi leaves Tuği at the point where Gürcü is deposed and Mere reappointed and shifts to Hasanbeyzade's third version. I insist on stressing the precise point in the *Fezleke* at which the shift from Tuği to Hasanbeyzade occurs because this shift and its location are meaningful rather than arbitrary.

Based on what has been shown thus far, then, the following general pattern emerges: up to the point in the chronological account where the grand vezirate changes hands from Gürcü Mehmed Pasha to Mere Hüseyin Pasha (end of 1622 to beginning of 1623) the *Fezleke* chiefly draws on Tuği's work; thereafter it is mainly based upon Hasanbeyzade's third version. We are now left with the last piece of the historiographic puzzle: Katip Çelebi's use of *Tarih-i Peçevi*. The basic observation in this respect is that Peçevi's work is not mentioned, not even once, in the *Fezleke*'s account of the Haile-i Osmaniye. Despite the absence of any explicit reference, there is evidence in the *Fezleke* to support two observations. First, it can be inferred that Katip Çelebi was familiar with Peçevi's account of the Haile-i Osmaniye but rejected the interpretation it offered. Second, it can be shown that he used *Tarih-i Peçevi* on certain occasions but chose not to acknowledge its author.

Like Tuği, Hasanbeyzade, and Peçevi, Katip Çelebi begins his account with an explanatory exposition, only he formalizes it as a special section under the heading "The Cause[s] of the Event" (*Sebeb-i vak'a*).[10] Like the introductions to his colleagues' accounts, Katip Çelebi's introduction is expected to explain how the enmity between the padishah and his kul evolved and what prompted the former to embark on his (in hindsight) self-destructive venture. Katip Çelebi's explanatory scheme comprises eight causes, and, most significantly, a distinction is drawn between the first two causes and the other six. The first two causes, about which Katip Çelebi says they "were put forward and recounted by the scribes of the event," are the inspection *(yoklama)* that Osman II imposed on the janissaries in the course of the Polish campaign under the pretext of granting incentives and the reproachful speech he delivered to the sipahis following the death of Karakas Pasha, during the same campaign.[11] The comparative analysis of Tuği's and Peçevi's explanations in the previous chapter makes it obvious that these two causes are in fact extracted from Peçevi's explanation, whereas the six that follow are Tuği's, somewhat modified.[12]

Very telling are the fact that Katip Çelebi separates these two sets of causes and the grounds on which he does so, though it should be stressed again that he does not intimate that one set (the first two causes) was Peçevi's and the other (the other six causes) was Tuği's. Following his discussion of the first two causes and preceding his discussion of the other six, Katip Çelebi inserts this revealing judgment: "But these [two] causes are of little authority *(zayıfdır)*. Because this sort of circumstance has always occurred between padishah[s] and kul."[13] Katip Çelebi, then, read Peçevi's account and begged to differ; also, implicitly, he on the whole approved of Tuği's explanation, as we shall see in greater detail later. The rejection of Peçevi's interpretation is supported by the scarcity of references to *Tarih-i Peçevi*, with or without acknowledgment, that characterizes the representation of the Haile-i Osmaniye in the *Fezleke*.

What Katip Çelebi does extract from Peçevi's history testifies to his scholarly perceptiveness. Peçevi's distinctive view and interpretation of the Haile-i Osmaniye, it might be recalled, largely derived from his vantage point on two occasions. One is the three turbulent days of the event in Istanbul (18–20 May 1622), and especially the dramatic third day (Friday, 20 May), when the two sultans, Osman II and Mustafa I, found themselves together at the janissaries' mosque, Orta Cami. Whereas Tuği and Hasanbeyzade, in describing this event, see everything through the kul's eyes, Peçevi's presentation is determined by a different perspective: that of Sıdkı Çelebi, secretary to the Grand Vezir Ohrili Hüseyin Pasha; and Kara Mizak, a janissary officer who was inside Orta Cami on that Friday and told Sıdkı Çelebi what he had seen and heard. Sıdkı Çelebi's comprehensive account is reportedly reproduced by Peçevi. The other occasion is the rebellion of Abaza Pasha concerning which Peçevi's vantage point is that of an Anatolian province rather than the capital.

Katip Çelebi employs Peçevi's insights on the first occasion and ignores the second. He inserts three points extracted from Peçevi, and with good reason, for all three throw additional light on what Tuği and Hasanbeyzade offer on the same instances. The first is Sıdkı Çelebi's questioning of his master, Ohrili Hüseyin Pasha, as to the wisdom of his advice to Sultan Osman to bribe the kul in order to make them abandon Sultan Mustafa and to regain their support.[14] The second instance is concerned with the appointment of Davud Pasha, who shortly afterwards became Genç Osman's executioner, as grand vezir. Whereas Tuği and Hasanbeyzade ascribe the appointment simply to Sultan Mustafa's decree, Peçevi, relying through Sıdkı Çelebi on Kara Mizak, who was present with other janissary officers, the two sultans, and the queen mother *(valide sultan)* at Orta Cami, reports that the appointment was the result of the valide's behest, which these officers sensed and consequently endorsed.[15] The third instance is the scene of the two sultans at Orta Cami, with the kul anxiously waiting outside (Friday, 20 May 1622). While Tuği and Hasanbeyzade depict the scene from the perspective of the kul outside the mosque, Peçevi's camera, again relying indirectly on Kara Mizak, is poised inside Orta Cami and therefore yields a different meaning.[16] Although there can be little doubt that Katip Çelebi extracted these insights from Peçevi, he seems to have been determined not to mention it. Introducing the first instance taken from Peçevi, Katip Çelebi states that its source was Sıdkı Çelebi. As for the second and third instances, he simply notes, "It is related by Kara Mizak that. . . ."[17]

Put in the jargon of modern historical scholarship, what Katip Çelebi does is to render what for him must have been a secondary source (Peçevi) as if it were a primary one (Sıdkı Çelebi and Kara Mizak). In this matter, however, one must urge a cautious judgment of Katip Çelebi, for accusing him of plagiarism might be anachronistic. The fact that discovering all this requires from the modern reader (myself at any rate) some substantial textual footwork, and that the modern reader would intuitively tend to question Katip Çelebi's scholarly integrity, does not mean that this was the case in the contemporary Ottoman discourse. It is possible that in Katip Çelebi's dialogue with his Ottoman audiences, or indeed any Ottoman historian's for that matter, he did not feel obliged by iron rules of precise and explicit reference to sources, and they did not expect it from him. It is also conceivable that what the modern reader deems a tangle of interdependency, which precisely because explicit references are occasionally absent requires a thorough sorting out, was obvious and transparent to the contemporary, well-educated Ottoman reader.

Bekir Kütükoğlu, whose study of Katip Çelebi is foundational, and, following him, Suraiya Faroqhi mention Katip Çelebi's fondness for Peçevi's scholarship as something that significantly determined his choice and presentation of sources. What has been shown thus far complicates this view. Although concerning the Haile-i Osmaniye Katip Çelebi was not oblivious to certain insights offered by Peçevi, it is odd that he at the same time chose not to acknowledge an author whom, according to Kütükoğlu and Faroqhi, he held in high esteem. Most important, Katip Çelebi chose to reject Peçevi's overall interpretation.[18]

KATIP ÇELEBI'S REPRESENTATION OF THE HAILE-I OSMANIYE

I now turn to examine more closely what Katip Çelebi did with his predecessors' accounts and how his interpretation of the Haile-i Osmaniye stands vis-à-vis these sources. To present this examination clearly I focus on three points, which follow the pattern of the comparison in the previous chapter between Tuği's work and *Tarih-i Peçevi*. I begin with the analysis of Katip Çelebi's explicit explanatory framework, his introduction to and concluding remarks on Osman II's reign. Second, I deal with the way Tuği's text was incorporated into the *Fezleke*, what I call Katip Çelebi's editorial approach to Tuği's work, and how it affected the interpretation conveyed by the *Fezleke*. Third, I focus on the view Katip Çelebi took of Mere Hüseyin Pasha and account for why it was precisely at the point of Gürcü Mehmed Pasha's removal and Mere's reappointment that Katip Çelebi abandoned Tuği's work and turned to Hasanbeyzade's third version.

The Formal Explanations

At first glance, Tuği's and Katip Çelebi's explanations might misleadingly seem so similar so as to be virtually interchangeable.[19] However, a more painstaking comparison reveals, side by side with the apparent similarities, significant and interesting differences both manifestly and latently. The explanations are similar, first, in that Katip Çelebi's arguments resemble Tuği's and at times are identical. Second, both attempt to answer the same explicitly defined questions: what stirred up the enmity between the sultan and his kul and what prompted the sultan's venture. But the way these arguments are phrased in each case, and especially the manner and order in which they are presented, produce significantly different, though not necessarily contradictory, explanatory schemes.

The six causes, which by implication are in Katip Çelebi's view valid, are the following.[20] The first, listed also by Tuği, was the result of a rivalry in 1620 between the janissary chief, Yusuf Ağa, and the bostancı başı (lit. "head of the gardeners," contextually head of one of the units of the sultan's retinue), Mehmed Ağa. The latter, to humiliate his adversary, made the young ruler patrol the city incognito with a group of bostancıs, raid the cafes, and inflict heavy punishments on the janissaries he seized there. "Because of that most of the janissaries had grief in their hearts."[21] The second cause, again mentioned by Tuği, was the sultan's payment of insultingly low incentives to the troops during the Hotin campaign. The third, to be found in Tuği's work but not as an independent cause, was that by attributing the failure of the Polish campaign to the kul's lack of zeal, the sultan "ostensibly manifested behavior that indicated his aversion to them."[22] The fourth cause, central in Tuği's presentation, was that the kul had been slandered to the padishah by "some ignorant confidants of his," whom Katip Çelebi, unlike Tuği, does not name. Consequently, Katip Çelebi further argues, "the notion of preparing a new army was awakened in his [the sultan's] inner consciousness."[23] The fifth cause, which again Tuği alludes to but not as an independent one, was that what was awakened in the previous cause prompted the sultan to bring the views of his confidants "from potentiality to actuality":[24] that is, his attempt to realize his venture. The sixth cause, the status of which in Tuği's presentation is identical to the previous one, was that the padishah, as a pretext to going ahead with his venture, set out to go on the hajj "without consultation."[25]

In Chapter 4 it was shown that the causes in Tuği's explanation were presented in the opposite order to the chronological order in which they had taken place. Katip Çelebi took more or less the same causes but presented them in a diametrically opposite order: that is, according to the chronological order in which they had occurred. The meaning produced by this alternative representation is explained in what follows in conjunction with the latent level in the *Fezleke*'s formal explanation. At the manifest level, the most marked difference between the two explanations is the way in which each set of causes accounts for the two chief questions mentioned earlier: what (or who) precipitated the animosity between the padishah and the kul and what (or who) brought Genç Osman to conceive his plan. Tuği, it may be recalled, through the introduction to his explanation and other means, deemed one cause the reply to both questions: Sultan Osman's unworthy advisers and confidants.[26]

In the *Fezleke* the replies to these two questions are not unrelated, but different causes are suggested for each. Through the first three causes listed above, Katip Çelebi accounts *only* for how the antagonism between the sultan and the kul appeared, and this part of the explanation does not involve the sultan's advisers. They come into the picture only in the fourth cause, when, according to Katip Çelebi, they exploited the already evident animosity to instill in the sultan's mind the notion that his present kul were useless and that he had to dispense with them and recruit others in their stead. This fourth cause is also where the *Fezleke* establishes a connection between the two aforementioned questions: the enmity ought to be explained by the treatment of the kul by their master, regardless of his advisers; the confidants exacerbated an already existing circumstance to manipulate the sultan, the result of this manipulation being Osman II's plan with its far-reaching ramifications.

Tuği's explanation, then, by identifying those who stirred up the animosity between the ruler and the kul and those who induced the padishah to conceive his venture as the same people (the confidants), produces a single grand cause for the whole event. Katip Çelebi presents a more complicated picture, in which there are different causes for the animosity and for the sultan's venture. What establishes a connection between them in this scheme are the advisers who exacerbated the mutual resentment, which they were not responsible for creating, to produce the sultan's plan. There is another interesting difference, also at the manifest level. Although Tuği is critical of Sultan Osman, his castigation focuses on—but is also confined to—one specific mistake: his bad choice of advisers who led him astray. It is for these advisers that his vehement, on occasion virulent, contempt and criticism are reserved.[27]

A careful observation of the fourth and fifth causes in the *Fezleke* reveals that its implied critique of the ruler is broader than that of Tuği's account. What Katip Çelebi does is subtly to distinguish the responsibility that rests with the confidants from that which belongs to the sultan. The fourth cause stresses the folly of the advisers, and in this respect Katip Çelebi subscribes to Tuği's view in both content and tone: their slandering of the kul's performance in Hotin he calls "nonsense" *(hezeyan)*; he describes the advisers themselves as "ignoramuses," "heedless," and "mindless," and what they advised as "perverse ideas" *(efkâr-i faside)*.[28] At this point, however, Katip Çelebi introduces an additional cause, the fifth in his explanation, which distinguishes the advisers' folly (giving bad advice) from the action for which the sultan ought to be held accountable. Sultan Osman should be criticized, in Katip Çelebi's view, for the fact that having heard "perverse ideas," he sought "to bring them from potentiality to actuality" *[kuvveden fi'le getirmek]*.[29] Katip Çelebi, then, holds the advisers responsible for the fact "that the notion of preparing a new army was awakened in [the sultan's] inner consciousness."[30] But once the notion was awakened in his consciousness, it was the sultan's responsibility that he accepted it and, more important, that he tried to execute it.

The *Fezleke* may emphasize the part of the causality that is independent of the sultan's confidants, and that is focused on the ruler himself, in another way, at the latent level of the text. The crux of this emphasis is that while drawing on the causes offered by Tuği, Katip Çelebi presents them in a diametrically *opposite* order. (Altering the order of presentation is a general editorial approach that Katip Çelebi seems to have adopted toward Tuği's text; I shall dwell on this policy shortly.) The central argument in Tuği's explanation is latently made plausible by the representation of time. The causes in this exposition are arranged in an order opposite to their occurrence on the time continuum: that is, chronologically from end to beginning: Tuği first reports the slandering of the kul by the chief black eunuch, his inducing the padishah to rid himself of them and prepare a new army, and then how and why Hoca Ömer Efendi allied himself with chief black eunuch and his scheme. Only then does Tuği list the causes that relate to what took place between the sultan and the kul before and during the Polish campaign.[31]

From the summary of the *Fezleke*'s explanation above, it can be readily seen that Katip Çelebi presents more or less the same causes, but in the "proper" chronological order: first the evolving antagonism between the kul and the padishah, a process that was kindled as early as 1620, and as yet without mention of the advisers. Their intervention and the sultan's venture that ensued are brought to the fore only in the latter part of the *Fezleke*'s formal explanation. The opposite order of presentation of roughly the same "facts" in Tuği's account and the *Fezleke* lends support to the judgmental emphasis each text puts at the manifest level. In the case of Tuği's work, it latently supports the judgment that the advisers, especially the chief black eunuch, were the cause both for the enmity between the sultan and the kul and for the sultan's venture. As for the *Fezleke*, the correlation between the order of presentation and the chronological order emphasizes its attribution of a smaller role in the causation, and the blame, on Sultan Osman's confidants, even if their actions are deemed reprehensible.

The argument that the representations of time in each of these explicit explanations latently support their judgmental emphases requires some elaboration. Tuği's presentation of the causes in an order opposite to that of their chronological occurrence masks the fact that the enmity might have been created *before* the chief black eunuch intervened and advised the sultan to embark on his ambitious plan. This masking, I think, is bound to be more effective in a speech situation because the hearers did not have a written text that they could read and reread and because it was more difficult for them, as the oral address moved on to another issue, instantly to pause and notice, let alone ponder, the fact that a series of causes was being presented in an order opposite to that of their chronological occurrence.

The consequence of the presentation of roughly the same causes in adherence to their chronological occurrence in the *Fezleke* can be formulated in two ways. One is that the latent meaning produced by Tuği's presentation is canceled out. The other is that the unmasking of what Tuği's presentation masked supports the judgmental nuance, which Katip Çelebi's explanation adds to Tuği's: that is, that not all of the blame should be pinned on the advisers. This is achieved because the mere correlation between the order of presentation and the chronological occurrence clearly brings to the fore the possibility that the enmity between the sultan and the kul was created independently of the advisers, however reprehensible their later exploitation of this enmity might have been.

In addition to the new dimension that Katip Çelebi introduces to what basically was Tuği's explanation—judging the padishah for his decisions and actions, not only for his choice of advisers—the *Fezleke*'s explicit explanation also contains a formal conclusion to Osman II's reign.[32] In this conclusion, Katip Çelebi's chief deviation from Tuği is the aura of astrological inevitability that he gives to the explanation: "Apart from the ascending star of the late padishah [Osman II] not having been favorable, he [also] ascended the throne at an ill-boding time in a day of perpetual inauspiciousness, which [astrologers] interpreted [as] 'the low-lying hour.'"[33]

As evidence of the destructive potential of the inauspicious horoscope for the days of both the sultan's birth and his accession, Katip Çelebi lists at the end of his conclusion a series of natural disasters that afflicted Istanbul in the years 1619–21. These included huge fires, heavy rains and great floods, and the freezing of the Black Sea, which was followed by dearth and famine.[34] The introduction of an element of preordained inevitability into Katip Çelebi's explanation poses a problem that is shared with Tuği's and other texts: the tension between the freedom of choice of human agency in history and the existence of a providential grand design. As in Tuği's text, in the *Fezleke* one gets the impression that these two elements do not create a tension but rather coexist and complement each other.

Katip Çelebi's attitude toward the possible tension in his explanation of the Haile-i Osmaniye, namely the elaborate criticism of Sultan Osman's decisions and advisers and the preordained dooming of his reign to failure, is implied in a sentence that precedes the presentation of the astrological framework: "In the realm of causes there are many spiritual *(ma'nevi)*[35] causes for everything."[36] As I understand it within the context of the formal explanation, this sentence suggests that to Katip Çelebi astrological causation was supplementary, rather than contradictory, to the causes presented in the introduction. Put differently, in Katip Çelebi's logic the immediate-human causation and the preordained-astrological causation, or the material and spiritual respectively, joined to yield a coherent explanation and were not mutually exclusive. Modern readers are advised to resist the temptation of applying their criteria of logic and causal deduction and of judging Katip Çelebi in their terms. After all, these criteria are as culture conditioned as Katip Çelebi's.

The Editorial Approach

I turn now from the formal explanation to what I earlier called Katip Çelebi's editorial approach to Tuği's work. First I will explain why I contend that this ostensibly technical issue is actually meaningful; then I will illustrate my contention through what I consider the most significant example of Katip Çelebi's editorial approach. As stated, the crux of the editorial approach is that whereas Tuği's text presents events and facts (or "causes") out of the chronological order in which they occurred according to Tuği himself—and, as was abundantly shown in Chapter 4, these occasions are numerous—the *Fezleke* arranges the same facts and events according to the chronological order in which they are said to have occurred. To use a variation on a familiar theme, Katip Çelebi edited Tuği according to the principle of "first happened, first presented." That the alteration of the order in which facts are presented yields a different, though not necessarily contradictory, meaning is evident from the comparison of the formal explanations. In this regard, the present case is another instance of a contention, adopted from Hayden White, that I have pursued throughout the study: that facts are where they are in a text not incidentally but because they sanction and make plausible certain interpretations.

The argument about Katip Çelebi's editorial approach and its effect cannot be based solely on the alteration of the order of the causes in the formal explanation discussed in the previous section; it is simply too broad a contention based on too little text. I shall therefore illustrate my contention through a more substantive example that shows how Katip Çelebi used and edited Tuği's text, and consequently how the *Fezleke* might latently reinterpret this text.

In the prose part of Tuği's work, two codes are employed: the chronological account and the digressions in time. Dwelling on several digressions, I earlier drew attention to their importance as loci of the text's interpretive aspect, and I stressed the significance not only of the content, form, introduction to, and conclusion of the digressions but also of their position in the text vis-à-vis the evolving chronological account. In the light of this reminder, let us now briefly survey the opening portion of Tuği's work, up to the point where the chronological account reaches the end of the first day of the Haile-i Osmaniye "proper" (18 May 1622) but before the kul's surge into the Imperial Palace, which took place on the second day (19 May).

Tuği's presentation begins in the morning of 18 May 1622 with a brief description of the initial assembly of the kul near the Süleymaniye, where they demanded that the padishah give up his venture. Then the chronological account pauses and the first digression—the formal explanation—is inserted. The chronological description is momentarily resumed but instantly goes back to late April 1622, when the preparations to implement the sultan's plan were set in motion. Still within the chronological account, Tuği's text returns to the growing gathering of the kul (noon, 18 May 1622), this time adding a demand for the execution of the hoca and the chief black eunuch to their list, allegedly sanctioned by a fetva of the sheyhülislam. Tuği then reports the assaults of the furious kul on the homes of the hoca and the grand vezir, firmly but to no avail demanding that these two intercede with the padishah on their behalf, and recounts their dispersal, resolved to reassemble next morning (afternoon and evening, 18 May

1622). At that point, most significantly, instead of proceeding with what happened on the next day (19 May), Tuği's text, going back to early May 1622, introduces a long digression that presents the padishah's dream and its final outcome: his resolute intention to carry out his plan despite earlier indications that he might abandon the idea.[37]

Essentially, what Katip Çelebi's presentation of the same facts and events does is to simplify Tuği's adroit maneuver on the time continuum. Before commencing the chronological account, Katip Çelebi provides a general introduction to the Haile-i Osmaniye and his sources, which is followed by the formal explanation (which in Tuği is the first digression). Then, in a chronologically ordered manner, each under a separate heading, he recounts the events up to the end of the first day of the dramatic climax (18 May 1622): the issuance of the preparatory decrees to the provincial governors in Anatolia (mid-April 1622); the padishah's dream and its consequences (early May 1622, in Tuği's text the second digression); and only then the first day of the Haile-i Osmaniye "proper" (with which Tuği's text begins): the kul's gathering near the Süleymaniye, their raids on the homes of the hoca and the grand vezir, and their dispersal in the evening (18 May 1622).[38]

The fact that the *Fezleke* was composed as a purely written text makes reasonable the assumption that Katip Çelebi's intention was to straighten Tuği's twists and turns on the time continuum. The effect of Katip Çelebi's editorial approach is twofold: first, it nullifies the dramatic effect of the digressions in Tuği's speech; second, by rendering the digressions part of the chronological account, it considerably reduces the manipulative power of the digressions in Tuği's text. That the combination of the chronological code and the digressions enhances the drama in Tuği's narrative seems obvious. For a brief moment the audience is allowed a glance at the kul's gathering and is then immediately drawn back to the intriguing of the chief black eunuch and the Hotin ordeal. Then the audience is readmitted to the growing kul assembly and follows their activities throughout the rest of that day, only to go three weeks back and be told a dream the sultan had one night. All these fluctuations in time and place vanish with a strict adherence to the chronological presentation.

The manipulative effect of the digressions in Tuği's text is so radically reduced in the *Fezleke* because the digressions simply disappear. In Chapter 4 I elaborated on the role played in Tuği's text by the digression that presented the sultan's dream. This digression and Tuği's explanation of why it was inserted convey most forcefully and effectively the kul-centrism that underlies his representation and constitute the high point of his text, having been essentially a defense of what the kul did in the Haile-i Osmaniye. The mere fact that the very same dream and its interpretation and consequence are in the *Fezleke* located elsewhere in the narrative, as just a part of the chronological account,[39] results in the dream losing the manipulative effect that it possessed when it was presented as an emphasized digression in Tuği's text. The disappearance of this digression, and hence also its effect, epitomizes the chief consequence of Katip Çelebi's editorial approach at the latent level of his text: it effectively tempers Tuği's extremely kul-centric way of looking at and presenting things and his strong pro-kul bias without contradicting the basic interpretation.

The Grand Vezirate of Mere Hüseyin Pasha

Let us now consider two issues that may initially seem unrelated but are in fact interchangeable: first, the reason why Katip Çelebi leaves Tuği's account as his chief source and shifts to Hasanbeyzade's third version at the point when Mere is reappointed as grand vezir and, second, Katip Çelebi's view of Mere and the support he was given by the kul and whether it is different from Tuği's view. As indicated earlier, I ascribe significance to the precise point where the shift from Tuği's work to Hasanbeyzade's third version occurs in the *Fezleke* because on the face of it this point does not seem to be the obvious place for this shift to be located. Had the *Fezleke* borne with Tuği's work up to the point where the latter is abruptly brought to conclusion (late March 1623) and then turned to Hasanbeyzade's third version, the shift would have been self-evident. But Katip Çelebi leaves Tuği's work and turns to Hasanbeyzade's precisely at the description of Gürcü Mehmed Pasha's removal and Mere's reappointment, disregarding Tuği's fairly detailed account of this important development and what followed it.[40]

Comparison of the three texts (Tuği's, Hasanbeyzade's third version, and the *Fezleke*) concerning Mere's reappointment suggests the reason for the point at which this shift occurs. Katip Çelebi must have found unacceptable Tuği's favorable view of Mere and his praise for the support lent to him by the kul and must have preferred Hasanbeyzade's account, which in its third version depicts an utterly different picture of Mere. Tuği's view on the matter can be thus summarized: the kul rightly demanded the removal of Gürcü from the grand vezirate because he was unwilling and unable to suppress Abaza's rebellion; they wanted Mere not only because they regretted having wronged him earlier but also because of his superior authority and administrative qualities; the latter point is presented by Tuği not as the kul's or his own view but as a generally held and accepted truth. Peçevi presents a comprehensively antithetical interpretation in this matter. More important to the present argument, Hasanbeyzade in the first version, in one of his very rare deviations from Tuği's text, inserts a sentence that implies reservations about Mere having been reappointed because of his superior merits and suggests that his reappointment derived solely from his being more masterful than his rivals in the art of winning over the kul.[41]

Hasanbeyzade's reservations about Mere, only hinted at in the first version, are vigorously and explicitly uttered in the third version. The marked difference between the first and third versions concerning Mere should be attributed, I think, not so much to the better historical perspective Hasanbeyzade had when he produced the third version, but rather to the fact that by that time Mere was most probably out of favor and power, perhaps even not alive. This must have meant that Hasanbeyzade could fearlessly say what he thought. Hasanbeyzade's account of Mere's second grand vezirate, in the third version, contradicts Tuği's in two ways: it contains a judgment that is opposed to what Tuği says, and it recounts a very significant event that is absent from Tuği's work even though it occurred within that work's time span.

To take the first point first, contrary to what Tuği says, according to Hasanbeyzade the kul's initial demand to dismiss Gürcü, presented to the janissary ağa by "forty experienced sipahis and many janissary company commanders (odabaşıs)," was based, not on Gürcü's alleged reluctance to deal with Abaza's rebellion, which is not even mentioned in this respect, but rather on his tormenting them: "Gürcü Mehmed Pasha, the present grand vezir, has unnecessarily killed and destroyed many of our comrades. After today, we do not want him in the [grand] vezirate."[42] Contradicting Tuği, Hasanbeyzade, like Peçevi, considers Gürcü's performance and personality commendable rather than deplorable. In his own explicit voice, he intimates that Gürcü was renowned for his correct judgment and praises him for the fact that "he caused the execution of Sultan Osman's killers according to what they deserved by the Şeriat."[43]

Further in conformity with Peçevi and in opposition to Tuği is what Hasanbeyzade says about Mere's role in Gürcü's removal. Tuği emphasizes that Gürcü was deposed as a result of the kul's initiative and says that only when asked whom they wished to become the next grand vezir did the kul point at Mere. Hasanbeyzade, like Peçevi, leaves no room for doubt that Mere was behind this initiative from its inception: "While he [Gürcü] was dispensing justice (ihkâk-i hak etmişken), it seems that Mere Hüseyin Pasha set out to become the grand vezir again."[44] Hasanbeyzade elaborates on Mere's contrivance and reports that a group of zorbas (thugs) raided the

Imperial Council and forced Gürcü's dismissal and the reinstatement of Mere. Furthermore, according to Hasanbeyzade, these representatives of the kul approached Gürcü in a confrontational manner *(bilmuvacehe)*, and the content of their ultimatum to him was more violent than even what Peçevi presented: "We do not want you in this vezirate. We do not accept that [an] impotent person is thus established in the grand vezirate. If as a result of this assault a change of vezirate does not occur, we shall draw [our] daggers and tear you apart."[45] To remove lingering doubts as to why Mere was reappointed, Hasanbeyzade concludes in his own voice: "In consequence of this seditious speech he [the sultan] granted the seal of the vezirate to Mere again and gave him precedence over all the vezirs."[46]

In the third version, Hasanbeyzade contradicts Tuği on not only the circumstances that brought about Mere's reappointment but also the nature of his second term in power. In a similar vein to Peçevi, and antithetically to Tuği, who praises the sense of justice shown by Mere in his second vezirate, Hasanbeyzade's characterization is succinctly conveyed through the following sentence: "In his vezirate this [the second] time Mere Hüseyin Pasha manifested a degree of wickedness and enmity, the expressing and explaining of which is impossible."[47] Like Peçevi, Hasanbeyzade recounts at length an event that all Ottoman historians viewed gravely but that Tuği does not mention, though it occurred (January 1623) within the time span of his work.[48] The event came to be known, in this as in other cases thanks to Katip Çelebi's naming, as "The Incident of the *Abu'lfeth* [Mehmed II] Mosque."[49] Briefly, this was what happened. On finding out that the ulema had gathered at Sultan Mehmed's mosque, where, with the padishah's approval, the sheyhülislam was to remove the grand vezir, Mere Hüseyin Pasha took action. He sent some janissaries and sipahis, who intercepted the sheyhülislam on his way to the mosque and detained him at the residence of the janissary chief *(Ağa Kapısı)*. Mere then repeatedly ordered those at the mosque to disperse. When this had no effect, a large force of kul was dispatched to the mosque. They surged into Sultan Mehmed's mosque and killed many ulema.[50]

What matters to the present argument is not so much the details of the incident as the fact that its mere presentation was bound to portray Mere unfavorably and that the incident is reported in Hasanbeyzade's third version but is absent from Tuği's. Finally, the account by Hasanbeyzade of Mere's removal perfectly conforms with Peçevi's; it points out what Mere's power base was and that he had devious intentions. Like Peçevi, Hasanbeyzade reports that the sipahis sensed that Mere was scheming to destroy them and demanded his dismissal. Mere resorted to his zorbas, whom Hasanbeyzade explicitly identifies as the janissary ward commanders *(odabaşıs)*, but eventually to no avail. He was removed and replaced by Kemankeş Ali Pasha.[51] It is essential to note that this particular depiction of Mere by Tuği, and his failure to mention the incident in the Sultan Mehmed Mosque, are confined to MS Flügel 1044. In other manuscripts of Tuği's work the depiction of Mere is different and the incident is reported. This is one of the reasons why I argue elsewhere that MS Flügel 1044 is an extant manuscript that represents the authentic oral address that was delivered amidst the unfolding Haile-i Osmaniye.[52]

It was most probably this contradictory judgment of Mere and the support lent to him by the kul that prompted Katip Çelebi to adopt Hasanbeyzade's third version at that point and to abandon Tuği's text before it ended. A comparison of the *Fezleke* and Hasanbeyzade's third version concerning the three points discussed above patently reveals Katip Çelebi's shift and adherence to Hasanbeyzade.[53]

A remark made by Naima suggests that he too was aware of the shift in the *Fezleke* from Tuği to Hasanbeyzade and what caused it. As will be shown later, Naima, with respect to the Haile-i Osmaniye, followed the *Fezleke* closely; even when he did introduce changes, they very rarely were in the form of direct citations from the *Fezleke*'s sources. One of these rare occasions falls precisely at the point where the above shift occurs—Gürcü's removal and Mere's second appointment. Naima inserts the following sentence that is absent from the Fezleke: "Hasanbeyzade says that the sipahis and janissaries made an assault upon the [Imperial] Council in agreement *(müttefikan).*"[54]

Naima's reference, doubtless extracted from Hasanbeyzade's third version,[55] has two implications. First, the mere fact that Naima found it necessary to refer directly to Hasanbeyzade, rather than be content with the *Fezleke*, suggests that he was well aware of the shift Katip Çelebi had made and perhaps sought to emphasize it. Second, the content of the reference indicates that Naima understood, in the same way that I do, why Katip Çelebi had turned from Tuği to Hasanbeyzade at that specific point. This reference is not a citation of Hasanbeyzade but Naima's concise summation of what he thought Hasanbeyzade intended to convey. The sentence quoted above, which Naima presents as "Hasanbeyzade says that . . . ," does not appear in Hasanbeyzade's text; especially, the word *müttefikan* ("in agreement") was not used by Hasanbeyzade. This subtly implies that Naima realized what Hasanbeyzade had wanted to say: that what was "in agreement" was a scheme that Mere and the kul who were loyal to him tried to carry out. With respect to Mere and the support he was given by the kul, unlike the Haile-i Osmaniye in general, Tuği's judgment stands apart. Whereas he praises Mere himself and the kul for supporting him, all the other historians surveyed here deplore Mere, his followers, and the way he won their support and wielded power.

The discussion of the historical representation of Mere Hüseyin Pasha occasions a final comment on the extant manuscripts of Tuği's work. In Chapter 4 I stated that I mainly used that version of Tuği's text, which is represented by the unpublished manuscript catalogued as MS Flügel 1044 (Austrian National Library, Vienna) for two reasons. One is that MS Flügel 1044, or a similar variant, was what the Ottoman historians read and used. The other is that MS Flügel 1044, or a similar variant, best represents the version of Tuği's text that circulated in great proximity to the occurrence of the Haile-i Osmaniye, perhaps even as it was unfolding.

In further support of my choice, MS Flügel 1044 is the only manuscript of Tuği's work I have seen that is categorically and comprehensively pro–Mere Hüseyin Pasha. In other manuscripts Mere is explicitly castigated, sometimes severely, and the incident at Mehmed II's mosque is reported. What this indicates, I think, is that in MS Flügel 1044 we get the Tuği who is a partisan not only of the kul in general but also of the particular—possibly Albanian (see Chapter 8)—household of Mere and the middle-ranking janissary officers in the barracks. In other—later, in my view—manuscripts, the unadulterated praise of Mere was probably unpalatable, so copyists and scribes introduced changes.[56]

CONCLUSION

The formation of the state narrative in Naima's history concludes the unfolding of the historiographical story of the Haile-i Osmaniye. In the next and final part of the book, the Ottoman state in the seventeenth century assumes center stage. Two historiographical issues—the alleged rebellion of Abaza Mehmed Pasha and Naima's particular comments—are highlighted in conjunction with the discussion on the state as a conclusion of the way history writing and the state were intimately related in the seventeenth century.

Before turning to the Ottoman state, a concluding remark on history and theory may be of some interest. The relationship between the *Fezleke* and Tuği's text in particular highlights another relationship—between Hayden White's theory and my interpretation—in several related ways.[57] First, White's argument that to change the form of the narrative may not change the information conveyed but does change the meaning produced is what drew my attention to Katip Çelebi's reordering of Tuği's text and to the fact that this reordering was meaningful. Second, White's view that the formation of a narrative discourse necessarily entails the appearance of alternative representations is enhanced in my analysis, which in turn enjoys the advantage of interpreting a corpus of texts. If one reads Katip Çelebi's history in isolation, it is difficult to notice that his strict adherence to the chronological ordering of events—ostensibly so obvious a choice as to be trivial—is actually a reordering of another form of representation, namely Tuği's. The constant consideration of a textual corpus contributes to White's theory in the sense that whereas for him it suffices that alternative representations can be imagined, here they actually exist and can be brought to the fore.

Finally, there is the recurring theme of Freudian latency that White, and I, informed by him, have employed. What can be safely argued is that Katip Çelebi's reworking of Tuği's text, or editorial approach, resulted in meaningful differences. It may be suggested that since Katip Çelebi was part of neither Tuği's context nor, especially, the oral address, and since he consciously produced a written text that he assumed would be read, there was no reason for him not to reorder Tuği's text the way he did. What is impossible to ascertain is whether through his "editing" of Tuği's text Katip Çelebi intended his own text to produce the meaning it did. The freedom from the author's conscious intention that the text may thus gain makes this level of the text latent.

PART III

The State

7. The Early Modern Ottoman State
History and Theory

The purpose of Part III is to establish possible relations between historiographical discourse in the seventeenth century and a major process in that period, namely the redefinition of the state. The chief argument is that this discourse, interpreted in detail in previous chapters, is a useful guide for understanding the process of redefinition, for it is a manifestation and part and parcel of the struggle over drawing and redrawing the state's boundaries. Put differently, the shaping of the historiographical discourse was part of the power and identity politics of the seventeenth century and, ultimately, part of the contest over being included in the state and having the power to exclude from it. The previous chapters showed that the Ottoman historical texts are not unstructured collections of facts; rather, examined as a corpus, they constitute a narrative discourse that is judgmental and interpretive. At this point I wish to take the historiographical discourse beyond the domain of both *Quellenkritik* investigation and literary interpretation to what is conventionally said to lie outside texts. Attempting to do this, however, I cautiously bear in mind that what is said to lie outside texts is ultimately accessible to us historians only in a textual way.

The present chapter selectively looks at two kinds of scholarly literature. The first consists of attempts to grapple with the state as a conceptual and historical challenge. The second comprises significant conceptualizations and interpretations of the early modern Ottoman state. The problem, I shall show, is that the first kind of scholarly literature has not had sufficient bearing on the second. Numerous substantial achievements notwithstanding, scholarship on the Ottoman state has, by omission, produced a lacuna. The Ottoman state has been substantively considered as institutions, rulers, and functionaries and as a reflection of material processes. The possibility that the Ottoman state—like all other states—is *also* a construction, a reified subject endowed with autonomous agency and ontological existence, has not been addressed. More important, the ways in which both contemporary Ottomans and modern scholars have thus reified the state have not been investigated. It would seem that the famous Ottoman slogan *Devlet-i Aliye daiman muzaffere* (The Sublime State is always victorious) has been curiously vindicated.

I suggest in this chapter that the literature discussed below may be highly instructive for thinking about the Ottoman state, and I offer in the next chapter a preliminary illustration of how the state might be interpreted by this line of thought "through" the historical texts.

THE STATE AS A CONCEPTUAL AND HISTORICAL PROBLEM

Reflections on and study of the state constitute a vast and elusive field, both historically and conceptually. The following discussion is instrumental. It is meant to lead to a problem in the conceptualization of the Ottoman state that I wish to address. Accordingly, the underlying theme that runs through the presentation is a critique of the binary way of thinking about the state whereby a line separates state and society into two concrete, identifiable objects.[1] The state as analytical unit was expelled from the study of politics in the 1950s and 1960s in favor of something called the political system, within which both state and society were included. The appearance of this particular trend might be explained, intellectually, by the dissatisfaction with the formalistic emphasis that prevailed at that point and, politically, by the Cold War.[2]

From the 1970s on, the Hegelian-idealist understanding of the state was rejuvenated, especially in American political science, in the form of a school of thought that came to be known as the statist approach, or the approach of "bringing the state back in." The statist school emerged as a reaction to the fact that the state had vanished in the ubiquity of the political system, hence the need to "bring it back in." The modus operandi of the statist school justifies the view that it is a rejuvenation of the idealist understanding of the state. The state is first grasped as an autonomous agency that lies outside of society, acts upon it, and is in a way independent of it. Then follows the demarcation of a clear boundary that separates the two entities, state and society, which are conveyed as concrete "things" rather than constructed abstractions. To render the boundary more dichotomous and less porous, the domain of the state is finally reduced to decision making. Instead of the Weberian emphasis on institutions that legitimize and execute violence and coercion, or the Marxist focus on the maintenance of social and capital relations, the new statist approach identifies the essence of the state "in the formation and expression of authoritative intentions." Construed as machinery of intentions—usually termed *rule making, decision making,* or *policy making*—the state becomes essentially a subjective realm of plans, programs, or ideas. In the words of a critic of the statist school, "The state appears to stand apart from society in the unproblematic way in which intentions or ideas are thought to stand apart from the external world to which they refer."[3]

Whereas the reappearance of the Hegelian tradition, in the form of the statist approach, hardly involved questioning or elaborating the tradition itself, some scholars from the Marxist school undertook a more serious stocktaking that, still within the framework of this school, opened new avenues for the understanding of the state. A significant locus of this venture, from the 1980s on, has been the *Journal of Historical Sociology.* One of the more stimulating contributions, by Philip Abrams, subverts the perception of the state as an autonomous entity, a thing that exists independently of its ideological abstraction. The effective collusion in the reification of the state, Abrams argues, underpins both Hegelian and Marxist schools. His critique of Marxist understanding of the state is particularly significant.[4]

Abrams observes an "ambiguity" in Marxist thinking in which "authors have both perceived the nonentity of the state and failed to cling to the logic of that perception." What Abrams points to is in fact a conceptual and historical paradox. On the one hand, thinkers such as Gramsci and Poulantzas did notice that the state was "an illusion" that masked social subjection or, at best, "an abstract-formal object." On the other hand, however, especially with regard to the capitalist case, they and others, "instead of directing their attention to the manner and means by which the idea of the existence of the state has been constituted, communicated and imposed," treated it "as a 'real-concrete' agent with will, power and activity of its own."[5]

The impact and significance of Abrams's essay stem, first and foremost, from the fact that his fundamental stocktaking—especially of the prevailing wisdom in his own paradigm—led him to ask different questions about the state.[6] I discern two main recommendations. First, he suggests that "we should recognize that cogency of the idea of the state as an ideological power and treat that as a compelling object of analysis. But the very reasons that require us to do that also require us not to believe in the idea of the state, not to concede, even as an abstract-formal object, the existence of the state."[7] The second recommendation, the only way to avoid the trap of reifying the state, "is to understand it as historically constructed."[8] One might surmise from this that the endeavor repeated by generations of scholars of politics to come up with a finite definition of the state (in itself and vis-à-vis society) is futile. What should be done instead is to follow the ways in which the idea of the state has been constructed and rendered effective in different times and places.

It is, of course, not enough to expose the state as an ideological reification and proceed happily ever after. To draw an obvious analogy, the same feeling of dissatisfaction with merely dismissing something as an ideological construct is what compels Benedict Anderson to reject the notion that the modern nation is "invented" or "fabricated" and to insist, first, that it is imagined and, second, that the prevalence of this imagining renders it real.[9] Similarly, the state may well be an ideological construct, but the fact that it is conveyed and grasped as a "real thing" and that people act as if it really existed as such makes the state very real indeed. Consciousness that results in action becomes a social fact in itself.

A concomitant problem to that of the reification of the state is the rigidly binary way of looking at the state/society complex and a host of related analogies, most notably superstructure/base, ideology/reality, and politics/economy. Perry Anderson, with whose *Lineages of the Absolutist State* (1974) Abrams concludes his essay to illustrate the observation that the state must be studied historically, comments on this problem. Judging by the content and references, however, Abrams fails to notice an illuminating passage in which Anderson censures Marxist historians for mindlessly adhering to the base/superstructure and economy/politics polarities.[10]

Anderson takes issue with the ahistorical tendency of Marxist historians to universalize feudalism as a mode of production, regardless of the particular legal, ideological, and political systems (i.e., superstructures) within which these purportedly purely economic structures operated. Thus, once economic relations are seen to have been morphologically similar (and the superstructures are discarded), feudalism is seen to have prevailed anywhere and everywhere. Anderson notices a resulting paradox, which is as fundamental as that which frustrates Abrams:

> Laws and states, dismissed as secondary and insubstantial, reemerge with a vengeance, as the apparent authors of the most momentous break in modern history. In other words, once the whole structure of sovereignty and legality is dissociated from the economy of a universal feudalism, its shadow paradoxically governs the world: for it becomes

the only principle capable of explaining the differential development of the whole mode of production.... A colour-blind materialism, incapable of appreciating the real and rich spectrum of diverse social totalities within the same temporal band of history, thus inevitably ends in a perverse idealism.[11]

Anderson then resorts to an independent reading of Marx. In this reading, in all precapitalist modes of production the base and superstructure, economy and politics, society and state, were inseparable, perhaps even inextricably intertwined, because the extraction of the surplus in all of them was achieved through extraeconomic coercion. Only in capitalism, according to this understanding, "the means whereby the surplus is pumped out of the direct producer is 'purely' economic in form—the wage contract: the equal exchange between free agents which reproduces, hourly and daily, inequality and oppression."[12] In a formulation that is directly pertinent to our discussion, what Anderson suggests is in effect the casting aside of "binarism." The nature and variety of precapitalist modes of production were determined by the incessant interplay between economy and society on the one hand, and politics, law, state, and ideology on the other. The latter realm was neither extrinsic to nor a reflection of the social formation but rather part and parcel of it. The view of "the economy as a formally self-contained order," Anderson insists, pertains only and for the first time in history to the era of capitalism.[13]

It is evident why even a critical historian such as Perry Anderson cannot go beyond, so to speak, the capitalist state, though he has clearly pinpointed the a priori commitment to a binary way of looking at the state/society complex, in a materialist garb in this case, as a fundamental flaw. The trouble is, of course, that Marxist scholars, whatever their particular field, have always been concerned with the capitalist state to the point of obsession. They have striven to highlight the extent to which it is unique, elusive, and powerful but also to reassure themselves that it is not invincible. Commending Anderson's work, Abrams voices this frustrating duality:

> If that sort of radical unmasking of the state is possible for absolutism, why not for more recent political arrangements? Of course there is a certain brutal candour and transparency about absolutism which subsequent constructions have not reproduced. "L'etat c'est moi" is hardly an attempt at legitimation at all; it so plainly means "I and my mercenaries rule—O.K.?" Yet on balance I think it is not the devious cunning of more recent political arrangements that has deceived us but rather our own willing or unwitting participation in the idea of the reality of the state.[14]

Timothy Mitchell develops the lines of thought suggested by Abrams and Perry Anderson, though without reference to them. Employing discourse theory, Mitchell rejects as ahistorical and idealist the attempts to draw a static dividing line between state and society and thus to understand the state as a coherent, autonomous agency that does all sorts of things with clearly identifiable intentions. Mitchell sees the modern state as a series of social practices that, through a complex process and a variety of technologies, is made to seem extrinsic to society and to seem a coherent, reified structure. In his understanding, this does not mean that the state is a phantom, an illusion, or an ideological mask. It is a "discursively produced effect," and this effect is the consciousness of the state as a coherent structure that shapes society and acts upon it from a "topographically" extrinsic and elevated location. In this concept, the state/society polarity is not only discursively produced but also historical. By *historical* it is meant that the polarity is constantly contested and redrawn and that trying to come up with a finite definition of it is a futile endeavor. What should be done instead is to follow the ways in which the polarity was constructed in different temporal and spatial circumstances.[15]

Mitchell's approach to the modern state was one of the main foci of a series of stimulating workshops he and Roger Owen organized. Thinking further along the lines proposed by Mitchell, Partha Chatterjee and Akhil Gupta raise several interesting points. Chatterjee succinctly explains why it has been difficult, even from a clearly critical awareness, to find a theoretical language that would constitute an alternative to the language through which the state represents itself: "[T]he self-definition of the state structures the discursive field in which the state itself can be talked about. Thus our images and theories of the state employ assumptions given to us by the language and practice of the state." Gupta goes even farther in appreciating the inherent difficulty of a critically extrinsic view of the state. In a way he echoes the frustrations of Abrams and Perry Anderson: "The critical tone of this debate should not obscure the fact that it serves as a mechanism for imagining the state and thus strengthening it as a symbolic construct."[16]

This instrumental survey of the study of the state might be concluded by positioning Mitchell vis-à-vis the main, older schools. Mitchell explicitly rejects both the liberal-modernizationist school (through the ubiquitous political system, it sidesteps rather than addresses the problem of the state) and the reappearance of idealist-Hegelian thought in the form of the statist approach (fundamentally ahistorical). Implicitly, by arguing that his discursive framework should not be confused with the view that the state is an ideological mask behind which lies real power, and by insisting that the effect of the state becomes a sort of reality, Mitchell's concept is an alternative to orthodox Marxism too. Mitchell's insistence that state and society should not be separated even—indeed especially—in the modern-capitalist case means that he also disagrees with critical Marxist scholars like Abrams and Anderson. I think, however, that in the same manner in which Foucault's philosophy is a certain reading of Marx, so Mitchell's theory of the state is dialectically indebted to the Marxist assessment of the same phenomenon that Abrams and Perry Anderson presented earlier.

THE PRICE REVOLUTION AND THE CRISIS OF THE SEVENTEENTH CENTURY

Before proceeding with an exposition of concepts and interpretations of the early modern Ottoman state, it is necessary to present the environment, so to speak, within which the history of the state unfolded. This "environment" was what modern scholarship has termed the price revolution (when the discussion is specifically economic) or the crisis of the seventeenth century (when social, political, and cultural concerns are added to the economic). These two terms are used here interchangeably. No neat separation between this process and the history of the state is possible.

The process in question consists of the rise of prices in Eurasia in the late sixteenth century and the attendant social and political features in the seventeenth century; the temporal focus tends to be 1580–1650. Şevket Pamuk offers a thoroughly illuminating reevaluation of the price revolution.[17] For modern scholarship the phenomenon was initially European, but it gradually came to be recognized as engulfing Eurasia. Also, the initial focus and explanations were strictly economic, but later social, demographic, and other dimensions were added. At least concerning Europe, Pamuk makes clear, "The debate about the Price Revolution . . . has not been about whether the price increases took place. Rather, it has focused on their causes and consequences."[18]

The various causal explanations of the price revolution have evolved along two simultaneous paths.[19] One has been to move from the exclusive explanatory force attributed to the supply of money to the velocity of its circulation and to demographic changes, urbanization, and the intensity of trading contacts and networks. The other has been to move beyond Europe and Eurocentric explanations. The explanation that prevailed for a long time was rigidly monetary and culminated in the quantity theory of money. It basically argued that the flow of precious metals from the Americas into Spain caused dramatic prices increases there, spreading to the rest of Europe and then to the Middle East and Asia. Refined versions of this argument emphasized that the Spanish inflation could spread through trade and that the actual exchange of bullion was therefore not a necessary condition for the monetary explanation to work.

In the 1980s and 1990s the monetarist approach was severely undermined in four related but distinct ways. First, evidence from the Low Countries showed that while the arrival of specie in Europe continued in the seventeenth century, prices actually declined. Second a series of studies on non-European regions, especially China, showed that while the phenomenon was global and Asia was part of it, their evidence and analysis rendered a simplistic and Eurocentric money-supply thesis unsustainable. Third, there was a new emphasis on the significance of the velocity of the circulation of money (roughly the demand for money), which the money supply thesis had deemed constant and conveniently ignored. Fourth, research brought to the fore demographic changes and urbanization, although the more crude manifestation of this argument, that demographic growth unaccompanied by the growth of agricultural production accounts for inflation in a monocausal fashion, has been questioned.

As occasionally is the case with the demise of authoritative paradigms, the fall of the monetarist theory did not result in an alternative monocausal explanation. The impression is that the supply of money was significant but that rather than having been a single cause it might participate in sustaining the rising prices; that the experience of the price revolution and the crisis of the seventeenth century varied spatially; and that extraeconomic questions need to be asked and addressed.

In the Ottoman case, the impact of the price revolution and its consequences played an important role in the decline paradigm. Ömer Lütfi Barkan accepted the monetarist explanation of the price revolution as a whole and argued that the emergence of the powerful "Atlantic economy" and inability of the Ottomans to sustain their supposedly self-contained economy resulted in an irreversible decline. Pamuk offers a comprehensive empirical and conceptual reconsideration of Barkan's thesis. Without going into a detailed economic discussion, it should be noted that Pamuk's achievement is quite remarkable. He successfully challenges Barkan's rigidly monetarist explanation and his narrative of consequential and irrevocable decline, which held sway for a quarter of a century. Furthermore, through meticulous documentation and sophisticated interpretation, Pamuk brings Ottoman scholarship on this subject to where European and other historical fields have been for some time.[20]

One of the scholars whose work Pamuk presents as alternative to the money quantity theory is Jack Goldstone. Pamuk highlights Goldstone's attempt to relate the increasingly dense urban population, the increasing velocity of money circulation, and, in light of this, how the supply of money might help sustain a resulting inflationary drive but not cause it. Interestingly, Pamuk refers to a host of publications by Goldstone but not to his ambitious comparative exercise that I wish to discuss.[21] Looking at three cases, Stuart England, the Ottoman Empire, and Ming China, Goldstone seeks a global perspective that would relate the crisis of the seventeenth century to—among other things—the transformation of states in Eurasia. He seeks, moreover, a causal framework that neither is Eurocentric (i.e., based on capitalism and the absolutist state) nor artificially isolates certain components of the seventeenth-century crisis and analyzes them separately (e.g., only the increase in prices or only the fiscal crisis).[22]

Goldstone's underlying causality is what he calls a major ecological change at the end of the sixteenth century and first half of the seventeenth: impressive demographic growth throughout Eurasia whose pace overwhelmed the slower rate of economic growth. This common cause led in turn to price inflation and fiscal crises of the states. The next stage in Goldstone's causal chain points to cleavages and conflicts within the elites and between them and the state and to comprehensive—rather than merely peasant—rebellions. The final stage was an ideological change in the shape of religious heterodoxies and radicalism.

According to Goldstone, the various components of the seventeenth-century crisis were not autonomous causes but aspects of a multifaceted process into which they all converged. Thus the English Revolution was not a uniquely Western phenomenon, a particular outcome of the crisis of either capitalism or absolutism, but part of a comprehensive process in Eurasia. Similarly, what Goldstone understands as the divergence between Western and Eastern civilizations after midcentury should not be attributed to a structural difference between "revolutions" in the West and "peasant rebellions" or "dynastic crises" in the East. Possible explanations should be sought in the common crisis of the seventeenth century and its manifestation in each region and state.[23]

Unfolding his causal framework, Goldstone offers some interesting observations that pertain to the Ottoman case. The first is an acute undermining of the monetarist theory of the price revolution alluded to above.

Goldstone rejects the ahistorical presupposition that a host of economic parameters—the velocity of money circulation in particular—can be discarded as constants and that only changes in money supply should be followed. In this historical case, he argues, velocity kept changing and what accounts for the seventeenth-century price revolution is not the extrinsic factor of silver from the Americas but primarily the fact that "between 1500 and 1700 price movements across Eurasia corresponded closely to the balance between population and food supply."[24] In this respect, however, Pamuk's reservation about an unmitigated causal connection between demographic growth, which was not accompanied by a similar rate of growth of agricultural production, and steep price inflation should be borne in mind.[25]

The second observation concerns the fiscal decay of the Eurasian states. Contrary to the accepted view of excessive taxation, Goldstone contends that in fact, relative to the resources of the various societies, the level of taxation was too low and, especially, that the state's share of it was decreasing. Existing technologies, among other reasons, made it difficult for state bureaucracies to come up with fiscal mechanisms that would be sufficiently effective to deal with the demographic growth. They could hardly update their records, to say nothing of actually levying the due taxes. The crisis was exacerbated by fiscal policies that were ad hoc and alienated the wealthy and powerful. The latter found ways to evade taxation, thereby forcing the system to exert more fiscal pressure on the have-nots.[26]

The third observation touches upon the social repercussions of the ecological change. Here two points are noteworthy. One was the problems faced by the elites, among them the overburdening of the systems of recruitment and socialization—Oxford and Cambridge are interestingly discussed by Goldstone—which devalued them and brought about a serious discrepancy between the increasing demand (of the systems' graduates) and static supply (of positions). The social repercussion was the popular uprisings, which were varied and comprehensive in their social composition and range (both rural and urban); most important, they marked "the broader breakdowns in the social order, not merely popular discontent with rising prices and landlessness."[27]

The merit of Goldstone's work lies in the comparative framework he puts forth and the common context he constructs. This, I think, should be particularly appealing to Ottomanists, whose referent—the Ottoman state and society—has for so long been marginalized, in stark contrast to its size, longevity, and complexity, by essentialism and particularism. Even if disputed with regard to particular arguments and concrete cases, the comparative framework offered by Goldstone might stimulate fresh questions on

Ottoman history.[28] My own disagreement with the concluding part of his work—the ideological change—is an example. Trying to account for what he calls the East/West divergence, Goldstone maintains that it was deeply affected by the differing ideologies that dominated the reconstruction of the state following the crisis of the seventeenth century.

Common to the three cases that Goldstone studies was the spread of literacy beyond the official classes and that of popular literature, as well as the appearance of radical, heterodox movements and ideologies. This phenomenon was by no means confined to the masses but included, and was frequently led by, merchants, state officials, and scholars. Goldstone stresses the striking similarities between the Academy and Puritan movements in China and England respectively. Both started as movements for the "purification of religious practice and public and private morals, continued by bemoaning the corruption of the state and failure of its official educational system," and their appeal to similar social classes stemmed "from the disordered social structure brought by increased mobility." In the Ottoman Empire, which in Goldstone's view did not correspond as neatly as China and England in this respect, the locus of the analogous phenomenon could be found in Sufism and orthodoxy's response to the activities of Sufi orders.[29]

Finally, the aforementioned divergence is attributed to the fact that the essence of the ideological change in its Puritan guise was apocalyptic—that is, oriented to the future—with the result being that "political change was to create a new, Protestant, world." In stark contrast, the ideological eruption in China and the Ottoman Empire was cyclical. "Thus, after 1650, the Ottoman and Chinese empires became more rigidly orthodox and conservative than they had been earlier; they turned inward and eschewed novelty, while rewarding conformity to past habits. State reconstruction on these terms was successful in restoring a measure of prosperity and prolonging the life of these States, but they entered the late-seventeenth and eighteenth centuries without the dynamism of England."[30]

So, after an instructive tour de force in the paths of comparative history and contextual emphasis, we are disappointingly forced back to the realm of cultural essentialism, biological metaphors of the rise and decline of states, and the East/West dichotomous division. Casting aside the notions that underpin this particular argument, I think that Goldstone's impression that the English and Chinese cases resembled each other while the Ottoman-Sufi case did not stems from the fact that he looks for a "Puritan" discourse in the wrong place. I would venture that the nasihat literature (formally literature of advice to rulers) in the Ottoman state, as it developed between the latter part of the sixteenth century and the middle of the eighteenth, might be interpreted as a "Puritan" discourse. It sought moral regeneration and the purification of state servants. It advocated return to a past that was ideologically constructed as a golden age. It bemoaned the breakdown of what it deemed the correct social order (embodied in the metaphor of *nizam-i alem*, the order of the world) and its concomitant, excessive social mobility in the seventeenth century. And the sociological profile of its authors, as members of the civil bureaucracy, resembled that of the Academy movement in China. I intend to pursue this argument elsewhere.[31]

CONCEPTS OF THE OTTOMAN STATE

For the present discussion, Goldstone's study has conveniently related to one another the crisis of the seventeenth century and the history of early modern Ottoman state. The study of the Ottoman state has made a significant leap in recent years. After decades of adherence to intellectually stifling and ahistorical concepts such as the Islamic state or the classical state (Hegelian essentialism), or an Oriental-despotic state that reflects the Asiatic Mode of Production (Marxist essentialism), the Ottoman state is being rendered increasingly historical in three related ways. Firstly, it is viewed synchronically—that is, it is compared to its contemporaneous dynastic states—rather than being treated solely as a diachronic evolution of the Islamic state. Second, the leading question has changed from what did not happen in the Ottoman state and why to what did happen and why. Third, the intuitive attitude has been altered as a result of the demise of the decline narrative: changes are instinctively felt to have been historically natural, given the longevity of the state's existence and the variety of circumstances it faced, rather than being deviations from or corruptions of a classical model.[32]

By far, the most influential concept of the Ottoman state as a classical model from which deviations occurred after 1600 is that of Halil Inalcik. It is manifested throughout his voluminous work and, most significantly as far as its impact is concerned, in *The Ottoman Empire: The Classical Age, 1300–1600* (1973). Inalcik's work is well known and thoroughly discussed; in the context of the present exposition of more recent and specific studies on the state in the seventeenth century, I wish to stress two basic traits of his conceptualization, traits whose imprint on Ottoman scholarship is evident.

The first is that Inalcik's understanding of the state is fundamentally idealist in two ways. The state is conceived of as an autonomous agency, or form, that is clearly separable from society (content) and acts upon it. Second, this agency has an ideological essence: that is, it is an "idea" that can be unfolded through normative texts (chiefly juristic and bureaucratic). The important things here are intentionality and institutions. By *intentionality*, it is meant that the state as agency has discernible intentions that certain policies are supposed to realize. The institutions derive from the state's ideational essence, and, in their ideal articulation, they manifest it in their daily operation.[33]

The second trait is "the classical age" as an organizing abstraction and its prevalence in Ottoman scholarship. It might be safely argued that without such abstractions the social and human sciences might not be thought or written. The issue is therefore not to question the mere use of a given cognitive filter but to try and draw the elusive line, regarding concrete cases, between two ways of using it. In the first, an abstraction makes intellectual discourse possible and may even enhance its insight, whereas in the second an abstraction (sometimes the same one) becomes a fetish, an end in itself that is repeatedly described and reproduced. The problem with "the classical age" is that it is closer to the second use than to the first. The consequence is twofold. Regarding the alleged classical period, it is rarely asked whether it was classical at all and if so in what ways; it is rather presupposed to have been so. Regarding the so-called middle period (the seventeenth and eighteenth centuries), the common starting point is, reductively, that it is "post" one thing (the classical age) and "pre" another (the Tanzimat). Thus the seventeenth and eighteenth centuries in Ottoman history, and the history of the Ottoman state in particular, suffer from the syndrome of the "middle child." Paradoxes and apparent contradictions abound. For instance, the classical model and its concrete articulations are implicitly assumed somehow to have always been there, at the Ottomans' disposal. Thus Geza David, in an overview of the Ottoman conquest of the Balkans and Hungary, gives the impression that the acquisition and administrative integration of these core territories were achieved along the lines of a classical, established pattern. The historicity borders on the absurd, for even if there was such a classical pattern it must have been formed and shaped while Rumelia was being acquired (roughly 1350–1550) and could not have already been there.[34]

In 1980 Inalcik published an impressive corrective to his "classical age" thesis. His article was a comprehensive interpretation of the "postclassical" period (the seventeenth century), but it nonetheless implied a modified view of the previous era (1300–1600). Although Inalcik endorses Barkan's explanation of the price revolution, he seems reluctant to interpret the significant changes of the seventeenth century as decline. He emphasizes the pressing need of the Ottomans to adjust to environmental changes and the consequent military transformation. The impact of this transformation on the fiscal system and on Anatolian society was the primary factor, in this exposition, that determined the course of Ottoman history in the seventeenth and even eighteenth centuries. The state as an autonomous historical agent continued to underpin Inalcik's interpretation; it might be even suggested that its omnipresence was reinforced. Inalcik, moreover, transmitted this idealist bias to some of his students, as we shall later see. Regarding the changes of the seventeenth century, however, Inalcik not only explains them but clearly deems them historically natural rather than the corruption of a classical age or decline.[35]

At the level of explicit conceptualization and in a more implicit way at the level of empirical historical research, there have been some interesting developments in the study of the Ottoman state and its environment in the seventeenth century. Several empirical studies, though not explicitly intending to conceptualize the state, open meaningful paths to doing that.

Metin Kunt's book on the upper echelon of the provincial administration, the ümera, sprang out of initial interest in the formation and spread of the elite household, the *kapı*.[36] As his study was based on the official documentation of the state, which acknowledged the kapı but did not deem it a formal institution, Kunt was led by his source material away from the kapı to the formal institutions, though the importance of the household did not go unnoticed. Kunt shows that the change in the period 1550–1650 in the structure of the ümera was threefold: a growing tendency to appoint senior officials from the central government, sometimes from the sultan's inner personnel (the *enderun*), to the position of beylerbeyi, the highest in the provincial administration; the ascendancy of the *beylik* (province—the administrative unit governed by a beylerbeyi) as the chief administrative unit at the expense of the *sancak* (subprovince—the administrative unit governed by a *sancakbey*) and, correspondingly, the rising power and income of the beylerbeyis at the expense of the sancakbeys; and the increasing prevalence of patronage and households.[37]

Kunt's findings point to a major change in the nature of the Ottoman state that is not unlike that undergone by other dynastic states in Eurasia. He is well aware that the change at stake was a passage from the *dirlik* [lit. "subsistence"—a stipend of the state to its servant that was estimated to be sufficient for his sustenance] system of provincial administration to one where the beylerbeyi supervised revenue collection in the provinces and made cash contributions to the central treasury. In its essence this was not a process of "decline"; it may even be referred to as "modernization," in the sense that it was a shift from a "feudal" arrangement to a monetary one. Furthermore, the shift was intended to increase the power of the central government, another feature of the "modern" state.[38]

Kunt, then, shows that a major change in the state—that is, the demise of the *timar* (a prebendal land grant and typical form of dirlik until the middle of the seventeenth century) and the subsequent monetarization of the fiscal structure—was a natural change within the Eurasian context of the Ottoman Empire. It was neither a sign of decline nor a corruption of a classical model. Still at the empirical level, Rifaat Ali Abou-El-Haj's article on the political households of the elite reveals another significant change undergone by the Ottoman state in the seventeenth century. He argues that from the middle of the century onward, a sociopolitical structure identified as the vezir/pasha household emerged as a major locus of power that recruited, trained, and socialized manpower into the Ottoman state. Moreover, the networks of patronage extended by these households became the sine qua non for participating in state politics and for attaining a successful career within it. Though gaining power at its expense, the vezir/pasha households coexisted with, rather than challenged, the sultan's.[39]

In different but related ways, Kunt and Abou-El-Haj, and numerous other scholars, are concerned with the oscillation of the early modern Ottoman state between the patrimonial and bureaucratic poles. The significance of Kunt's work in this respect is that it shows the movement of the state in the seventeenth century from the dirlik basis of its foundational phase to a substantially more monetary structure in its sedentary existence. Dirlik and monetarization may be seen as specific articulations of the patrimonial and bureaucratic state respectively. Abou-El-Haj's observations are in a way analogous. The change alluded to by Abou-El-Haj highlights the demise of the *devşirme* (a recruitment mechanism of Christian youth from the Balkans that distinguished the sultan's household from the rest and augmented its power), the diversification of what was considered legitimate sources of recruitment for state service, and the relative decline of the sultan's household as an institution of recruitment and socialization. The state, in other words, became more bureaucratic and less patrimonial because the dynastic household and the state became much less coterminous than they had previously been.

This change too, however, is not construed as decline or deviation from something classical. Interestingly, this change did not undermine the fundamental notion that the kul were a pivotal institution of the Ottoman state, though one feels that it gradually acquired a different meaning. A member of the kul institution became less the sultan's servant (the original, literal meaning congruous with the patrimonial end of the above continuum) and more the state's servant (the metaphorical meaning, more congruous with the increasingly bureaucratic state).

An insightful elaboration on the ubiquity and importance of the household is Jane Hathaway's work on Ottoman Egypt in the seventeenth and eighteenth centuries. Hathaway has tackled head on an important thesis that was born out of the forceful—if curious—combination of Orientalism and Middle Eastern nationalism. This thesis argued that Egypt, like the rest of the Middle East and North Africa, not only hopelessly declined under the Ottoman yoke but also promptly became "neo-Mamluk" and continued to be Ottoman nominally at best. Hathaway not only obliterates this implausible thesis but also brings Egypt—a province of singular importance in the imperial structure—and its provincial elite back into the fold of Ottoman history in fresh and innovative ways. Moving comfortably between the provincial and imperial sources and perspectives, she shows the variety of elite households, their formation and development in an Ottoman province, and perceptively teaches us how to identify these elusive structures that, precisely because they did not constitute a formal category, are difficult to discern. Hathaway's comparison of Egypt to other provinces as well as to the center, particularly with regard to genealogies and their political meaning, sustains the suggestion that the households were a nexus that tied together the central and provincial elites, thereby creating a more tightly knitted imperial space.[40]

At the level of explicit conceptualization, and within a Marxist framework but critical of the universal pretense of both Marxist and liberal scholarship, Tosun Aricanli and Mara Thomas, in "Sidestepping Capitalism: On the Ottoman Road to Elsewhere," see in the Ottoman state the site of dynamic history. They argue that this scholarship deals with "what the east was not" and that our knowledge of the eventual integration of the Ottoman Empire into the capitalist system often imposes the presupposition that that route was inevitable.[41]

More concretely, Aricanli and Thomas contend that because of a Eurocentric bias the sphere of production is automatically examined as the locus of change and dynamic history. Once this is not found, and in the Ottoman case it might not be, the conclusion is that stagnation prevailed and the question is why what was putatively supposed to happen did not happen. The authors suggest that perhaps it happened elsewhere. Offering an interesting analogy, they maintain that whereas the site of dynamic history in the early modern history of some European cases was indeed production, the analogous site in Ottoman history was the state. Aricanli and Thomas focus their analysis on three categories: class definition, the concept of property, and the distribution of the surplus. By dissociating these categories from production and associating them with the state, they illustrate the extent to which "Ottoman history sheds its petrified cloak and the Ottoman state comes to life."[42]

The basic notion espoused by Aricanli and Thomas, that class, property, and the distribution of the surplus are comprehensible in the Ottoman case only when associated with the state, yields interesting propositions. One concerns property. They argue that the prevalent view is misleading, for it assesses property anachronistically, in terms of the modern notion of private property. This leaves the state out and exclusively stresses the "feudal" mode of production: landowners versus peasants. In the Ottoman Empire, however, "Domination came from outside the productive organization of the peasant community, and was defined without reference to property." They insist: "Restriction of the analysis [of property] to the sphere of production fails to capture the motion of the system."[43]

To the fact that only by looking at the state does the dynamic history of property come to the fore, I would add that perhaps we ought to consider what property meant for the Ottoman state officials at that period. We might find, I suspect, that for them it was neither land nor houses but as secure as possible possession of state-derived dirliks. In other words, a tight hold over, for instance, the office of beylerbeyi with minimal or no periods of *mazul* (being made temporarily redundant) might be considered by these Ottomans a worthwhile investment. Within this logic, the office itself might be deemed property.

Another specific insight is the way Aricanli and Thomas relate the practice of the distribution of the surplus to the site of the state rather than to that of production. They point out that whereas in early modern England the practices of both appropriation and distribution took place at the site of production, in the Ottoman Empire there was a meaningful separation: while appropriation indeed occurred at the site of production, "Distribution was strictly a political process embedded in the state."[44] It is in this embeddedness, they suggest, that the dynamism of Ottoman history can be found, for it contained two processes of redistribution of the surplus, which were conflictual: one between the center and its functionaries and the other among the functionaries who struggled to maintain and increase their share of the surplus via the state.[45]

The conceptual framework propounded by Aricanli and Thomas might be seen as a particular case that lends credence to Perry Anderson's theoretical overview discussed earlier, though they make no reference to his work. Anderson, it should be reminded, censures Marxist scholarship for erroneously identifying a universal, ahistorical feudalism. This misconception stems from ignoring the superstructure, the state first and foremost, and the consequent blindness to the fact that in precapitalist formations, society and state, economy and politics, base and superstructure were inextricably intertwined. Moreover, it is precisely this incessant interplay that creates the variety of historical cases and renders the excessive application of feudalism reductive and unsatisfactory. Clearly, the dissociation of a variety of practices from production and their association with the state, the essence of the Aricanli / Thomas proposal, is an application of Anderson's insight, and the former might have benefited from the latter.

Aricanli and Thomas's article stimulates my own attempt to examine the state with and through the historical texts owing to what the article has and what it lacks. What it does have is a convincing argument, at least as a conceptual proposal, that the Ottoman state in the early modern period was a site of "hot" history and that its understanding entails—in the spirit of Perry Anderson's contention—the discarding of the binary view of society/state and economy/politics. What it lacks is twofold. First, there is no serious grappling with, to use Marxist terminology, the state as superstructure, not only as the site of material conflicts and changes but, concomitantly, also as the site of discursive strife. Second, there is no discussion—so vital for the historian—of the pertinent sources and how to approach them, lest we forever remain in the realm of conceptual pondering. The first absence is important because it is rather typical of this school of thought. Although critical and wary of the crude materialist causality of previous generations of Marxist scholarship, numerous current scholars too seem to find it difficult to deal with the superstructure adequately. Aricanli and Thomas, to be sure, go a long way toward rectifying crude materialism, but it still, I think, hinders them: one always senses the unuttered supposition that once things are shown to be valid at the base level, the superstructure will take care of itself correspondingly.

Highly aware of the merit of comparative history, Rifaat Ali Abou-El-Haj makes a significant contribution to the fresh attempts to understand the Ottoman state in the seventeenth and eighteenth centuries.[46] He points out three problems that apply to the study of the Ottoman state more than to that of other early modern states: a particularism that hinders its analysis in a comparative perspective; the assumption that it was an unchanging entity; and its anachronistic judgment by the criteria of the modern nation-state. Abou-El-Haj then proposes the seventeenth century as a period that illustrates the merit of the comparative perspective and the extent to which the Ottoman state and its counterparts shared the same history in two ways. One was the possibility that the seventeenth century witnessed a socioeconomic revolution before the integration into the capitalist world economy, and the other was a process in which the state's nature altered radically.[47]

As regards the ongoing discussion of the conceptualization of the state in that period, Abou-El-Haj discerns at least four alternatives: (1) the state was an extension of the ruling class; (2) the state was based on the ruling class but retained its autonomy; (3) the state was part of the ruling class but at the same time forged independent alliances with provincial and regional elites; (4) the state was entirely autonomous, not based on any class, and its functionaries' self-image was that in this capacity they were beyond class frictions.[48] At the end of his discussion, Abou-El-Haj sees two basic, apparently contradictory, interpretations of the process of state formation. In the first, the developments in the seventeenth and eighteenth centuries are perceived as leading to the formation of a modern, centralized state that eventually became autonomous vis-à-vis the society it ruled. According to the second, which is favored by Abou-El-Haj, there emerged in that period a ruling class that gradually became independent of the state, both economically and to a lesser extent politically, though it should be examined within the context of the state.[49]

Along the way Abou-El-Haj offers two interesting observations. The first draws attention to the connection between the history of the state and that of its environment, most notably the Eurasian crisis of the seventeenth century. Emphasizing the relatedness of intrinsic and extrinsic factors, he sketches what amounts to a fundamental transformation in the seventeenth century of Ottoman state and society and notes that the notion of immobility is so deeply ingrained in Ottoman scholarship that even historically minded scholars have found it difficult to grasp such substantial changes in that particular period.[50]

The second observation concerns a foremost source for the study of the Ottoman state: the nasihat (advice to rulers) literature that flourished in the sixteenth to eighteenth centuries. Abou-El-Haj emphasizes the way this literature has been misused within much of the textualist-philological tradition of Orientalist scholarship and misinterpreted as conclusive evidence of the decline of the Ottoman Empire, as well of the fact that a golden, classical age once existed. He suggests, and to a rather limited extent implements, a more historical and contextual way to read the nasihat literature. Using mainly Koçu Bey's treatise and Naima's introduction to his history, Abou-El-Haj points out possible connections between the writers' context—both personal and sociopolitical—and the ideological and normative views they convey. He observes, for example, that the biological metaphor employed by Naima was meant to lend credence to the ascendancy of the civil bureaucracy, to which Naima belonged, at the expense of the military men. In this metaphor, the Ottoman state was in its midlife, a stage in which the former flourish at the latter's expense according to some "law of nature" that guides the life of states.[51]

I now turn to a slightly more detailed presentation of what I consider the two most coherent and thought-through interpretations and conceptualizations of the early modern Ottoman state. Each of these is consistent with the school of thought to which it adheres. They represent, moreover, the two main approaches in Ottoman scholarship in general: the idealist and materialist.

THE DIALECTIC OF "CENTRIPETAL DECENTRALIZATION": ARIEL SALZMANN'S POLITICAL ECONOMY

Mainly and directly inspired by the pioneering work of Mehmet Genç, Ariel Salzmann's research on the early modern Ottoman fiscal system has produced what in my view is the freshest and most insightful interpretation of the history of the state at that period.[52] The underlying result of her thoughtful argument is a possible coup de grâce to the prevalent metaphor of centralization/decentralization as the explanatory framework for the passage from early modern empires to modern nation-states. This metaphor applies—unwittingly perhaps—Newtonian mechanical physics to the state-society relationship, and it has found forceful expression in the teleological narrative of the nation-state and in developmentalist theories of the formation of the modern state (the two are, of course, not easily distinguishable). Crudely put, the presupposed logic of this metaphor is that decentralization bespeaks—indeed is a nicer way of saying—decline, whereas centralization is its diametrical opposite.

Salzmann is not averse to the mere use of this metaphor, nor does she object to decentralization as a possible way of looking at the eighteenth century, but she perceptively undoes the Gordian knot between decentralization—as "venality," "corruption," "state breakdown," or any combination thereof—and the disintegration of the imperial state structure. Her counterproposal is that, in fact, the success of decentralization actually facilitated "the peculiar institutional centralization that ushered in the modern state in the early nineteenth century."[53] Since she is well aware that the contours of Ottoman history are comparable to those of the empire's contemporary states in Eurasia, her interpretation might be significant beyond the confines of Ottoman history.[54]

Salzmann's dialectical interpretation emerges out of her study of the fiscal system in the eighteenth century and, within it, the life-term revenue tax farm *(malikâne muqataa)*. She first follows the ways in which the crisis of the seventeenth century, the substantial military changes, and the global Eurasian-Atlantic economy brought on the monetarization of the fiscal system and, in particular, the introduction of tax farming *(iltizam)* in the seventeenth century. A host of related reasons, beyond the scope of this study, ushered in at the end of the seventeenth century the era of the malikâne (Salzmann's precise periodization is 1695–1793). The malikâne was actually an elaboration of the general fiscal notion of (the shorter term) tax farming. Like the iltizam, this contract was publicly auctioned, but it awarded the successful bidder the right to collect taxes for life. The official payment to the fisc was twice or thrice the anticipated annual profit, but Salzmann remarks that it was actually much higher. The contractor had to remit the fixed annual payments, so his exclusive hold over all surplus extraction for life yielded attractive profits. "Shares on *malikâne* holdings could be traded privately," Salzmann notes, "with provisions made for inheritance of shares pending payment of a new *muajjele* [what the successful auctioneer had to pay in advance] by his sons or other male relatives."[55] It is understandable that she calls the bottom line of this fiscal process "privatization."

In this exposition the malikâne was also related to the ascendancy of the political household *(kapı)* and to the accumulation of power by the central-state elite[56] at the expense of the dynastic household and the provincial elites, though the latter were not completely excluded from this dialectically peculiar state-owned, increasingly privatized, fiscal market. Those who gained from the malikâne system not only controlled its market through their effective households but also successfully exerted pressure to extend the scope of the malikâne. This they achieved in four spheres: the geographical reach of the malikâne, the financial liquidity of malikâne-derived assets, the variety of surplus yielding sectors of the economy that became eligible for bidding in malikâne auctions, and the allowance that there could be Istanbul-based absentee malikâne contractors. The fiscal development had a curiously inclusive consequence, for although from 1714 only Muslims had direct access to malikâne contracts, Jews, Greeks, and Armenians joined the enterprise as bankers, accountants, and financial advisers.[57]

The extent of the process charted by Salzmann was meaningfully articulated in the development of the households. They grew from what Abou-El-Haj terms "the vezir/pasha household" of the late seventeenth century into Salzmann's "vizirieal firm": "In administrative terms, one may think of the larger *malikâne* contracts as a firm composed of at least one active partner, sometimes a subcontractor or agent, and his staff on site as well as several silent partners based in Istanbul or serving in senior military and administrative posts elsewhere in the empire."[58]

How is all this related to the state and to the centralization/decentralization metaphor? The answer, in a nutshell, is the dialectic of "centripetal decentralization." An assortment of liberal and nationalist—in the Ottoman case, add Orientalist—presuppositions have combined to instill in scholarly discourse two synonyms. One is decentralization and the weakening—or decline—of the state, and the other privatization and "less state." Salzmann's original argument amounts to a fundamental refutation of both. She skillfully shows how a pivotal fiscal process that was ostensibly decentralizing might actually have a centripetal trajectory, how the imperial state structure might become more tightly knitted, and how privatization might actually go hand in hand with "more state."

We may conclude with Salzmann's concise formulation of the dialectic of centripetal decentralization:

> Given the web of fiscal, legal, political, and cultural obligations which underlay relationships between direct producer, revenue contractor, and the state, life-term revenue contracting was rarely a net devolution of state power. For the state, granting *malikâne* contracts on relatively insignificant revenues from tithes on villages and fields was a means of tapping into the cultural authority of provincial notables. In an expanding economy marked by strong urban growth during the first half of the eighteenth century, *malikânization* provided special political immunities for contractors while associating them in a long-term and formal fashion with the provincial state apparatus. Over time, quasi-venal offices, especially those which oversaw the local *malikâne* auctions, turned certain notables into state brokers, enabling the state to reorganize tax farming and administration from the base.[59]

THE ULTIMATE REIFICATION: KAREN BARKEY'S IDEALIST STATISM

The work of Karen Barkey has the same concern as Jack Goldstone's, discussed earlier in this chapter: the relations between the crisis of the seventeenth century and the state. She too uses comparison (with France), but she ultimately reaches the opposite conclusion: that the Ottoman state emerged from the crisis of the seventeenth century stronger and more centralized.[60] Barkey's work is the most comprehensive attempt both to conceptualize the Ottoman state in the seventeenth century within an idealist framework and to construct a narrative of the state in that period in order to render the conceptualization plausible. The dimension I propose to add to the thinking about the state is meaningfully stimulated by a critique of Barkey's approach.

Cognizant of the seventeenth-century crisis and of similar processes in contemporary states, Barkey refutes the view that this period witnessed the breakdown of the Ottoman state, which purportedly collapsed under a combination of external and internal pressures. In particular, the activities of the bandits *(celali)*, and the way the state dealt with them, were interpreted as indications of the alleged breakdown. This view, she contends, emanated from contemporary Ottoman historians and nasihat authors, contemporary foreigners (historians and consuls), and modern Ottomanists and sociologists of "primitive rebellions." Barkey offers and substantiates a counterinterpretation whereby the intriguing relations between the state and the bandits bespeak the strength and flexibility of the former. Applying a variety of means, which ranged from bargaining through cooptation to annihilation, and which were employed according to changing circumstances as perceived from Istanbul, the state emerged from this period not only unscathed but en route to further centralization and consolidation.

My contention with Barkey's work is concerned not so much with the conclusion that there was neither "decline" nor "breakdown" of the state in the first half of the seventeenth century, with which I agree. Conceptually, however, Barkey's overall framework has two problems. One is the way she understands the state and, concretely, her reification of the state as an independent subject, and her binary opposition of bureaucrats/bandits as an instance of the larger state/society binary opposition. The other is the uncritically positivist way in which she employs the Ottoman historical texts. Barkey's approach has in common with the idealist school the notion that the state is an autonomous and coherent agency, clearly distinct from society, an agency that possesses identifiable essence, tendencies, and, most important, intentions that yield policies.

Barkey's is the most systematic and coherent articulation of an idealist understanding of the Ottoman state I have hitherto seen. Its expression is threefold. First, the state is reified into an omnipresent being. Second, the state/society binary opposition is presupposed and reproduced. Third, the state as agency is both accorded intentionality and, when it becomes historically tricky to discern who is inside or outside the state, identified as the locus where intentions/policies are produced.[61]

The reification of the state to the extent that it becomes an omnipresent, coherent being underlies all of Barkey's work. This impression can be gained from the syntax that abounds throughout her text: the state is always the subject that does all sorts of things to and with others, which are obviously not it. The magnitude of what this omnipresent "thing" can do is illustrated, indeed encapsulated, in a passage that summarizes Barkey's understanding of the celali phenomenon:

> For all intents and purposes, the state invented and manufactured banditry, and when it was no longer useful the state disposed of it. This is not to say that the state created banditry per se, ordering shady individuals to become bandits. Rather, it created disenfranchised groups, with access to weaponry, whom it directed toward actions consistent with the state's goals of increased coercion and control at the central and regional levels.[62]

That to Barkey's mind state and society are two separable entities is amply evident. Her observations, almost page by page, are replete with various expressions and formulations to the effect that the Ottoman state imposed its will upon society, was autonomous of societal forces (such as elites and peasantry), and controlled and manipulated society.[63] More concretely interesting is the way in which a particular articulation of the wider binary opposition, the one between state and bandits (as "society") adversely affects historical interpretation. The main problem comes to the fore with regard to the combination of the bandits and the political households *(kapı)*: the binary opposition in its idealist guise is inherently static; the result is that while Barkey's reified state does change its intentions and policies, they remain socially inconsequential because the underlying concept is so static. Thus she herself observes that there were two phases of celali activity and that the second phase (roughly the 1620s to the 1640s) was significantly different from the first, yet, without explanation, the bandits of the second generation are excluded from "the state" and forever remain within "society."

These people, however, survived the wrath of the grand vezir Kuyucu Murad Pasha earlier in the century, and many of them were recruited and coopted into the state via the households of high-ranking Ottoman officials following the defeats of the celali armies. Aided by their patrons' intisap, they themselves became officeholders and, the more successful, also heads of their own households. Barkey herself shows that regarding the competition over positions in the Ottoman administration the bandits were not different from governors sent by the palace in their politicized rhetoric and political action.[64] The possibility, in other words, that the line that separates state and society was dynamic and always contested, and that the household was a sociopolitical structure that rendered this line porous and diffusive, is missed because the idealist notion of the state lacks historicity by its very definition.

Finally, there is the issue of intentionality and of the state as the locus where intentions are conceived. To begin with the latter, it is palpable from Barkey's analysis that she narrows down the state to the realm of intentions/policies/decision making. Implicitly this narrowing down underpins her narrative, which is constructed around the state as the chief—almost anthropomorphized—protagonist. The state-as-protagonist then interacts with all sorts of groups and institutions that may be located inside or outside the state but are clearly not the state. Thus Barkey's state applies a variety of policies that refer to the kul, the provincial administration, the kadis, and the bandits. These policies are the intentions translated into action by state officials, vezirs, and the sultan; but neither the latter nor the former are the state, which by implication remains a reified, omnipresent being. On one occasion Barkey explicitly and concisely states this: "While the contested sources of various decisions within the state might be fascinating to analyze, my purpose here is to consider the state as an integrated set of institutions that exhibited a variety of policies resulting from exchange, debate, and political rivalries. The policies and their impact are of more interest to this work."[65]

Barkey is aware that intentionality is a thorny question but ends up ascribing it to the state. In a revealing passage, she manifests this awareness:

> The question of state action has often been confused with that of intentionality. I clearly provide the Ottoman state with agency, but I do not argue that all state practices were deliberately or accurately calculated by state officials to achieve increased control. Often, various narratives of state action exist simultaneously because many diverse events that may or may not be causally connected occur all at once. Nevertheless, what gets chosen as the actual narrative of state action is that which

seems most rational for gaining state control and imputes perfect intentionality to state actors. That is because it is easier to relate events in a temporally and causally connected fashion and attribute straightforward intentions to individuals. But to those actually carrying out actions, events often look as if they have been pieced together in quite an ad hoc fashion.[66]

The problem is that the subtle awareness is cast aside when it comes to actual historical interpretation. Thus in an article that deals with the scheduling of appointments and positions of officials as a mechanism that enhanced the control of the state over these officials, to the extent that it determined their time conception, Barkey is adamant, rather than cautious, about intentionality: "Both rotation [of officers in the provincial administration] and limited regional authority were certainly products of intentional, direct state action," and "Differences in rotation schedules applied to governors and governors general demonstrate the intentionality of state action in the control of regional officials."[67]

In addition to an idealist concept of the state, the other reason for which the state in this view appears to have been static rather then contested and historical is Barkey's uncritically positivist use of the historical texts. These constitute the basis of both her narrative and her interpretation.[68] She sometimes alludes to them directly and occasionally alludes to their problematic amalgamation by von Hammer. There is, first, a problem at the level of *Quellenkritik*, for, as I hope was amply shown in this study, these texts constitute a historiographical corpus in which each text is intimately related to another or to others. Even scholars who wish to use this historiography only as a source for extrinsic reconstruction have to grapple with its tangle of interdependencies. Second, these texts are not transparent reflections of external events but a discourse whose inscription, certainly with regard to the state as a contested site, is an integral part of that which it also represents. To extract the informational layer that these texts certainly contain without regard to the concomitant ideological-political layer is to miss the wealth of this type of source.

CONCLUSION

The critique leveled by Abrams and Perry Anderson at Marxist scholarship on the state and Mitchell's critique of idealist statism in effect deconstruct the binary opposition of state and society as separate entities and underlie the dimension I propose to add to the study of the Ottoman state. Abrams and Mitchell in particular draw attention to the extent that the state is not a given thing but a contested field of a variety of human actions both material and ideological. They urge us to analyze the ways the state is constructed to appear as a real object, outside and even topographically above society, but at the same time to bear in mind that it is fundamentally a construction, which gains "realness" because enough people act as if the construction were always already there. They further stress, especially Mitchell, that the state as construction (or "a discursively produced effect" in his terminology), is historical: its boundaries, nature, ways of exclusion and inclusion, and identity of those excluded/included all keep changing and being contested, in varying degrees of intensity, in different times and places. Ottoman scholarship has not considered these observations, and I think they ought to be heeded.

The dimension I propose to add to the interpretation of the Ottoman state is twofold. First, cognizance should be taken of the simple—yet at the same time not so simple—fact that the state is a constructed reification. The Ottomans themselves constructed the state as an autonomous and abstract agency, by writing it, among various other ways, and modern scholarship has reproduced it. Whether by assuming that the line that separates state and society is an easily identifiable and unchanging location or that "state" and "society" just ontologically exist, even theoretically conscious scholars such as some of those surveyed here fail to address the question of "constructedness." This does not mean that several attempts to conceptualize and interpret the Ottoman state have not advanced our understanding in a very substantial way. It does mean, however, that a significant dimension of the Ottoman state might be missing and that adding it might make its historical interpretation more comprehensive. I cannot overemphasize that what I propose is to add a dimension rather than to offer a comprehensively alternative concept.

Second, I think that mere cognizance of reification does not suffice. Rather, my aim is to begin an investigation into the discursive historicity of the state, into how it was reified, how the line that divided state and society was drawn and redrawn, how the state as a contested site of inclusion and exclusion was written. This also means attention to clearly ideological source material such as historiography and a different way of interpreting it. Salzmann, for instance, makes an intriguing statement: "For the state, granting *malikâne* contracts . . . was a means of tapping into the cultural authority of the provincial notables."[69] This statement is neither explained nor rendered empirically plausible. More generally, as innovative an interpretation of the state as Salzmann's doubtless is, it still retains the state/

society binary opposition. With all her awareness of the fact that the distribution of the surplus gave rise to conflict and cleavage, Salzmann nonetheless adheres to a state (as the central elite) that acts upon a society (as the provinces).

Mitchell examines a host of social practices that, construed in a certain way, render the state a discursive effect. Informed by him, I look at a social practice he does not consider: the writing of history as a discourse within which the state as a contested field was written. The next chapter is thus a tentative and preliminary attempt to historicize the early modern Ottoman state not only materially and institutionally but also ideologically and discursively.

8. The Ottoman State as a Discursively Contested Field

THE STATE AND THE OTTOMAN POLITICAL IMAGINATION

We may continue where we left off in the previous chapter. Although without explicit theoretical elaboration, Cemal Kafadar seems to be well aware of the contested "constructedness" of the Ottoman state from its formative phase. It is not coincidental that Kafadar's awareness is amply manifested in a masterful study that simultaneously interprets the formation of the Ottoman state and the formation of Ottoman historiography in the period 1300–1500.[1] In Chapter 2 Kafadar's contribution to the scholarship on Ottoman historiography was discussed; here I naturally focus on his understanding of the state. In a way what in principle Kafadar shows about the early history/historiography I apply to the seventeenth century: "In other words, it [the Ottoman state's] was a history of shifting alliances and conflict among various social groups which themselves were undergoing rapid transformation while constantly negotiating their position within the polity."[2]

Skillfully oscillating between the historiography (mainly in the second half of the fifteenth century) and the history of the formation of the state and its expansion, Kafadar also specifies the conflicts and constant vying for position that he describes more generally above. Granted that the line between historical continuity and crude historicism is indeed fine, I nonetheless think that some of these rifts and cleavages, at least their morphology, are pertinent to the renegotiation of the state's boundaries in the seventeenth century. The fundamental rupture, embodied in the historiography, was the one between what might be termed the gazi-dervish milieu and the drive toward a sedentary, bureaucratic state that radiated from the House of Osman and was "ideologized" by orthodox ulema and courtiers. When the state was inscribed in the historiography, the context was that the imperial drive had won the day while the frontier historical ethos expressed bitter acceptance of the marginalization of its social representatives and their relegation to fief-holding provinciality.[3]

The reign of Murad I (r. 1362–89), especially the 1360s and 1370s, is retrospectively considered a turning point in the history of the state as a contested field. At that period the passage between Ottoman Anatolia and Ottoman Thrace was severed because of the temporary loss of Gallipoli to Amedeo of Savoy. This led groups of gazis already in Thrace to challenge Ottoman authority, not an uncommon practice in the frontier (uc) politics of the northeastern Mediterranean. When the Ottomans regained Gallipoli in 1376, Murad I appointed some prominent gazis, for the first time in Ottoman history, as "governors of the frontier" (uc beyleri), thereby, in the historical consciousness of the Ottomans as well as in modern retrospect, transforming the traditional perception of politics in which the Al-i Osman had the status of primi inter pares among bands of gazis. The House of Osman now began to distinguish itself, as a center of sovereignty and authority, from its dependencies and appointees. Kafadar captures the retrospective significance of that moment brilliantly: "The appointment of begs of the frontiers also indicates the emergence of a schizoid mental topography in Ottoman political imagination in the same old pattern that divides the land between a core area (iç il?) and an uc [frontier]."[4]

This "schizoid mental topography" attained a concrete manifestation—one of several—and a particular symbolism, both of which meaningfully pertain to the seventeenth century. The concrete manifestation was the gazi/kul resentment, and the particular symbolism was that of other cities—especially Edirne as the center of gaza—versus Istanbul. The rise of the kul following the conquest of Constantinople and their growing hold over the central army and bureaucracy, as well as the marginalization of the gazis and the sense of betrayal among them, became irreversible under Sultan Mehmed II (r. 1451–1481, the Conqueror or Fatih).[5] But while the power struggle had been decided, its evocative power endured. Thus Prince Cem (1459–95), in his unsuccessful bid for the Conqueror's succession against his brother Bayezid II, based the ideological aspect of his venture on an attempt to appeal to the gazi circles through commissioned historiography, naming one of his sons Oğuz, and on an alleged promise to return to Edirne, "the abode of gazis." He lost to Bayezid precisely because the high-ranking kul constituted his main opposition.[6]

The symbolism of an alternative capital, usually related to dissatisfaction with the kul, remained meaningful. Kafadar mentions several episodes: Osman II's plan to move to Bursa, Damascus, or Cairo; the Edirne/Istanbul controversy of 1703 that forced Mustafa III to abdicate and his successor Ahmed III to promise to stay in Istanbul; Mahmud II's reported threat in the 1810s that if the janissaries did not behave he and his family would leave Istanbul; and, of course, the shift of the capital from Istanbul to Ankara with the establishment of the Turkish Republic. "These incidents," Kafadar remarks, "do not have anything to do with the gazi circles; it would be an anachronism to talk of the frontier warriors as a political force after the sixteenth century. Yet the thread binding these incidents, from Cem's promise to reside in Edirne to the choice of Ankara as the capital of the Turkish republic . . . is clear: in the 'longue durée' of Ottoman political history, the political tension of 'Istanbul versus another city' represented a symbolically potent axis that defined different sociopolitical interests, preferences, and visions."[7]

The "schizoid mental topography" proposed by Kafadar leads to the illustration of my concept of the state as a discursively contested field and as a reified agency. What I show is that the unfolding of the historiographical discourse simultaneously surrenders the discursive struggle and the fact of reification. I first focus very specifically on the representations of Abaza Mehmed Pasha's alleged rebellion and then conclude with an overview of the historiography of the Haile-i Osmaniye as a whole.

ABAZA MEHMED PASHA, HISTORIOGRAPHY, AND THE STATE

As might be recalled from previous chapters, the trauma of the Haile-i Osmaniye did not end with the restoration of Sultan Mustafa I. His second reign (May 1622–September 1623) was marked by unrest and instability, particularly in the eastern provinces and in the capital itself. Eastern Anatolia is where our protagonist assumes center stage. It is alleged in some accounts that Abaza Mehmed Pasha, the governor *(beylerbeyi)* of Erzurum, was motivated by his desire to avenge the killing of Sultan Osman, for which he held the kul responsible. He recruited a sizable army of sekban (irregular, mercenary troops whose immense significance will be discussed later), extended his rule to adjacent provinces, and persistently harassed the janissaries, both those sent from Istanbul and those localized in the provinces *(yerliye)*. Under severe pressure from the kul in the capital, the sultan's staff first ordered that Abaza be transferred to another province. Then, as this order was ignored, a force was sent against him. This force, however, failed to encounter Abaza and returned to Bursa without having engaged him in battle.

The Abaza affair was to end only under Murad IV (1623–40). Following two serious campaigns, the second of which was led by the grand vezir Hüsrev Pasha (1627), Abaza finally surrendered. Significantly, the grand vezir treated Abaza and his troops with pomp and ceremony. He was assigned to Bosnia, where he continued to persecute the kul and fought on the European front. Abaza later returned to Istanbul and is reported to have been close to Murad IV. He was nonetheless executed in 1634, when the sultan was asserting his authority. Again significantly, or perhaps as an instance of the Ottoman imperial sense of humor, Abaza was ceremoniously buried next to Kuyucu Murad Pasha, the grand vezir who had annihilated Abaza's celali "ancestors" under Ahmed I (r. 1603–17).[8]

Let us begin with the construction of Abaza's identity. The bottom line should be registered first. The sociopolitical identity of Abaza Pasha that was inscribed in Ottoman collective memory, and as such came down to us, was that of a rebel *(ası)* rather than a provincial governor, a member of the ümera (the high echelon of the military provincial administration).[9] This was basically because Tuği's perspective and judgment, however much re-read and rewritten, rather than Peçevi's, was adopted by Katip Çelebi and consequently also by Naima. The latter's institutional position as the first state historian rendered his narrative official. Interestingly, Abaza's identity as rebel was retrospectively sealed long before the historical episode itself ended, for Tuği's text deals only with the initial phase of this episode; the decade-long activities that followed had no impact in the final analysis.[10]

The alternative constructions of Abaza's sociopolitical identity are to be found in Tuği's (rebel) and Peçevi's (ümera member) texts. It is worthwhile following in some detail the textual ways in which these identities were constructed, especially with regard to Tuği, whose text might misleadingly seem "flat" and transparent. My contention is that in Tuği's text Abaza's activities are perceived and represented from two viewpoints. The broader one is that of the capital at large toward provincial events. The narrower, more complicated, and more significant viewpoint is that of the janissaries in the capital, who grasped the "rebellion" on the basis of what their comrades and envoys had reported. The representation in Tuği's account is consequently (like the rest of the text) pro-kul and anti-Abaza as well as retrospectively scathing of Sultan Osman's venture. By contrast, Peçevi represents the same event from the perspective of some Anatolian ümera.

This alternative angle yields a meaning very different from, at times even antithetical to, Tuği's.

The most basic constituents of Tuği's perspective, which might ostensibly look meaningless, are verbs that denote motion. They are critically important for determining the place from which events are seen because we have in this story two centers of activity: Erzurum and the Anatolian provinces in general, and Istanbul. The three most frequently used verbs of motion are *gitmek, gelmek,* and *varmak.* I ignore *varmak* not only because it appears less frequently than the other two but chiefly because in Ottoman, unlike modern, Turkish it can mean either "to go somewhere" or "to come from somewhere"; this, of course, cannot serve to indicate the place from which a certain motion was seen. By contrast, since the other two verbs clearly specify the direction of movement and since both are abundantly used, it is possible to identify the position of Tuği's "camera": that is, the angle from which events are perceived and narrated.

According to Tuği's account, the rebellion in Erzurum erupted when the governor, Abaza Mehmed Pasha, began violently to abuse the janissaries sent there from the capital as well as the localized ones *(yerliye).* After apparently accepting some sort of reconciliation negotiated by the local notables *(ayan),* Abaza suddenly seized the fortress of Erzurum, drove out the janissaries, and detained the yerliye. He then proceeded to recruit a sizable army of sekban with which he was able to extend his rule to include neighboring provinces. His audacity grew to such an extent that he ignored explicit orders from Istanbul to vacate his office and turned away the sultan's envoys.[11]

The pattern that underlies this account is that the expelled janissaries always *come to* Istanbul and that the envoys *go from* Istanbul *to* Erzurum and *come back.* This clearly shows that Tuği's "camera" is always positioned in either Istanbul at large (the wider angle) or, at other times, in specific locales there, such as the official residence of the commander of the janissary corps *(Ağa Kapısı)* or the janissaries' barracks (Yeni Odalar). It was there that complaints and reports from the provinces were digested, reproduced, and translated into such forms of action as meetings or demonstrations and written or oral petitions. These petitions, in turn, constituted the basis for Tuği's representation of Abaza's revolt. Thus the expelled janissaries "came that day and complained of Abaza Pasha in Istanbul" *(yeniçerileri . . . ol gün gelip Asitanede Abaza Paşadan şikayet eylediler);* "repeatedly, complainants about the governor of Erzurum, Abaza Pasha, came and notified [the authorities], with certainty, that he was a rebel" *(Erzurum beylerbeyisi olan Abaza Paşadan tekrar şikayetciler geldiler ve ası olduğun muhak-*

kak ilam eylediler); and "the janissary unit commander who had gone over [to report on] Abaza Pasha in Erzurum came and notified [the authorities] in Istanbul of Abaza's rebellion" *(Erzurumda Abaza Paşa üzerine giden çorbacı gelip Asitanede Abazanın isyanı ilam eyledi)*.[12]

The interpretation constructed in Tuği's account is founded, then, on a vantage point that can be defined as the janissaries' perspective on Abaza from the capital, seen through the "lens" of the reports submitted by their expelled comrades and envoys. Consequently, Tuği's interpretation establishes several allegedly causal connections, two of which are particularly pertinent. The first is the classification of the state of affairs in the eastern provinces under the trope of *fitne ü fesad* (sedition and disorder) and the assertion that it was caused by Sultan Osman's venture and its disclosure throughout the region by the decrees *(emirler)* dispatched by the sultan to his trusted governors in Anatolia. Especially destructive was the impact of the clause that ordered doing away with the existing kul and replacing them.[13]

Bearing in mind that it might also be an oral address, the way Tuği's text lures the audience into following this line of causality is quite remarkable. The account of Abaza's rebellion begins with an explicit assertion of the causal connection, delivered in an objective narrator's voice, as a mere statement of fact: "In what was previously told it was noted that Sultan Osman Han had secretly sent messages everywhere, saying that the janissary corps would be destroyed. For that reason sedition appeared in some provinces."[14] This statement is immediately followed by three illustrations of the state of civil disorder *(fitne ü fesad)*. The first is a feud in the city of Aintab between a reportedly tyrannical kadi, Baki Efendi, and the janissaries who—as usual by now—have been victimized and seek to restore justice. The second is yet another feud, in Baghdad, this time between the kul and the beylerbeyi. And the third is Abaza Pasha's seizing the fortress of Erzurum and thereby launching his revolt.[15]

By binding together with Abaza incidents that occurred elsewhere and might be of a different nature, Tuği's representation renders the former the epitome of a more general state of fitne ü fesad rather than a particular incident. The portrayal of Abaza's actions as the nadir of a wider pattern of civil disorder that evinced the disastrous potential of Sultan Osman's venture is an emplotment made in Tuği's text rather than a relation found in (or among) the events themselves. This causal structure, essentially literary in my view, seems to emanate naturally from the order in which things happened as long as the latent kul-centric, Istanbul-based viewpoint goes unnoticed.

Two additional narrator's statements then reinforce this causality: one follows the above incidents, and the other, more effective because of its position in the text, is inserted in the conclusion of the prose part of the narrative. There, in the narrator's voice, the whole Haile-i Osmaniye is concluded with the statement that after Sultan Osman had taken a niyet (a formal resolution to perform a religious act) to exterminate the current kul and recruit sekban in their stead, Abaza launched his revolt, and his cause attracted brigands *(eşkiya)*, who, according to Tuği, manned his army.[16] The fact that the narrative ends on this note is also an indication that the immediate context shared by Tuği and his kul audience was the tangible threat posed by the ascendancy of Abaza Pasha.

The second causal connection established by Tuği's text is forged by the definition of Abaza's activities as "rebellion" *(isyan)* and Abaza himself as "rebel" *(ası)*. In my understanding, unlike less clear-cut terms, such as *fitne ü fesad* or *hilaf* (contravention), in the political discourse of the seventeenth century *isyan* specifically meant an "official" rebellion, or coup d'état, against the legitimate sovereign: the reigning padishah and, more generally, the House of Osman.[17] Needless to say, an isyan was also considered an overt attempt to undermine the central authority, and the center's viewpoint typically (with the occasional exception of Peçevi) dictated the perception of events in provinces that we find in the Tarih-i Al-i Osman works of the seventeenth century in general.

Significantly, in Tuği's text, throughout the narration as well as the alleged speeches and petitions of the kul, the term *isyan* is exclusively reserved for Abaza's actions, while the other incidents in the eastern provinces are described mostly as indications of fitne ü fesad. Tuği's account seems to follow, naturally as it were, the practice of the kul in Istanbul and their recently expelled comrades from Erzurum, who simply refer to Abaza and his actions as *rebel* and *rebellion* respectively without feeling the need to explain why.[18] The ostensible explanations provided by the narrator on numerous occasions are actually just repetitions of statements uttered previously in the kul's voice but reiterated in the guise of narrative objectivity. For instance, the narrator concludes the digression in which a brief vita of Abaza Pasha has been given with a statement whose grammar encapsulates the way in which language and text transform a perspectival logic of causality into an objective state of affairs: "With his [Abaza's] spiteful persecuting of the janissary corps, he became a rebel against the blessed padishah (V*e yeniçeri taifesine husumet etmekle saadetlu padişaha ası oldu*)."[19]

Peçevi's alternative representation is, like Tuği's, the product of his perspective on it. Whereas Tuği's picture is underlain by a combination of an

Istanbul perspective and kul-centrism, Peçevi's is that of an Anatolian province and its ümera. Peçevi described many events from a provincial perspective because he spent much of his career in the provincial administration. The alternative meaning that this noncentral—and non-kul—perspective produces is revealed with special clarity in the representation of the Abaza Pasha affair.

Peçevi intimates that when Abaza Pasha made his first move (it is significant that he never applies the term *isyan* to these events[20]), he himself was the director of finances *(defterdar)* of Diyarbekir under the governorship of Hafiz Pasha. Using the first-person voice, Peçevi discloses having learned at the time that the ümera in the provinces around the capital had grown concerned about and dissatisfied with prevailing conditions in Istanbul, especially the increasing power of the kul. Closer to home, in Diyarbekir, Peçevi noticed that frequent traffic was going back and forth between Hafiz Pasha and Abaza Pasha: "I realized that an understanding had been established between them. Thus Abaza Pasha made his first bid." He adds that Abaza, before killing the janissaries he had captured, would often tell them: "You are the slayers of the caliph of the era and the padishah of the world." In Peçevi's reading of the situation, "Hafiz Pasha's intention was to unite all the beys in governorship and in commanding positions, secure the approaches to Üsküdar, and demand the slayers of the padishah."[21]

Peçevi's representation is a meaningful alternative. According to Peçevi, Sultan Osman's plan did not inflame the ümera against the kul; the former were already unfavorably inclined toward the latter. After Osman's deposition and death, the ümera observed the growing power and influence wielded by the kul with even greater concern. Abaza Pasha's initiative was not, in Peçevi's view, the result of Genç Osman's ambitious venture; nor did the sultan's assassination do more than add fuel to the fire and suggest vengeance as an expedient rationale. Rather, this initiative was a concerted effort by the ümera to counterbalance the powerful position of the kul in the center. Effectively contradicting a claim made by Tuği, Peçevi, from his position on the spot, contends that the Anatolian ümera were not coerced into cooperating with Abaza Pasha but supported him wholeheartedly.

To further the interpretation, let us return to Barkey's understanding of the Abaza affair within the framework of what she calls "the second phase" of celali activity (1623–48). She sees Osman II's venture as an attempt to continue the centralizing policies of Ahmed I (1603–17). Barkey is adamant that even the deposition and assassination of the young ruler should not be construed as breakdown. In her view Abaza's revolt was the most notable example of the modus operandi of the bandits in that period: their bargaining with the state took advantage of the rupture between the central standing army and the provincial units of sekban. What distinguished this generation of bandits from the first was their "politicized rhetoric of bargaining." Adopting an anti-janissary, pro-sekban rhetoric, they sought to legitimize their demands and position in ways that would make their cause more compelling within the discourse of the Ottoman polity. This phase ended with the steps taken by Murad IV from 1632 on, which according to Barkey represented the most ambitious attempt at state consolidation since Kanuni Sultan Süleyman.[22]

It is precisely concerning Abaza's political bid that the difference between Barkey's concept of the Ottoman state and my own becomes acute. In another formulation, her exclusion of the "bandits" of the second generation from the state, wrongly in my understanding, stems from the two problems pointed in the previous chapter: the idealist, inherently static, notion of the state and the positivist use of the contemporary historiography as a transparent amalgamation of facts. Both Abaza's bid and the kul's furious reaction to it contested the drawing of the state's boundaries at a given historical moment: the former manifested the attempt of the celali who had become provincial governors to assert their inclusion within the state and their acquired Ottoman identity; the latter endeavored to make sure that exclusion prevailed. The state was revealed in this affair as a *historical* site of both material and discursive conflict, as a site whose boundaries could be drawn, contested, and redrawn. And what Barkey calls "politicized rhetoric" was in fact a declaration of identity by a group that had acquired an Osmanlı sociopolitical identity and strove to affirm its place *within* the *Devlet-i Aliye* (Sublime State).

Important issues of continuity and change are involved here. Another junction at which the definition of the state was contested—again, at once historically and historiographically—was naturally the period of the formation of the Ottoman state. As soon as Gallipoli had been recaptured in 1376 (after a decade), Çandarlı Kara Halil, then chief judge *(kazasker)* and founder of the famous lineage of grand vezirs, proposed to the sultan a new levy, the *pencik* (fifth). According to this levy, one-fifth of the prisoners taken in gaza activities should be passed to the ruler's household. One Kara Rüstem had proposed the levy to Çandarlı Kara Halil. The pencik was obviously levied from the leading gazis of Rumelia, the main frontier, and might be interpreted as Murad I's reaction to the gazis' autonomous aspirations when the link between Rumelia and Anatolia had been severed

(1366–76). Kara Rüstem was duly appointed *pencik emini* (inspector of the fifth) in Gallipoli, the point through which the gaza booty passed from Rumelia to Anatolia.[23]

In retrospect, that event can be seen a formative phase in the foundation of the janissary corps and the kul institution in general. Retrospect is the key here. What probably had been in the second half of the fourteenth century a conflict within a frontier principality was appropriated, a century later, by the politics and historiography of the imperial project. The pencik controversy came to symbolize the conflict between the marginalized gazis, once the center of the Ottoman enterprise, and the kul, "products of the pencik" and now themselves the center of an increasingly centralized, dynastic state.

Closer to the period under discussion is the formation of the bandits as a social category, the dynamic historicity of their interaction with the state, and the incongruity of this historicity with Barkey's concept of the state. Directly, the bandits/sekban formation should be understood in the context of the military transformation explained by Inalcik. The growing need for large infantries was what led to the recruitment of tax-paying Anatolian peasants. Their importance, increasing power, and conflict with the janissaries were central features of the seventeenth century. In 1687–89, under Yeğen Osman Pasha's leadership, the power wielded by the sekban reached its peak, and they dominated the central imperial institutions.[24] More generally, the context was the price revolution and the crisis of the seventeenth century throughout Eurasia.[25]

One of the notable results of this comprehensive crisis "was the increased number of vagrant youths in the Anatolian countryside: that of the movement of villagers, young men moving away from their fathers' homesteads toward a life of religious education, military service, or banditry."[26] In Barkey's interpretation, the process whereby out of this multitude of people, whether religious students *(suhtes)* or just disenfranchised peasants, the bandits/sekban emerged as the most significant social group was, again, driven by the state's centralizing intentions. The state militarized the countryside and temporarily recruited and demobilized the Anatolian peasantry, but it severed their ties to agricultural life irrevocably. By attempting to control, manipulate, and eventually coopt these people, the state manufactured a new—and artificial, according to Barkey—social group, namely, the bandits/sekban. They were recruited in two ways. One was directly into the central state army. The other was into the Ottoman elite households, to the extent that "the need for and more men drove power holders to enlist peasants [as *kapı halkı*, retinue], shifting the source of retinues from traditional slaves to peasants."²⁷

This highly significant change had numerous repercussions, some of which pertain to the state as a contested field. One was the tension it created between the more conservative-minded bureaucrats and the kul (the janissaries especially) on the one hand and the sekban on the other. Though the latter enjoyed much less prestige and were underprivileged, they nonetheless expected to become part of the state's armed forces and reacted bitterly and violently when demobilized; they also developed cohesive internal organization and esprit de corps.²⁸ The way the kul reacted is amply demonstrated throughout Tuği's text. Inclusion prevailed, however, and here I fully agree with Barkey, who stresses that, antagonism notwithstanding, "by Osman's reign, the idea of a permanent sekban army was fully formed in the minds of some state bureaucrats"²⁹ and, it might be added, reportedly in the mind of the sultan himself.

Another result of this change is that making the Anatolian peasantry a chief reservoir of recruitment for elite household strengthened their position vis-à-vis the dynastic household. From the introduction of pencik sometime in the 1370s, through the development of the devşirme and çıkma (selective recruitment, classification, and promotion of palace trainees and graduates), the sultan's household became unique and the most powerful in the realm. The demise of the devşirme in the seventeenth century and the further diversification of the recruitment mechanisms—devşirme had never been the only one—and of the legitimate recruitment reservoirs are key to understanding the ascendancy of the elite household and the way in which it subverted the boundaries of the state and rendered it an increasingly inclusive "creature."

To return to Mitchell, this process was embodied in a symbolic act whose meaning points to the state as a "discursively produced effect." Until 1654 the office of the grand vezir was only one among others within the confines of the sultan's household and palace, though it was the most important. Then the grand vezir took both his household and offices to a palace of a former pasha near, but outside, the Topkapı palace, and it became his permanent and official residence. It would later gain universal fame as *Bab-i Ali* (the Sublime Porte). This is an instructive example of a discursively produced separation between the private and the public, a discursively produced "announcement" that the state was no longer coterminous with the sultan's household, that the state was becoming less patrimonial and more bureaucratic.³⁰

In her study on the Ottoman finance bureaucracy, Linda Darling highlights another change with analogous discursive meaning.[31] Early in the seventeenth century the finance department became too large to remain within the Topkapi and the empire's chief comptroller (*baş defterdar*) too powerful to want to stay there. The result was that the whole finance department moved out of the palace to separate quarters, called the Residence of the Chief Comptroller *(Defterdar Kapısı)*; this resembled what the grand vezir and his retinue would do half a century later. It was accompanied by the separation of the sultan's expenses from those of the government, thereby constructing the discursive dichotomy—in the financial domain in this case—between private and public. More generally, this is another instance of the process in which, as the seventeenth century unfolded, the dynastic household and the state ceased to be coterminous. The observation stressed in this study on several occasions seems to echo Darling's: "If the Ottoman Empire had once fit the description of a patrimonial state, it was now approaching a bureaucratic model, at least in the case of the finance department."[32]

The third result is the emergence of what Barkey terms "banditry as a social type."[33] In contention with the bulk of scholarship—much of which is romantically "Robin Hoodized"—on "primitive rebellions" and social banditry, she persuasively argues in favor of change: the bandits were *not* part of the peasant community, even if they had originated from that stratum. Barkey convincingly shows "that an analytical distinction has to be made between the peasant and the brigand. Even if the brigand was originally from the same village, the transformations I have described refashioned him to benefit from new conditions and new alternatives. In the process, he developed a new persona, disloyal to his origins and even helping to repress members of his village."[34] All this noteworthy awareness of the bandits/sekban's historicity, however, comes to a halt when the static idealist state interferes. This group may have altered its position and identity in the course of two or three decades, from peasants to bandits/sekban and even to ümera. The ahistorical state/society barrier prevails, however, and the bandits remain a metonymy that stands for society in this dichotomy. Crudely put, the bandits were free to roam in the meadows of "society," as they did in changing from peasants to bandits/sekban, but they could not enter "the state" even when they were recruited into elite households and became provincial governors.

With the textual and contextual dimensions provided, it is now possible to conclude the interpretation of the Abaza affair and its relation to the state as a discursively contested and historical field. As a young man, Abaza

Mehmed Pasha fought in the army of Canbuladoğlu Ali Pasha, one of the most prominent celali leaders based in northern Syria and eastern Anatolia. Abaza was captured sometime between 1607–9 and might have been executed. He was saved, however, by being recruited into the household of Halil Pasha, one of the Ottoman commanders in the campaigns against the celali, led by the grand vezir Kuyucu Murad Pasha. Halil Pasha's successful career—he was to become grand vezir and kapudan paşa (admiral of the navy) in the late 1610s and early 1620s—launched Abaza's own career. Later on, Abaza consolidated his sociopolitical network *(intisap)* by marrying into the household of *Gürcü* (the Georgian) Mehmed Pasha, another grand vezir during Mustafa I's second reign.

Significantly, Tuği gives much information on Abaza's life. In meaningful places in the narrative, he digresses from the chronological account and presents certain details from this life that within his kul-centric logic justify a particular course of action the kul took.[35] Thus the successful pressure applied by the kul to dismiss Gürcü Mehmed Pasha from the grand vezirate was justified by the information that Abaza was related to Gürcü: that is, he had married the daughter of Gürcü's brother and thus was reluctant to suppress the rebellion as required by the interests of the Exalted State (not the kul, of course).

All this means that by the time he "rebelled," Abaza and many of his colleagues were no longer bandits, just as they were no longer peasants. Their recruitment, careers, socialization, and acculturation must indicate that they had become provincial Osmanlıs. Abaza's career in particular—and here a prosopographical study of the sort advocated by Metin Kunt would be very interesting—also illustrates the extent to which the rise of the elite household altered the rules of the game. That a social group like Abaza's would contest its inclusion within the state, whose boundaries were determined chiefly by the dynastic household and its members, was almost inconceivable. The seventeenth-century household was a structure that subverted and rendered porous the state's boundaries; it was instrumental in eventually redefining the state as a more inclusive field, at least for much of the seventeenth century (1610s to 1680s).

The Ottoman historiography of the period, composed as it was in such proximity to the events it represents, simultaneously reflects and constitutes the struggle over the redefinition of the state. Tuği's kul-centric text was part of the kul's effort to exclude the ümera of peasant-bandit origin and the sekban troops from the state. The energy invested in this text to render Abaza a rebel rather than an ümera member is a cultural signifier whose political signified was that he was not, as either an icon or a concrete person, part of the state. Peçevi's text gives us what Barkey calls "the politicized rhetoric" of the bandits' second generation, and what I deem the self-assertion of, particularly, the ümera of celali origin as provincial Osmanlıs, as a social group that had redrawn the boundaries of the Ottoman state.

A final note should be made on how "the state" handled Abaza in the first phase of his "rebellion." Tuği, precisely as the kul's voice, offers a key insight in this regard. The details on Abaza's vita and intisap in his text, in addition to justifying the kul's dismissal of Gürcü Mehmed Pasha, are presented also to lend credence to their suspicion that "the state" was not particularly inclined firmly to suppress Abaza Pasha. We may now take "the state" apart and observe, regarding this event, three pertinent agencies within it: the kul, the Anatolian ümera, and several high-ranking vezirs. I think that the kul, as their voice is brought in Tuği's text, were perceptive. What numerous modern scholars interpret as weakness and incompetence seems to have been an exercise in good old Ottoman politics of balance and counterbalance. The vezirs might be happy to let Abaza keep the kul threatened and insecure, because their power and audacity had grown so much. These vezirs could not, of course, explicitly endorse Abaza's actions. They were content with dispatching envoys and decrees, which were turned away and ignored, and with sending the odd military force, which, inexplicably, failed to encounter Abaza. The governor of Erzurum, it would seem, could take a hint.

THE HAILE-I OSMANIYE AND THE STATE

One of the simultaneously confusing and fascinating facets of the seventeenth-century historical discourse, as well as that of the advice literature, is that the general ideological line articulated in Tuği's text kept winning the day, whereas Peçevi's Anatolian perspective was not accepted. At the same time, the recruitment of Anatolians into what was conceived of as the state through the elite households and the army continued. The result is that what were cleavages within the state and constant struggles to redraw its sociopolitical boundaries are interpreted at worst as decline or breakdown, deviations from a golden age classical model, and at best as a state/society binary opposition. I would now like to offer an explanation for the construction of what became the official state narrative of the Haile-i Osmaniye in Naima's history. The explanation is conveyed through two illustrations of the state as at once a reified thing and a contested field. One is yet another concrete instance of what Kafadar identifies as "a schizoid mental topography in Ottoman political imagination in the same old pattern that divides the land between a core area and an uc." The other is a cleavage within the Ottoman establishment along ethnic-regional *(cins)* lines, and the possible positioning of Naima in particular vis-à-vis this cleavage.

A simple but significant biographical fact must be stressed before we proceed (see Chapter 2). Three of the five historians discussed in this study, Tuği, Hasanbeyzade, and Naima, came from kul families. As far as can be traced, these kul families originated from the Balkans, the traditional area of recruitment, and Tuği himself may have been born in Belgrade.

The account of Katip Çelebi in his *Fezleke-i Tarih* was incorporated, with few alterations and additions, into *Tarih-i Naima* and thus became the official narrative of the Haile-i Osmaniye.[36] Naima's additions to the *Fezleke* can be found in his introduction to and conclusion of Sultan Osman's reign. In the introduction Naima discusses the sources and pays tribute to Katip Çelebi's historiographical prowess.[37] The conclusion has two significant additions. One, on which I do not dwell here, is a further elaboration of Katip Çelebi's exposition of the astrological inauspiciousness that doomed Osman II and his reign. The other is a severely critical assessment of Sultan Osman and the errors that brought about his downfall. In these concluding remarks Naima forcefully expresses the disapproval of Genç Osman that pervades the histories of his earlier colleagues, with the exception of Peçevi.[38]

Naima is the only one who explicitly suggests that Sultan Osman's inability to choose the right advisers had to do with his age: "Besides having ascended the throne in the first bloom his youth, and not having been successful in attaining experienced, intelligent, and faithful companions, he [Osman II] also met only fools and those who humored his whims."[39]

Naima, again uniquely, goes back as far as Istanköylü Ali Pasha's grand vezirate (1619–21) and identifies it as the first occasion on which this inability manifested itself with irreversible consequences. Ali Pasha, Naima explains, became grand vezir through bribery and, even worse, augmented the sultan's treasury through ruthless means of collecting revenues. He not only made the young ruler "accustomed to injustice and confiscation" but also "distanced his [the sultan's] faithful old retainers." The impact was fatal: "The world-adorning padishah was puffed up and completely abandoned the path of good harmony and diplomacy that are necessary for conducting the realm." Naima also explicitly blames the sultan for the enmity between himself and the kul and attributes to his attitude the kul's indifferent performance on the battlefield: "He [Osman II] cooled the ardor in the troops' hearts with coercion and subjugation." Finally, Naima is the only one who points out Sultan Osman's ignorance in political tactics, exacerbated by "kingly vanity" (nahvet-i mulukâne). The sultan's failure in this respect, Naima argues, was his confident assumption, bolstered "by the deficient ideas of some people of weak judgment," that he could carry out a contentious venture without having on his side at least one estate (sınıf) within the army (presumably either the imperial cavalry, the altı bölük, or the janissaries).[40]

Neither Tuği's account nor Hasanbeyzade's is incorporated into the Fezleke, hence into Tarih-i Naima, uncritically, in toto, or verbatim. The altruistic motivations that Tuği's text ascribed to the kul are drastically tempered in the Fezleke. Katip Çelebi and, even more, Naima in his conclusion also temper Tuği's vituperative criticism of Sultan Osman's advisers, particularly the chief black eunuch, by the mere fact that they pin a much larger portion of the blame on the sultan himself rather than on those who, according to Tuği, led him astray. Nonetheless, with the exception of Tarih-i Peçevi, the historical discourse before us is underpinned by a common, largely unspoken, assumption that Sultan Osman's venture had to be stopped lest the empire suffer its disastrous consequences and that this venture was so impracticable as to be ludicrous.

To further the explanation of the ultimate, official judgment of the Haile-i Osmaniye, let us accurately define what, in the Ottoman historians' own perception, the sultan's venture was about. In their understanding, what Osman had essentially wanted—and for this he and his advisers were vehemently deplored—was, first, to shift the reservoir of the kul's recruitment from the traditional places to inner Anatolia, Syria, and—in some accounts—Egypt; to focus on inner Anatolia, he had intended to transform the sekban into the backbone of the kul institution and central army. Concomitantly, he had wished to transfer the capital from Istanbul to a major city in one of these regions or, some say, to Edirne, "the abode of gaza." Of equal significance is what the padishah did not have mind according to the historians' own presentation of his plan: he did not want to abolish the kapı kulları as a pivotal institution of the Ottoman state. The strongest indication that this is how the Ottoman historians understood it is that all of them, when presenting the plan, say that the sultan's intention was to create a body of *"new kul"* (yeni kul).

What is deemed so objectionable in Osman's venture is very effectively conveyed in a metonymy that is copiously repeated in Tuği's dialogue with his audience. The sultan, it is reported, intended "to move into Anatolia" (Anadol[u] semtine geçmek) or "to go in the direction of Anatolia" (gitmek instead of geçmek); this is frequently followed by "with the pretext of performing the hajj." It was this intention that the kul and high officials ceaselessly demanded the sultan to abandon. It was the impression that this intention might be carried out, when a rumor spread that the imperial pavilion had been transferred to Üsküdar and erected there, that ignited the explosion of the kul. I shall return to consider the fundamental meaning of this metonymy in the Epilogue. Here I confine the discussion to its more immediately political signification.

Freud argues in *The Interpretation of Dreams* that concrete metaphors are more effective than abstract ones because they contain a richer web of associations. In a similar vein, Tuği's metonymy was so effective in its own context because it was meaningful both literally and figuratively. It embodies the reason for which the other historians too, who shared neither the context of Tuği and his audience nor its underlying kul-centrism, disapproved of Sultan Osman's venture, again both literally and figuratively. They comprehensively rejected not only the sultan's actual attempt to realize the intention "to go in the direction of Anatolia" but also the figurative meaning of the metonymy: that is, turning away from, first, Istanbul and, second, what lay to its west, and seeking Bursa and what was to its east and south.

To return to Kafadar's "schizoid mental topography in Ottoman political imagination" as a *longue durée* structure, I would suggest that Tuği's metonymy signifies its manifestation in the seventeenth century. On the one hand, the demarcation of the state never ceased being contested, and "a schizoid mental topography" whose formation is noticed by Kafadar in the period from the 1370s to the 1480s resurfaced, in its own contextual guise, in the first half of the seventeenth century. On the other hand, however, our historiographical discourse occurred one a and a half or two centuries after the gazi/uc suspicion of the notion of "state-ness" had succumbed to the drive toward a dynastic state, identified with Istanbul and the various imperial institutions that could change but at the same time developed established characteristics. This was deeply ingrained in the worldview of the Istanbul-based bureaucrat-historians, to the extent that they could not entertain as radical a change as they attributed to Sultan Osman. Recruiting sekban was for these historians one thing; endorsing an ideology and policy that, in the "schizoid mental topography," would radically alter the prevailing distinction between "core area" and "frontier" was quite another. It is instructive that none of the historians felt the need to ask what was so bad about Osman II's venture and then to supply a well-argued reply. "To move into Anatolia" seemed to suffice, and the answer was assumed to be in the description of the venture. Not that there was a conspiracy to prevent such questioning: the limits that the hegemonic discourse imposed rendered the questioning unthinkable and the answer taken for granted.

There are two more subtle points. One is that it would be ill advised to construe crudely a perfect correlation between location (Istanbul/Anatolia in this case) and the stance taken on the core area/frontier mental topography. The correlation has certain validity of course, but not a comprehensive one, for the Ottoman state was a complex, schizoid field indeed. It must be borne in mind that in the formative period of the latter part of the fifteenth century one of the foremost cultivators and propagators of the gaza/uc path was Prince Cem, neither a resident in the frontier nor your average gazi. Similarly, the notion embodied in "to move into Anatolia" emanated from, no less, "the padishah of the era" and his advisers, not from the Anatolian ümera and sekban. The other point involves the delicate, often elusive, balance between continuity and change as well as that between historical awareness and crude historicism. Like Kafadar, I am cautious not to argue that the sekban and ümera of celali origin were a seventeenth-century reincarnation of the old gazis or that Anatolia and northern Syria at that period were literally frontier zones. Rather, I think that the "schizoid mental topography" is a useful guide for the cultural and political contours of the Ottoman state. It is a *longue durée* structure of consciousness whose underlying morphology is where historical continuity lies. At the same time, its variously particular appearances, as in the history and historiography of Haile-i Osmaniye, should be interpreted in their constantly changing circumstances.

For the part of the explanation of the official narrative of the Haile-i Osmaniye that is concerned with the ethnic-regional *(cins)* affiliations of the Ottomans, I return to the grand vezir Mere Hüseyin Pasha and the exceptionally favorable view Tuği takes of him (presented in detail in Part II). Metin Kunt, in an article on ethnic and regional tensions within the Ottoman establishment, offers the contextual framework for this part of the explanation.[41] Kunt sets out to refute the view that those recruited to the Ottoman establishment, especially the devşirme recruits, lost their previous ethnic-regional attachments. After all, more than modern nation-states, the Ottoman collectivity was a true melting pot. One of his examples, which suggests that the mother tongues of these people were not forgotten, is the following: "Mere Hüseyin Pasha, a grand vezir in the early 17th century, would give the order for the removal of guilty persons in his native Albanian; the order 'take him,' 'mere' in Albanian, stuck as his nickname."[42]

More generally, Kunt has an interesting observation. Drawing on the poet Veysi (first half of the seventeenth century) and the historians and contemporaries Naima and Silahdar Mehmed Ağa, he suggests that throughout the seventeenth century there developed in the Ottoman establishment a cleavage along ethnic-regional lines between "westerners" and "easterners." By *westerners* he means those recruited to imperial service from Albania and Bosnia, whereas the easterners were originally Abkhasians, Circassians, and Georgians. Kunt further identifies a process in the seventeenth century wherein the westerners gradually came to dominate the Ottoman establishment. It is indicative, Kunt notes, not only that this domination is noticed in Veysi's poetry but also that the histories of Naima and Silahdar are scattered with remarks that point to an ethnic prejudice against high officials of eastern origin. The lack of such remarks on westerners, Kunt concludes, testifies to the Albanian-Bosnian ascendancy, which had already existed in the first half of the century but was enhanced in the second half under the grand vezirs of the Köprülü household. It is also significant that neither Silahdar nor Naima was directly involved in cins frictions but that both allude to their existence and point to the members of the group that became dominant within the imperial system.[43]

Paradoxical though it may seem at first, Kunt's observation helps both to account for Tuği's exceptional view of Mere and to offer a complementary explanation for the official narrative of the Haile-i Osmaniye. As was observed in Part II, it is plausible that Tuği was a partisan not only of the kul as a whole but specifically of an Albanian barracks-based household that comprised janissary officers of middle ranks and Mere. The fact that the chief rival of this possible household, hence a prime target of Tuği's wrath, was a Georgian grand vezir, as the nickname *Gürcü* indicates, conforms with Kunt's westerners/easterners cleavage.

However, although this division seems to explain Tuği's view, which stands in stark contrast to that of all other historians, Naima's stance on this matter raises a problem. While Kunt holds that as a product of the palace system Naima favored the westerners and manifested a prejudice against the easterners, in this case he does the opposite: he endorses the castigation of a westerner (Mere) and the praising of an easterner (Gürcü). The ostensible contradiction, I think, does not invalidate Kunt's argument. He draws his references from the sixth and last volume of *Tarih-i Naima* (in the standard edition of 1867), which covers what were for Naima current events and personae. Therefore, most—if not all—of the officials whom Naima alluded to in that volume were most probably his contemporaries, part of the politics of his time, concerning whom his reflective prejudices must have been vivid and personal. The case of Mere and Gürcü was much more distanced from Naima, the personality and deeds of the former understandably objectionable, and Tuği's partisanship too blatant; all this seems to have resulted in the fact that Naima just accepted the judgment of Hasanbeyzade and Katip Çelebi on this particular matter.[44]

In addition to the "schizoid mental topography," the ethnic-regional friction suggested by Kunt and the increasing domination of the westerners during the seventeenth century might be another context within which the official narrative of the Haile-i Osmaniye could be seen. This applies to Naima in particular. If not taken strictly formally, his was not just an appointment as state historian *(vakaniüvis)* but an appointment to the *vakanüvislik* (post of state historian) by the Köprülü household. Naima owed it to his affiliation to this powerful household, and he was a loyal member. At crucial points, Naima's household affiliation and historical writing were inextricably intertwined. His historiographical defense of the Köprülü foreign policy toward the Hapsburgs at the end of the seventeenth century, by constructing an analogy to the Prophet's political tactics, is an outstanding example.[45] The domination of the Albanian recruits seems to have become overwhelming under the Köprülüs. Thus this friction might explain, in a way that pertains to Naima in particular, the preconception of Albania and Bosnia as the chief, and natural, reservoir of manpower for the Ottoman state as well as the fact that "moving into Anatolia" was dismissed as ludicrously inapplicable.

There is another way in which Naima's context might be pertinent, though not in a strictly biographical fashion. As several studies on the imperial center in the late seventeenth and early eighteenth centuries suggest, that period witnessed the consolidation of an assertive bureaucratic elite, confident in its power and beliefs, which for all intents and purposes ruled the empire or at least oversaw its day-to-day management. Naima was a member of that elite. His use of the biological metaphor to show that the Ottoman state had reached maturity, and should therefore be entrusted at the hands of its bureaucratic managers, is highly suggestive in this regard. This was a period in which the imperial bureaucracy and military did not hesitate to tame enterprising sultans.[46] To borrow again Weberian terminology, the relative fluidity of the charismatic era to which the crisis of the seventeenth century had given birth no longer pertained to Naima and his contemporaries. If "moving into Anatolia" had seemed conceivable to Genç Osman and his advisers, in Naima's zeitgeist it might be deemed a naughtily youthful whim.

Weighing the two explanations for what became the official narrative of the Haile-i Osmaniye, I think, first, that they are not mutually exclusive but complementary. Second, these two explanations illustrate the state as a contested field, the extent to which the historical discourse was part and parcel of this contestation, and therefore, the extent to which the historical discourse helps, so to speak, to decipher the state. Third, the first explanation, based on the notion of a schizoid topography as an underlying *longue durée* structure of consciousness and political imagination, seems to capture in a more comprehensive fashion the historical discourse as a whole. The second explanation, which draws on the ethnic-regional friction, is especially applicable to Tuği's unique stance on the Mere/Gürcü struggle over the grand vezirate and to Naima's perspective.

CONCLUSION

Historiography has revealed itself through the foregoing analysis as a type of source that makes possible a dialectical observation: of the appearance of the state as an independent subject and of the fact that this appearance is a historically constructed reification. To invoke Philip Abrams and relate theory to concrete historical analysis, historiography as a source makes it possible for us to recognize the "cogency of the idea of the state as an ideological power and treat that as a compelling object of analysis. But the very reasons that require us to do that also require us not to believe in the idea of the state, not to concede, even as an abstract-formal object, the [independent] existence of the state."[47]

If, for instance, one reads only Naima's account of Abaza Mehmed Pasha's "rebellion" or uses the whole historical representation of that event in a rigidly positivist way, one may easily accept the fact of reification and the state/"rebels" (i.e., society) dichotomy as objectively given. If, however, one brings to the fore the contested and ideological historicity of the way this historiographical discourse was constructed until it became the state narrative, one should be able simultaneously to observe the discursive "constructedness" of the state and to historicize it.

Finally, it seems appropriate to end this chapter with a note on history writing as a dialogue between present and past and between context and text. Baki Tezcan shows that precisely what most seventeenth-century Ottoman historians had found deplorable in Sultan Osman's ambitions, Turkish historians writing within the new realities of the unfolding nation-state considered praiseworthy. For the latter, Genç Osman had made a gallant attempt, alas premature, at Turkifying the Ottoman state at the expense of its cosmopolitan nature embodied in Istanbul and epitomized by the domination of the devşirme recruits. They saw in the young ruler's venture the beginning of a process that was successfully completed two hundred years later by Sultan Mahmud II. By destroying the janissaries in 1826, he turned Haile-i Osmaniye (the Ottoman Tragedy) into *Vak'a-i Hayriye* (the Auspicious Event).[48]

Epilogue: Poetics of Ottoman Historiography
Preliminary Notes

I would like to end the present study with a general remark on Ottoman scholarship and a few preliminary notes on the poetic deep structure of Ottoman historiography.[1] Concerning the second undertaking, concrete observations based on the texts I have thoroughly read seem to me preferable to the most modest generalizations on Ottoman historiography, to say nothing of prose writing, as a whole. At the present state of the study of Ottoman literature, any generalization is bound to be unhelpful at best. Being derived from the mood and tone of the present book, the concluding discussion contemplates a possible agenda—which is by no means intended to exclude other interests and preferences—for Ottoman history. The gist of this agenda is an approach to the record left to us by the Ottomans (their archival documents, literature, and buildings) that would find in this record engaging interlocutors, not only transparent informants.

NOT ONLY WARS, NOT ONLY TAXES

If, until recently, a stranger attended a convention of Ottoman studies, he or she might have emerged with the impression that what was earlier termed—courtesy of LaCapra—a documentary paradigm of knowledge dominated the field, not only because this was a prevalent scholarly preference, but also because the Ottomans lent themselves to such an approach. This impression would be likely to have two main causes. One would be the fascination with the depth and wealth of the archival documentation that the Ottomans bequeathed to their researchers. The other would be the Orientalist narrative of "the decline of Islamic civilization" after the late Middle Ages, most effectively articulated by H. A. R. Gibb and Gustav von Grunebaum. In this narrative, high culture in particular reached its zenith in the late medieval period, especially, according to von Grunebaum, with the Muslim scholars who preserved for Europe the cultural treasures of antiquity until the Renaissance men could reclaim and develop them. "The Turks," and here Kawakibi's ethnic taxonomy in *Umm al-Qura* and Gibb's work seem to converge, might arrest "the decline of Islam" in political, military, and administrative ways (until the sixteenth century), but they had an adverse impact on the further development of "Islamic civilization" and made no significant contribution to it.

While that Orientalist narrative has become obsolete for most Ottoman historians (though this is truer for social and economic studies than for cultural investigation), what might be figuratively called the fetish of the defter has prevailed. The problem is of course *not* the infinite wealth of the archival material in locations that were the imperial capital and important provincial centers. The problem is rather the rigidly documentary framework within which these documents are used. This rigidity has already given rise to serious stocktaking that is concerned precisely with archival material that used to be regarded as purely and essentially informational. The Şeriat court records are a good example of such stocktaking.[2]

By this observation I do not mean to suggest that all studies henceforth should interpret literary texts (though a few would be welcome) and that they should eschew documentation and reconstruction. My hope is rather that this book will point to future research that is aware of two premises. One is that to make the overall portrayal of Ottoman history more multidimensional, comprehensive, and balanced, literary, cultural, and ideological questions ought to be addressed and given more attention. The other premise is that a more dialogical and less documentary approach to the sources, be they defter-like, literary, or visual, is crucial for fresh questions and insights on what the Ottomans were all about. They must have amounted to more than levying taxes and waging wars.

WHAT WAS TRAGIC ABOUT THE HAILE-I OSMANIYE?

In the Introduction I stressed that my use of Katip Çelebi's heading *Zikir Vaka-i Haile-i Osmaniye* as "Ottoman Tragedy" is neither simple nor straightforward. The present discussion occasions an explanation.

It is best to begin lexicographically. The host of dictionaries and lexicons that issued from the pioneering work of Sir James Redhouse, first published in 1890, offer various meanings for the word *haile*. In the exclusively modern dictionary the variety of meanings that the word conveyed in older usages has disappeared, and *hail* denotes only "barrier, curtain, screen."[3] The earlier Redhouse rendering, which is already modern but attentive to the Ottoman cultural and linguistic heritage, offers a greater variety of meanings. Thus *hail* also means "fearful" or "frightful." *Haile*, whose Arabic origin is registered, is explicitly related to theater and denotes "tragedy" or "drama." The adjacent term *haileniivis*, literally a writer of *haile*, indicates "tragedian."[4] In his historical dictionary of Ottoman terms, Mehmet Zeki Pakalın too defines "*Haile Nüvis*" as a writer of tragedy and "*Haile*" as tragedy.[5] The founding Redhouse *Turkish and English Lexicon*, most conscious of the Arabic origin, notices the adjectival gender difference (*hail*, masc.; *haile*, fem.) and translates *hail* as "fearful" or "frightful;" tragedy according to that lexicon, however, is not mentioned as a possible meaning.[6]

In Arabic, *hā'il* is an adjective (morphologically an active participle) derived from the root *hwl*. It has a substantial variety of meanings—some of which the Ottoman retained—ranging from "dreadful, frightful, and terrible" through "formidable and prodigious" to "grim and fierce." It is noteworthy that while *haile* as tragedy is the main meaning in dictionaries that contain the Ottoman Turkish of the early twentieth century (the "New" Redhouse and Pakalın), the *Turkish and English Lexicon*, which was first published in 1890 and presumably reflects a slightly earlier state of the language and culture, does not mention tragedy at all as a possible meaning. It is therefore evident that *haile* did not come to mean tragedy, specifically in the context of a dramatic discourse, until the very end of the nineteenth century.

Although this is not the chief concern of the present investigation, it might be of interest to venture the impression—and impression is all it is—that *haile* acquired the theatrical meaning of tragedy thanks to the writing of Abulhak Hamid Tarhan (1851–1937). Hamid had a successful ambassadorial career in the main European capitals at the Ottoman Foreign Service and, as a disciple of Namik Kemal, was also a renowned poet and playwright. Inspired by Corneille and Shakespeare, tragedy seems to have been a genre Hamid favored. One of the products of his stint in London (1886–1908 with a two-year interruption) was an eight-stanza poem Hamid dedicated to Fatma, whom he had hoped to marry but did not. The poem's title was *Haile*, and it revolved around a tension between the tomb and alcove. Alessio Bombaci transcribed the title as *Hag'le* and translated it as "L'Alcova" ("The Alcove").[7] While "The Alcove" might convey the spirit of the poem faithfully, I think that by translating *haile* as "alcove" Bombaci took unwarranted liberty. If my observation is correct, it may account for the absence of *haile* as "tragedy" in Redhouse's *Turkish and English Lexicon* and its appearance in the later dictionaries, for at the time the former was compiled, that meaning could not have gained currency linguistically or culturally.

Whatever the precise time at which *haile* began to mean dramatic tragedy, this was not what it denoted to seventeenth-century Ottomans, at least not in a straightforward way. An eighteenth-century lexicon does not contain the word, though strikingly it does convey dramatic awareness by including terms such as *theater* and *comedy*.[8] More suggestively, a seventeenth-century dictionary, Franciszek Meninski's, includes the word *hail* but renders a translation that is closer to the Arabic and to the *Turkish and English Lexicon* than it is to the "New" Redhouse and to Pakalın. Meniniski translates *hail* mostly as "terrible or horrible" or "strange." In close resemblance to Katip Çelebi's heading, Meninski illustrates the use of the word by translating *vaka-i haile* as "a strange and terrible event."[9]

As he himself indicated, Meninski's source for this illustration—*vaka-i haile* as a possible use of *hail*—was the venerated history composed by the sixteenth-century scholar and sheyhülislam Hoca Sadüddin Efendi and entitled *The Crown of Histories (Tacüttevarih)*.[10] As mentioned in Chapter 5, owing to their reverence for Hoca Sadüddin, the Ottoman historians of the seventeenth century who wrote state histories, beginning with Hasanbeyzade, started their works where *The Crown* had ended (1520). Searching through *The Crown*, I was unable to find a heading that read *vaka-i haile*, though it might appear in one of the extant manuscripts or not as a heading. The closest I came to Meninski's example was *vakaat-i acib* in the original Ottoman and *garip olaylar* for the same heading in the "translation" of *The Crown* to modern Turkish. *Acib* and *garip* have several meanings, but the one they share is "strange." The full heading was "Strange Events That Were Seen When the Padishah [Murad II] was in Edirne." In that section Hoca Sadüddin listed four events, which he numbered, that occurred immediately before or after the conquest of Thessaloniki by Murad II in 1430.[11]

Katip Çelebi did not explicitly mention *The Crown* as one of his sources, but there can be little doubt that he knew it thoroughly. It is therefore possible that Katip Çelebi was influenced by *The Crown*'s heading in entitling our event *Haile-i Osmaniye*. On the basis of the foregoing attempt to historicize the meaning of the word *haile*, it would seem that to Katip Çelebi and his contemporaries, unlike educated Ottomans ca. 1900, *Haile-i Osmaniye* probably meant "a strange, or terrible, Ottoman event." In the next and final section I shall address the question of what might be poetically strange and terrible about the Haile-i Osmaniye. One feels, however, that whatever the precise meaning of the title Katip Çelebi gave this series of events, the Ottoman historians had their own sense of what a tragedy, or a tragic plot, was and that it has something in common with our own sense of dramatic tragedy.

There are two related tragic elements in the historical discourse of the Haile-i Osmaniye. One is the constraint of inevitability. The other, which applies especially to Tuği's text, is that the narrative is structured in a way that highlights a climactic turning point, after which the unfolding of the plot toward its tragic conclusion seems irreversible and unavoidable.

The underlying constraint of inevitability has been mentioned on several occasions in this study. The inauspicious astrological constellation at the time of Sultan Osman's birth and ascension to the throne, and occurrences such as the freezing of the Bosphorus, famine, and fire that were presented as ominous signs of this inauspiciousness, underlie the portrayal of Sultan Osman's attempts to escape his predicament in a familiar tragic vein. The fate of the tragic protagonist is conveyed as obvious and inevitable from the perspective of the knowing narrator and audience, no matter how hard he tries to fight it and himself, and the steps he takes become increasingly desperate, self-destructive, and fatal. This is enhanced by a prayer made by the child-prince whom Sultan Osman had killed before the Hotin campaign, which the narrator and audience already know would be answered.

Owing to his frequent digressions, Tuği's narrative in particular emphasizes a climactic turning point in a way that is reminiscent of a tragic plot. At the point where the chronological account is about to present the explosion of the kul and what followed it (18 May 1622), Tuği digresses to late April/early May 1622. At that point, he informs his audience, it seemed that Sultan Osman was ready to abandon the chief black eunuch and the royal mentor, as well as the perilous plan they had made him embrace, and to heed the advice of responsible state officials. Then, however, came the sultan's dream, after which he became even more determined in his original course and tried to carry out his destructive plan. Thenceforth Sultan Osman went into a speedy downward spiral, and within three weeks or so he lost his throne and simultaneously his life. The detailed and graphic account by Tuği of the actual killing enhances the sense of a futile and tragic struggle against an already sealed fate. At the dungeon in Yedikule, Tuği describes how Sultan Osman struggled to hold off his executioners; he is not content, however, with reporting that the sultan was unsuccessful and was eventually killed. Instead Tuği recounts that in reaction to his struggle, the executioners brutally squeezed Sultan Osman's testicles; as he momentarily froze in astonished pain, they strangled him.

A possible source of this sense of tragic plot might be the *Shahname*. In Chapter 5 I analyzed the use of one episode in Firdausi's *Shahname* by Hasanbeyzade and showed how it made sense within the context of the Haile-i Osmaniye. Numerous stories in the Shahname may be interpreted as tragic in various ways, and the Ottomans were very fond of this medieval Persian epic. To point out a concrete instance, the tragic possibilities of the plot of the Haile-i Osmaniye are reminiscent of the story that led the hero Rüstem to slay his own son, the hero Sohrab, with their fatal and tragic encounter having been assisted by the conniving of Afrasiyab.[12]

This story represents a particular type of tragic plot in the *Shahname* (there are others): the inevitable fate of virtuous protagonists and a course of events they cannot avert no matter how hard they strive to do so. Firdausi masterfully makes the reader feel right from the moment Sohrab's looks are described that his striking similarity to his father Rüstem will lead to a mammoth confrontation between father and son. This feeling is enhanced when Princess Tahmina divulges to her son the identity of his father, and it is brought to the fore through the agency of Afrasiyab. The description of the duel between Rüstem and Sohrab by Firdausi underscores the tragic emplotment of divinely ordained fate. The heroes suspect each other's identity, but this does not alter their fatal actions. It might momentarily seem that the fight could be resolved without killing—alas, to no avail. The scene of the slaying of Sohrab by Rüstem is prolonged and typically marked by the confirmation—desperately late—of the combatants to each other of their identities. "When evil Fortune is stirred with wrath," Firdausi says upon the duel reaching its tragic peak, "then granite rock is softened like wax."[13] Not unlike Sultan Osman's, Sohrab's fate too had been sealed long before he died; youth plays a significant role in accounting for how this death came about in both cases; and the scenes of both deaths are temporarily delayed till destiny runs its course.

Finally, the question of tragedy is interesting because, like the narrative, it too might be a universal, cross-cultural way of telling stories and making sense of reality. We of course instinctively associate the term with "Western culture;" with classical Greek drama and Shakespeare's plays most notably. This, however, should not preclude the possibility that there were other notions of tragedy and, perhaps more important, that there were cross-cultural uses and interpretations of these notions. After all, the historical varieties of cultural products should matter no less than their temporal and spatial origin. This hermeneutic conundrum is magnificently demonstrated by Jorge Luis Borges, in his attempt to grapple with the way Ibn Rushd (Averroës) grappled with Aristotle's *Rhetoric* and *Poetics* and especially with the meaning of *comedy* and *tragedy*. In writing his *Tahafut al-Tahafut*, Borges says, Ibn Rushd was frustrated because "two words had halted him at the very portals of the Poetics. Those words were 'tragedy' and 'comedy.'" No assistance was forthcoming from earlier thinkers, and "the two arcane words were everywhere in the text of the Poetics—it was impossible to avoid them."[14]

Entering his library at dawn, Ibn Rushd felt he had deciphered the meaning of the elusive terms: "Aristu gives the name 'tragedy' to panegyrics and the name 'comedy' to satires and anathemas. There are many admirable tragedies and comedies in the Qur'an and the *mu'allaqat* of the mosque." Borges concludes his essay with a feeling of failure and defeat: "I felt that Averroës, trying to imagine what a play is without having ever suspected what a theater is, was no more absurd than I, trying to imagine Averroës yet with no more material than a few snatches from Renan, Lane, and Asín Palacios."[15]

THE FORCE OF A SYNECDOCHE: POETICS AND POLITICS

In Chapter 8 I emphasized the significance of a phrase that is profusely used in Tuği's text to allude concisely to Sultan Osman's "evil" plan: "to go in the direction of Anatolia" *(Anadol[u] semtine gitmek)* or "to move into Anatolia" *(geçmek* instead of *gitmek)*. Defining the phrase as metonymy, I explained how it underlay what the historians—not only Tuği—had found objectionable in Osman II's alleged intention and the attempt to carry it out. I further related this argument to Cemal Kafadar's characterization of the Ottoman political imagination as a "schizoid mental topography" in which there was a dichotomous separation between a core area and the frontier.

In the final discussion of this study I would like to suggest that Tuği's narrative of the Haile-i Osmaniye, and, owing to its status as urtext, the whole historiographical discourse, was cast in the form of a *synecdoche*. This synecdoche form may constitute a deep structure that establishes a possible nexus between the political and the poetic and between the historiographical and the mythic. I further propose that "underneath" Kafadar's insightful observation there may be a deeper layer of poetic and mythic meaning that sustains the schizoid nature of the political imagination.

It is helpful to begin by explaining why Tuği's phrase "to move into

Anatolia" should be figuratively understood as synecdoche rather than metonymy. I earlier used metonymy (Chapter 8), which in regular parlance needs less elaboration than synecdoche, because a precise presentation of the theory of tropes would have been unnecessarily obtrusive at that point. In this theory there are four tropes: metaphor, metonymy, synecdoche, and irony. Hayden White, whose definitions I follow here, points out that the latter three tropes "are kinds of Metaphor, but they differ from one another in the kinds of *reductions* or *integrations* they effect on the literal level of their meanings and by the kinds of illumination they aim at on the figurative level. Metaphor is essentially *representational*, Metonymy is *reductionist*, Synecdoche is *integrative*, and Irony is *negational*."[16]

The difference between metonymy and synecdoche is subtle but instructive for the present discussion. Some theorists, White clarifies, consider synecdoche a form of metonymy. Metonymy is reductive in the sense that although it reduces the whole to one of the parts, that part does not presume to stand for the essence of the whole. Thus "fifty sail" for "fifty ships" is a metonymy because in it a significant part indicates the whole without embodying any inherently essential quality the whole may have. The synecdoche does precisely that, as in the expression "he is all heart." The heart here is not just a part that has a crucial role in the functioning of the whole, as the sail has in a ship, but something that in some cultures symbolizes kindness and therefore embodies an essential quality of the person who is thus described in the form of a synecdoche.[17]

The expression "to go in the direction of Anatolia" or "to move into Anatolia" was a synecdoche precisely because it embodied the essence of Sultan Osman's intention as it was construed by Tuği and presumably his audience, and later by the other historians who read his text. It was effective because it was both literally meaningful—to carry out his plan Osman II had to cross the Bosphorus, move eastward, and be joined by the Anatolian governors loyal to him—and figuratively explosive. The latter signified to the Ottomans a reorientation toward Anatolia and the Middle East and a redefinition of what was to be "core area" and "frontier." The word *semt* in particular means "direction," in the navigational sense of azimuth. The whole discourse was cast in the form of a synecdoche because the explanation that this synecdoche sustained was integrative: the whole of Osman II's regime had to be brought down because "to go in the direction of Anatolia" was its essence.

The force of this synecdoche lay, I believe, in the nexus it established between the manifestly political and historiographical and between the deeply poetic and mythic. To consider the poetic first, the political dichotomy espoused by Kafadar between the core area and the frontier might be an exterior articulation of the poetic dichotomy between the garden (*bağ, bostan,* and *gülistan* appear frequently but are not the only words) and the wilderness (*sahra*) analyzed by Walter Andrews in his work on high-culture Ottoman lyric poetry.[18] In general, Andrews's project is an impressive attempt to rescue Ottoman culture, especially poetry, from the oblivion to which it has been doomed. His awareness of and interest in Ottoman poetry as an integral part of politics, society, and culture, as well as his historical sensitivity, should make his approach highly stimulating to those whose primary concern is not necessarily poetry.

At the risk of oversimplifying Andrews's complex theory of lyric Ottoman poetry, I wish to isolate two related arguments of his overall view and suggest that they are highly pertinent to the historiography of the Haile-i Osmaniye, especially to the underlying synecdoche "to move into Anatolia" or "to go in the direction of Anatolia." The first argument is concerned with the poetry as occurrence within a certain environment, what Andrews terms "Ecology of the Song." The lyric poetry—together with other forms of culture—is concerned with the party of friends in a clearly demarcated and confined space, the garden. The orderly and ritualized activity of the closely knit circle of friends within the garden is what makes them a group with distinct identity; this activity defines the parameters of inclusion within the group and exclusion from it. In addition to the relations among the members of the group, the primary relation is vertical, between the "ordinary" member (the lover) and the patron (the beloved). Every proper Ottoman ought to have had a patron/beloved, who might be a Sufi master, the ruler, or God. The underlying activity of the group is the actual gathering of the members in the confines of the garden, which is presented as an ideally ordered articulation of nature. A central dimension of the gathering's activity is *interpretation*. The interpretation is of what the group does as well as of the world outside the confines of the group. Significantly, knowledge of the rules through which the correct interpretation is attained is exclusive to members of the group, and this *correct interpretation* is constantly contrasted with the *misinterpretation* of hostile outsiders.[19]

To return to Tuği's text as an oral address to gatherings of the kul (the janissaries and the imperial cavalry in this context), I contend that it can be also interpreted poetically. As an affirmation of the kul's identity and esprit de corps, Tuği's address was a simulation of the gathering of the group members in the garden in which they established the correct interpretation of their own actions as well as of pertinent external events against the misinterpretation of the same activities and events by hostile outsiders. Put differently, Tuği's is a (primarily) prose text that simulates the collective-identity–shaping quality of the lyric poetry interpreted by Andrews. If my observation is plausible, then the force of Tuği's text as a contextual performance derived from the socially and poetically familiar ritual it was simulating.

Envisaged as such, Tuği's address contains the essential poetic and social ingredients highlighted by Andrews. Tuği tirelessly repeats the act of gathering and assembling, to the exclusion of other groups and as something that is meaningful as such. On two highly significant occasions, the location of the gathering is reminiscent of the poetic garden in the sense of being a secure sanctuary. One occasion is after the kul have taken Sultan Mustafa out of his confinement at the Imperial Harem and are about to carry him to the Old Palace. However, as a result of a rumor that Sultan Osman might assault him, the kul instantly decide to take Sultan Mustafa with them to the janissary barracks (Yeni Odalar) and end up guarding him at their own mosque (Orta Cami). The description of the kul's decision and of these sites clearly portrays them as safe sanctuaries, to the extent that one can almost hear the kul's sigh of relief once they are there.

The second occasion is the arrival and processing of the reports and complaints on Abaza Mehmed Pasha (see Chapter 8). In Tuği's text the sites where these reports are digested and translated into such forms of action as oral and written petitions and ultimata are either the janissary barracks or the residence of the janissary chief *(Ağa Kapısı)*. I shall shortly dwell on the pivotal significance of the interpretation/misinterpretation polarity, but concerning these sites as the poetic garden the point is that it was there, and only there, that the correct interpretation of Abaza's actions as rebellion *(isyan)* and the nadir of sedition and disorder *(fitne ü fesad)*, prompted by Osman II's intention "to move into Anatolia," can be constructed.

Then there is the lover-beloved relationship. Love in the lyric poetry is clearly carried over from the notion of a beloved patron—in a stably ordered society everyone should have a patron—in the pattern of the Sufi orders.[20] Love given to a patron can be both orderly and, when it becomes obsessive and excessively sexualized, disorderly and destabilizing. Tuği's text poetically construes the increasingly acrimonious relations between the kul and Sultan Osman as the disorderly type of love in which the beloved strays from the expected behavioral pattern because hostile outsiders have led him astray. The semiotic sign of this disorderly love is, again, the state of sedition and disorder *(fitne ü fesad)* in the provinces. The poetic purpose of the kul's surge into the Topkapı palace, and within it into the Imperial Harem, is to restore the orderly and stable type of love by finding a new beloved. Here the text offers highly suggestive clues to the possibility of interpreting it as a poetic situation. The kul ostensibly find Sultan Mustafa by coincidence, but truly it is destiny's agency that make the kul echo a mysterious voice that says, "We want Sultan Mustafa." The emotional burst after Sultan Mustafa has been rescued, which compels the narrator directly to elicit the audience's ovation, and the poem expressing devotion to that sultan, lend credence to the poetic-Sufi understanding of the kul's action as a beloved-seeking mission.

I mention the Sufi-poetic possibility of a lover-beloved relationship also because it may have an implication that is wider than the interpretation of the Haile-i Osmaniye. Ottoman scholarship has for some time been interested in the question of the vertical relations between master and dependents in the elite households, of which the dynastic household and the sultan-kul relationship were the most notable instances. The social and poetic example discussed above may be one possible key to the understanding of this question, and the expressions of love and devotion of the famous seventeenth-century traveler Evliya Çelebi to his master Melek Ahmed Pasha may be another useful example.

Pivotal is the construction of the correct interpretation as a significant dimension of the group activity, for, in a way, this is what Tuği's text as speech was all about. Earlier in the book it was shown that the immediate context Tuği and the kul shared was the fact that the latter were held responsible for the killing of Sultan Osman and that they were persecuted in the provinces. The purpose of Tuği's text was thus to establish and convey an interpretation of the Haile-i Osmaniye that would depict the kul favorably, would reassure the kul and convince others that they had acted as loyal members of the Ottoman state rather than as partisans, and would appear as the true state of affairs rather than as the kul's perspective. Almost every action of the kul was meticulously accounted for and justified along these lines, and at the same time, explicitly or implicitly, it was also contrasted with the misinterpretation of hostile outsiders, whether they were the chief black eunuch, the sekban, or the Anatolian governors led by Abaza Pasha. Thus, for example, when the chief black eunuch severely and repeatedly rebuked the kul (addressing the sultan) for their incompetent and lackluster performance at the Hotin campaign and proposed to do away with them and recruit a new body, Tuği's text did not deny the quality of the performance or the manifest lack of zeal. Rather, it instantly offered *the correct interpretation* of the kul's behavior that justified it, an interpretation that stood in stark contrast to the misinterpretation of Süleyman Ağa without disputing its outward appearance.

The outward appearance brings us to the last essential ingredient that supports the view of Tuği's address as a simulation of the social and poetic garden party. This ingredient is the distinction between the correct mystical-esoteric interpretation, to which only the inner members, the *erbab-i batın*, are privy, and the misinterpretation of those who may know only the outward appearance of things, the erbab-i zahir. Andrews stresses the significance of this distinction. He identifies the term *ehl-i batın* as one among several that define the inner group of the garden party and explains them as "those who accept the rules of the emotional (mystical) interpretation and the party activity."[21] Andrews then highlights the explicit distinction and observes that "the *erbab-i zahir* are, in the mystical context, the religious literalists as opposed to the mystics *(erbab-i batın)* and, in the party context, are those who never get into the jug (i.e., never drink wine), and condemn the party and its transcendent interpretation."[22]

Tuği's text echoes this distinction in a meaningful way. Accounting for the magnitude of pain inflicted upon Sultan Osman, the narrator submits a list of infamous tyrants who were far worse than the slain sultan yet had not had pain of a similar magnitude inflicted upon them. The reason, it is intimated, was the supplication of Prince Mehmed, before having been killed by his brother Osman, that the latter might suffer a similar fate. Those who thought that the whole affair should never had taken place, especially the killing of Sultan Osman, held that view according to Tuği because they were erbab-i zahir, because they interpreted people and actions literally and by their outward appearance. What Tuği is implying to his audience is that they themselves are erbab-i batın, aware of the inner and mystical essence of things and possessors of the correct interpretation. Most fundamentally, they understand correctly the meaning of the synecdoche "to go in the direction of Anatolia" and therefore the essence of Osman II's reign and plan.

Tuği and his audience were well disposed to simulate a Sufi social pattern and a Sufi-informed poetic theme. The long and solid association of the janissaries with the *Bektaşi* dervishes is well known, and in 1591 it was officially endorsed by the appointment of a master *(baba)* as a janissary officer and the lodging of dervishes in the barracks. "In consequence of this type of relationship," Andrews observes, "belonging to any of these groups involved initiation into the peculiar rituals and religious or mystical-religious interpretation accepted by the group. This, in turn, provided a framework for interpreting the areas of shared concern in a consistent cosmic, moral, and spiritual context."[23]

If the first argument extracted from Andrews's work informs the possibility that Tuği's text performed as a familiar social and poetic occasion, the second argument pertains to the whole historiographical discourse. The argument is that the lyric poetry establishes and perpetuates a dichotomy between interiority and exteriority expressed in the imaginary distinction between the garden and the wilderness. Informed by Deleuze and Guttari, Andrews sees this as a case of the "closely related oppositions of *smooth/striated* space, and *nomadic/royal* approaches to human behavior."[24] In this framework, "smooth spaces are steppes or deserts (as experienced by nomadic peoples), the sea (prior to or opposed to gridding—or striation—by navigational terms concepts such as mapping by latitude and longitude), pressed fiber textiles such as felt. Striated spaces might include a woven or knotted rug or textile, land dominated by agriculture or the imperial state, or a garden (as opposed to wilderness)."[25] Andrews stresses that both the nomadic and the royal/state categories are constructed idealizations. The nomadic follows its own trajectory in the smooth space, unconstrained "by a state-culturally supported semiotic order. In contrast, the state or royal ideal represents an order that striates space (through geometry, hierarchy, private/state property ownership, agricultural division of land, division of labor)."[26]

To return to the synecdoche "to go in the direction of Anatolia" or "to move into Anatolia," I argued earlier that it underlay the whole historiography of the Haile-i Osmaniye up to the state narrative, not only Tuği's text. Here I propose that because this is how the essence of Sultan Osman's intention was understood, and because this essence was what prompted the fundamental rejection of his plan and reign by most Ottoman historians, who were not part of the context Tuği and his kul-audience had shared, the whole discourse was cast as a synecdoche. This synecdoche was a deeply meaningful signifier whose signified was multilayered.

At the level of political imagination the signified was the core area versus the frontier *(uc)* or the provinces *(taşra)*, the schizoid mental topography that Kafadar formulates. This political signifier, however, is sustained by Andrews's poetic distinction presented above. At that poetic level, I wish to propose, the signified of "to move into Anatolia" (as a synecdoche) was intuitively felt to be the violation of the established boundary between interiority and exteriority, garden and wilderness, striated and smooth spaces; the signified might be, to adhere to Andrews's terminology, a monarch/beloved who exhibited an approach to human behavior that was more nomadic than royal. Crudely casting this argument, I would venture that at that level of deep collective consciousness what the synecdoche signified was the intention to transfer the imperial state from its proper space, the striated garden, into the smooth space, the libidinal domain of the nomad. This might be a cognitive disorientation that seventeenth-century Ottomans, from Tuği to Naima, could not tolerate.

The final note is a comparative speculation on the mythic layer of the historiography. The deeply felt opposition to "going in the direction of Anatolia" might be underpinned by a formative myth of water crossing that possibly united the Ottomans from the time the imperial project became paramount and the gaza ethos was subverted and rewritten. European historians have variously studied the crossing of water as a mythically formative event whose inscriptions in collective memory have literary conventions that are comparable across time and place. For reasons of subtlety and precision I prefer to call this phenomenon a myth of formation rather than—or as distinguished from—a myth of origin. The water crossing was primarily concerned, not with the original site of the said collective, but with a shared experience whose grandeur had formed that collective.

Two pertinent instances may be presented. One is Herwig Wolfram's study of the Germanic peoples of the Roman era, and especially of the literary genre of the *Origo Gentis*, the generic story of a tribe's origins and formation.[27] In his exposition of the shared conventional motifs of the various *Origo Gentis*, Wolfram highlights the importance of crossing: "First, once upon a time there was a small people—the Goths, the Saxons, the Longobards. As their homeland could no longer feed them, they set out under divine guidance. The first test demanded the performance of the primordial deed, be it the crossing of a sea like the Baltic or the North Sea or a river like the Rhine, Elbe, or Danube, be it a victorious battle against mighty enemies—or both, as it was in most cases."[28]

The other study is entirely focused on the connection between migration that involved water crossing and myths of formation: Nicholas Howe's interpretation of mythic constructions in the historiography of medieval England.[29] The formative myth of migration and crossing was founded in Bede's *Historia Ecclesiastica* (completed in 731). It was in this historical text that the actual migrations of the Germanic tribes from the mid-fifth century A.D. onward were mythically molded into the Anglo-Saxon collective, with emphasis on their conversion to Christianity initiated by Augustine. Howe insists that "although Bede's narrative of these settlements is ordered sequentially, the history of each tribe reveals an archetypal pattern: migration across the sea and then settlement on the island."[30]

The force of the mythic migration and crossing was such that in Bede's rendering there could be no collective identity without crossing. He supplied the speakers of four languages—British, Pictish, Irish, and Latin—with a story of crossing. "There are no aboriginal inhabitants of the island [in Bede's *Historia*]; there are only those who have, within historical memory, journeyed across the sea."[31] This mythic force was such, furthermore, that it also hierarchically subjected *genealogy* to its internal logic: "Genealogy became a paradigm of migration because the past must be set in another place."[32] As Christianity gained prevalence, Howe's argument continues, mythic crossing became paramount through the incorporation of the journey of the Israelites across the Red Sea in the Book of Exodus. This analogy between the Israelites and the inhabitants of the British Isles was foundationally articulated in a poem entitled *Exodus* and written in Old English (the dates of its composition have not been ascertained). Like the Ottoman synecdoche to which we shall immediately return, the Old English word for *journey* in that poem too is meaningful both literally and figuratively, for "it means the historical passage across the borderlands and the Red Sea as well as the symbolic passage through life to salvation."[33] Howe underscores the central significance acquired by the act of water crossing in the Old English poem and states that for the poet "the crossing is the exodus."[34]

How is all this related to the additionally mythic code that the synecdoche "to go in the direction of Anatolia," as the essence of Sultan Osman's intended plan, might signify to seventeenth-century Ottomans? As a possibility for future research, the comparative stimulation may lie in the investigation of a similar, or analogous, Ottoman myth of formation. That myth, I suggest as a working hypothesis, may be the significance in the Ottoman historical consciousness of the crossing of the sea from Asia Minor into Europe, perhaps with the first meaningfully recorded crossing to Gallipoli in 1354 as a focal point. I am aware of the Ottoman dynastic myth with its elaborate genealogical component, analyzed and clarified by Colin Imber among others. The existence and importance of this myth are of course undeniable. As Imber points out, it served to legitimize the dynasty, especially vis-à-vis its Turkish-speaking competitors in Anatolia, the Caucasus, Iran, and the Middle East.[35] It was not, however, nor was it meant to be, a myth that would explain the formation of the Ottomans as a whole collective. It was, after all, the southeastern European venture that was the marginal advantage of the Ottomans, and their success there distinguished them from other Turkish-speaking frontier principalities and made them a world empire.

In this context the synecdoche "to go in the direction of Anatolia" or "to move into Anatolia" is suggestive and begs the investigation of a possible myth of crossing in the way of inversion. The Ottomans in the seventeenth century objected deeply and intuitively to what they historiographically construed as Osman II's intention because, at the level of mythic consciousness, it signified a *countercrossing*, a crossing "in the wrong direction," and hence a countermyth.

Glossary

Adalet: Justice. Creating and maintaining a just order were pivotal in legitimating the Ottoman dynasty.

Ağa Kapısı: The official residence of the chief of the janissary corps.

Altı Bölük: The six regiments that together constituted the Ottoman imperial cavalry.

Aman: Protection and security granted to a party that either seeks refuge or is willing to capitulate.

Arz Defter: A document formally defined as a petition, which the highest-ranking officials of the Ottoman Empire were permitted to submit to the sultan in order to communicate with him.

Ası: A rebel against the authority and sovereignty of the Ottoman dynasty and state.

Bahşiş: A gift or bonus.

Başçavuş: One of the most senior officers in the janissary corps.

Başdefterdar: The chief comptroller of the Ottoman Empire, equivalent of chancellor of the exchequer in England.

Baştezkereci: A head clerk or secretary.

Batın: The inner essence of things.

Beylerbeyi: The governor of a province.

Beylik: In early Ottoman history the word denoted a frontier principality, whereas later it meant a province.

Biat: The oath of allegiance given to a Muslim ruler.

Birun: The outer service of the imperial household.

Bostancı Başı: Head of (lit.) the corps of gardeners, one of the main units of pages within the royal household.

Cariye: A concubine in the imperial harem.

Celali: A collective term for those defined as rebels in Anatolia in the late sixteenth and early seventeenth centuries.

Çıkma: Formally the graduation ceremony of pages in the palace system; effectively this was also the culmination of a process of selection and promotion that could determine the graduates' careers.

Cins: The ethnic-regional affiliation of people recruited into the Ottoman military-administrative system.

Cülus Akçesi: Accession bonus given by a new sultan to the troops. It was rather important not to use "bad coins" on these occasions.

Damad: A son-in-law via marriage to an Ottoman princess.

Darüssaade Ağası: The chief black eunuch of the imperial harem.

Dava: An allegation against a state official.

Daye Hatun: A wet nurse, especially of an Ottoman prince.

Defter: A register.

Defter Emini: Head of the office of cadastral registers.

Defterdar: The director of finances.

Deli: Mad.

Devlet-i Aliye: The Sublime State, the self-designation of the Ottoman Empire.

Devşirme: A recruitment system for the imperial household whereby a human levy was imposed on the Christian youth in the Balkans.

Dirlik: A state-derived grant to officials, which was meant to be sufficiently large for subsistence.

Divan: A council in the realm of government, and in the sociocultural domain a salon or a collection of poems.

Dua: A personal prayer.

Eğerliname: The book of [the conquest of] Eğerli in Hungary, an example of a historical work dedicated to a single event.

Ekberiyet: Seniority as the mechanism of the Ottoman dynasty's succession; it replaced fratricide ca. 1600.

Enderun: The inner service of the imperial household.

Erbab-i Batın: Those who see the inner essence of things.

Erbab-i Zahir: Those who see [only] the outward appearance of things.

Eşkiya: A collective noun for brigands and outlaws.

Farr: The quality of divine majesty in Persian dynasties.

Ferman: A sultan's edict.

Fethname: A book of conquest: that is, a historical work focused on the conquest of a given site.

Fetva: A legal opinion issued by a jurisconsult.

Fitne ü fesad: Sedition and disorder, a trope that signified, from the imperial vantage point, provincial unrest.

Gaza: In strictly doctrinal terms, war intended to expand the Abode of Islam; in certain historical contexts, it often meant the raiding battles at the frontier.

Gazi: A warrior who engages in gaza.

Harem-i Has and Haremi-i Hümayun: The private or imperial harem.

Haremlik: The family section of a household.

Haseki Sultan: The sultan's favorite consort.

Hatime: The formal epilogue of a prose text.

Hatt-i Şerif: A noble (i.e., sultanic) decree.

Hazine-i Hümayun or Hazine-i Amire: The imperial treasury.

Ilmiye: The men of knowledge, or the estate of state officials trained as ulema in the Ottoman Empire.

Iltizam: Tax farming. It became a central fiscal institution after 1600.

Inşa: An elegant and adorned style of prose writing.

Intisap: A sociopolitical network of relations that might facilitate, or sometimes hinder, the furtherance of careers in the Ottoman system.

Isyan: A rebellion against the authority and sovereignty of the Ottoman dynasty and state.

Kadi: An Islamic judge.

Kafes: The "golden cage," or chamber within the imperial harem in which Ottoman princes dwelt from the late sixteenth century onward.

Kalemiye: Men of the pen, or the scribal service of the Ottoman Empire.

Kanun: A sultanic or state regulation that, conceptually, was not supposed to contradict the holy Islamic law.

Kanuni: The Lawgiver—the epithet of Sultan Süleyman (r. 1520–66), whose other epithet was the Magnificent.

Kapı: Lit. "gate," denoting either the residence of a high-ranking official or the political elite household in the Ottoman Empire.

Kapı Halkı: Lit. "people of the gate," a collective term that denoted either the outer service of the imperial household (birun) or the retinue of an elite household in general.

Kapı Kulları: Lit. "slaves of the gate," the sultan's servants in the imperial household and the standing army in the capital.

Kapudan Pasha: The grand admiral of the Ottoman fleet.

Kaymakam: A deputy, especially of a grand vezir who left the capital on a war campaign.

Kazasker: A military judge, and from the end of the fifteenth century the title of the judges of the core regions of Rumelia and Anatolia.

Kızlar Ağası: Another term that designated the chief black eunuch of the imperial harem.

Kul: Short for kapı kulları.

Lala: Tutor, especially of the Ottoman princes.

Mahlas: A literary pseudonym.

Malikâne Muqataa: The life-term revenue tax farm.

Menakib: Gaza tales that articulated the ethos of the frontier.

Mihrab: The niche in a mosque that indicates the direction of Mecca.

Mühimme Defterleri: A chronologically ordered series of registers that, in effect, constitute records of the deliberations of the imperial council.

Münşeat: In general, collections of texts written in the inşa style. A specific case was collections of chancery documents in that style, which were considered authoritative manuals.

Muqaddima: Prolegomena in which authors presented their thoughts on the essence of history, as distinguished from accounts of actual historical events.

Nasihatname: A treatise in the literary genre of advice to rulers.

Nişancı: Formally the affixer of the sultan's cipher, effectively the chancellor.

Niyet: A formal resolve to perform a religious act.

Odabaşı: An officer of a ward in the janissary barracks.

Osmanlı: An Ottoman formally and culturally.

Padishah: A generic term for the Ottoman sovereign.

Pencik: The human levy whereby one-fifth of what was taken through gaza belonged to the sultan's household.

Pencik Emini: The official in charge of levying the pencik.

Reisülkuttab: The secretary-in-chief of the imperial council.

Şagird: An apprentice in the Ottoman scribal service.

Şeriat (Arabic Shari'ah): Islamic holy law.

Şerif: A prestigious lineage whose holder was considered a descendant of the Prophet through his grandson Hasan.

Sancak: A subprovince in the Ottoman administrative structure.

Sekban: A collective term for the musket-bearing irregulars in Anatolia.

Serdar: The commander-in-chief of a military campaign.

Shahanshah: King of kings, a prevalent title of a sovereign, including the Ottoman sultan.

Shehname: The Ottoman rendering for the book of kings.

Shehnameci: The writer of shehnames, a position established by Kanuni Sultan Süleyman and abolished after his death.

Sheyhülislam: The chief jurisconsult of the Ottoman Empire and from the late sixteenth century the head of the ilmiye hierarchy.

Sikke ve Hutbe: The name on coins and the name mentioned in the sermon following the Friday prayer respectively—the Islamic symbols of sovereignty.

Silsila: An authoritative chain of transmission.

Sınıf: An estate in the medieval-corporate sense of the term.

Solak: A guardsman of the sultan.

Suhte: Student of an Islamic school in the Ottoman Empire; such students were usually associated with unruly social groups at the end of the sixteenth and early seventeenth centuries.

Süleymanname: The book of Süleyman, a historical work dedicated to the reign and persona of Kanuni.

Taşra: The outside: that is, the provinces and the frontier as distinguished from the imperial center.

Tekbir: The call "God is Greatest."

Telhis: A condensed report prepared by the scribal service for the sultan.

Tezkereci: A secretary.

Timar: A prebendal land grant that sustained the Ottoman provincial administration until the seventeenth century.

Uc: The frontier in early Ottoman history.

Ulema: The learned religious institution.

Ümera: A collective term for the high echelon of the Ottoman provincial administration.

Vakanüvis: The Ottoman state historian.

Valide Sultan: The queen mother, mother of the reigning sultan.

Yeni Odalar: The janissary barracks in Istanbul.

Yerliye: The janissaries localized in the provinces, as distinguished from those newly sent from the center.

Yoklama: An inspection of the army that, effectively, sought to purge the military from payrolls that sustained the janissaries' civilian networks.

Zahir: The outward appearance of things.

Zorba: A thug or bully.

Notes

INTRODUCTION: THE CONTENT
AND FORM OF THIS STUDY

1. Cemal Kafadar, *Between Two Worlds: The Construction of the Ottoman State* (Berkeley: University of California Press, 1995); Dominick LaCapra, "Rethinking Intellectual History and Reading Texts," in *Modern European Intellectual History*, ed. Dominick LaCapra and Steven Kaplan (Ithaca, N.Y.: Cornell University Press, 1982), 47–86; Dominick LaCapra, "Rhetoric and History," in *History and Criticism* (Ithaca, N.Y.: Cornell University Press, 1985), 15–45; Nancy F. Partner, "The New Cornificius," in *Classical Rhetoric and Medieval Historiography*, ed. Ernst Breisach (Kalamazoo, Mich.: Western Michigan University, 1985), 5–59. Gabrielle Spiegel's pertinent work is conveniently assembled in her *The Past as Text* (Baltimore: Johns Hopkins University Press, 1997), esp. 3–83.
2. LaCapra, "Rethinking Intellectual History," 53.
3. LaCapra, "Rhetoric and History," 18.
4. LaCapra, "Rethinking Intellectual History," 78–81, and "Rhetoric and History," 35–41.
5. Partner, "The New Cornificius," 26.
6. Ibid., 26–27. Partner's field of interest is history writing in medieval England.
7. Ibid., 34–35.

1: THE PLOT

1. A. D. Alderson, *The Structure of the Ottoman Dynasty* (New York: Oxford University Press, 1956), and Leslie P. Peirce, *The Imperial Harem: Women and Sovereignty in the Ottoman Empire* (New York: Oxford University Press, 1993).

2. Tuği Çelebi (Hüseyin bin Sefer), *Tarih-i Tuği*, MS Flügel 1044, Austrian National Library, Vienna (other manuscripts of this text are mentioned and discussed throughout this study); Hasanbeyzade, *Tarih-i Al-i Osman*, MSS Flügel 1046 and 1049, Austrian National Library, Vienna; Ibrahim Peçevi, *Tarih-i Peçevi*, 2 vols. (Istanbul: Matbaa-i Amire, 1863–64); Katip Çelebi, *Fezleke-i Tarih*, MS Rawl. Or. 20, Bodleian Library, Oxford University; Mustafa Naima, *Tarih-i Naima*, 6 vols. (Istanbul: Matbaa-i Amire, 1864–66).

3. The description of Sultan Mustafa's first accession in the histories examined here is in keeping with the more general pattern sketched by Alderson, *Structure of the Ottoman Dynasty*, 40–42.

4. Katip Çelebi, *Fezleke-i Tarih*, MS Rawl. Or. 20, 304a.

5. Peçevi, *Tarih-i Peçevi*, vol. 2, 361.

6. The Topkapı was built under Mehmed II in 1468 and was called *Saray-i Cedid* (New Palace) to distinguish it from the *Saray-i Atık* (Old Palace). Until the reign of *Kanuni* (Lawgiver) Sultan Süleyman, the harem was located in the latter. The unification of the whole royal household, both the family component and the public-administrative one, within the confines of the Topkapı was the initiative of Süleyman's powerful consort/wife, Hurrem Sultan; after that, the Old Palace gradually became the site to which senior harem ladies retired when they lost public identity.

7. Peirce, *The Imperial Harem*, 97–112.

8. Ibid., 97–103.

9. In addition to the histories referred to above, see Peirce, *The Imperial Harem*, 99–100, 258.

10. Ibid., 57–113.

11. Ibid., 106.

12. Ibid., 127, 129, 233, 248–49.

13. In addition to Peirce's scattered remarks, see Jane Hathaway, "The Role of the Kızlar Ağası in Seventeenth-Eighteenth Century Ottoman Egypt," *Studia Islamica* 75 (1992): 141–58, and Jane Hathaway, *The Politics of Households in Ottoman Egypt* (New York: Cambridge University Press, 1997), 139–65.

14. Hasanbeyzade, *Tarih-i Al-i Osman*, MS Flügel 1046, 303b. Peirce, *The Imperial Harem* (248–49, 249n.), also notices this gender-charged statement but attributes it to Katip Çelebi's *Fezleke*. She is not mistaken in that it does appear in the latter text as well as in Naima's history (*Tarih-i Naima*, vol. 2, 160); but originally the statement certainly appeared in the first version of Hasanbeyzade's history, which both Katip Çelebi and Naima knew and employed.

15. Naima, *Tarih-i Naima*, vol. 2, 231–32.

16. These two modes of displaying sovereignty should be understood to be two poles of a continuum rather than dichotomous ideal types. Further, they refer to the whole royal household, not only to the sultan. On this issue, see Peirce, *The Imperial Harem*, 153–219, and Christine Woodhead, "Perspectives on Süleyman," in *Süleyman the Magnificent and His Age*, ed. Metin Kunt and Christine Woodhead (New York: Longman, 1995), 164–91.

17. Rhoads Murphey, *Ottoman Warfare, 1500–1700* (New Brunswick, N.J.: Rutgers University Press, 1999), 134–41.
18. Cemal Kafadar, *Between Two Worlds: The Construction of the Ottoman State* (Berkeley: University of California Press, 1995), 152.
19. The information for my argument that there was a structural weakness on the harem flank of Osman's "administration" is drawn from the Ottoman histories and Peirce, *The Imperial Harem*, 106, 233.
20. On the marriage, see Peirce, *The Imperial Harem*, 71, 106, 143.
21. That the memory was alive and evoked is mentioned by Peirce, *The Imperial Harem*, 106. That it might add to the gazi image is my own speculation.
22. Kafadar, *Between Two Worlds*, 64–90.
23. Ibid., 87.
24. Naima, *Tarih-i Naima*, vol. 2, 235.
25. Peirce, *The Imperial Harem*, 183.
26. Tuği, *Tarih-i Tuği*, MS Flügel 1044, 27a. Peirce refers this quotation to Naima, *Tarih-i Naima*; a similar statement does appear in Naima's history, but the true source is Tuği's text (Peirce, *The Imperial Harem*, 103, 103n.).
27. Peirce, *The Imperial Harem*, 101–2.
28. Tuği, *Tarih-i Tuği*, MS Flügel 1044, 5a.
29. Peçevi, *Tarih-i Peçevi*, vol. 2, 380–81.
30. For a published version of the Dresden MS of Tuği's text, see Fahir İz, "XVII. Yüzyılda halk dili ile yazılmış bir tarih kitabı: Hüseyin Tuği, "Vak'a-i Sultan Osman Han," *Türk Dili Araştırmaları Belleten* (1967): 119–55. The cited passage is on 124 (27a-b).
31. Murphey, *Ottoman Warfare*, 135.
32. Ibid., 134–38, 162–63.
33. Peirce, *The Imperial Harem*, 106.
34. Tuği, *Tarih-i Tuği*, MS Flügel 1044, 7b.
35. Murphey, *Ottoman Warfare*, 20–21.
36. Ibid., 16–17, 46–49, 57.
37. Tuği, *Tarih-i Tuği*, Dresden MS in published version (İz, "XVII"), 132.
38. Ibid., 136.
39. Ibid., 137.
40. Ibid. The citations in notes 37–40 can also be found, with slightly different formulations, in the MS of Tuği's work published by Midhat Sertoğlu, "Tuği Tarihi," *Belleten* 43 (June 1947): 498, 501, 502.
41. Peirce, *The Imperial Harem*, 263.
42. Peçevi, *Tarih-i Peçevi*, vol. 2, 385–86. Peirce refers to Naima (249, n. 80), who must have read it in Peçevi's history simply because the other historians do not relate the story from a perspective inside Orta Cami; they attribute Davud Pasha's appointment to Sultan Mustafa.
43. Peçevi, *Tarih-i Peçevi*, vol. 2, 387.
44. Ibid., 389.
45. This request is noted by Peirce, *The Imperial Harem*, 264.

2: THE FORMATION AND STUDY OF OTTOMAN HISTORIOGRAPHY

1. For another very useful survey of Ottoman history writing, see Suraiya Faroqhi, *Approaching Ottoman History: An Introduction to the Sources* (New York: Cambridge University Press, 1999), 144–74.

2. Cornell H. Fleischer, *Bureaucrat and Intellectual in the Ottoman Empire: The Historian Mustafa Ali* (Princeton, N.J.: Princeton University Press, 1986), 214–35.

3. Cemal Kafadar, *Between Two Worlds: The Construction of the Ottoman State* (Berkeley: University of California Press, 1995). Although Kafadar's views on historiography and his conceptualization of the state are inseparable in his presentation, I discuss the former in this chapter and dwell on the latter in Part III. For an informative survey of the repository of sources on the early period—both Ottoman-Turkish and Greek-Byzantine—see Colin Imber, *The Ottoman Empire 1300–1481* (Istanbul: Isis Press, 1990), 1–15.

4. Kafadar, *Between Two Worlds*, 91–98, 112.

5. Halil Inalcik, *Fatih Devri üzerinde Tetkikler ve Vesikalar* (Ankara: Türk Tarih Kurumu Basimevi, 1954).

6. The Kafadar/Lindner controversy ought to be seen in the context of Lindner's challenge to a thesis, Paul Wittek's, that dominated Ottoman studies for almost half a century. See Paul Wittek, *The Rise of the Ottoman Empire* (London: Royal Asiatic Society, 1938); Rudy Lindner, "Stimulus and Justification in Early Ottoman History," *Greek Orthodox Theological Review* 27 (1982): 207–24 (for a critique of Wittek); Rudy Lindner, *Nomads and Ottomans in Medieval Anatolia* (Bloomington: Indiana University, Research Institute for Inner Asian Studies, 1983) (for Lindner's alternative thesis). From his interpretive standpoint, Kafadar, *Between Two Worlds* (29–60), offers a thorough and well-referenced exposition of the debate among modern scholars.

7. Lindner, "Stimulus and Justification." For Kafadar's critique on this issue, see Kafadar, *Between Two Worlds*, esp. 98–99.

8. Kafadar, *Between Two Worlds*, 98. Kafadar rejects the way Lindner and a host of other critics of Wittek understand what gaza is all about. They see gaza as the canonical and doctrinal war of Islam against "the infidels" according to the foundational Islamic texts. They deny gaza to the early Ottomans, arguing that they were hardly Muslims. Kafadar identifies this view as essentialist and, more cautiously but not unlike Wittek, interprets gaza as a historically concrete reality of a frontier society. He also insists that regardless of the extent to which their ethos and behavior were congruous with textual-legalistic dogma, the image the early Ottomans had of themselves should matter to the modern historian.

9. On this historian's life and work, see also Halil Inalcik, "How to Read Ashik Pasha-Zade's History," in *Essays in Ottoman History* (Istanbul: Eren, 1998), 31–55.

10. Among his numerous contributions, the most pertinent to the present

discussion are V. L. Menage, *Neshri's History of the Ottomans: The Sources and Development of the Text* (New York: Oxford University Press, 1964); "The Beginnings of Ottoman Historiography," in *Historians of the Middle East*, ed. Bernard Lewis and P. M. Holt (New York: Oxford University Press, 1962), 168–79; and "The Menaqib of Yakhshi Faqih," *Bulletin of the School of Oriental and African Studies* 26 (1963): 50–74.

11. On the unstable period that followed the defeat of Bayezid I in Ankara (1402), see Imber, *The Ottoman Empire*, 55–69.

12. Kafadar, *Between Two Worlds*, 101. See also Menage, "The Menaqib." One of Menage's most significant contributions was to rectify a crucial scholarly error: up to that point, Yahşi Fakih's menakib had been identified as the passages in Apz's history that conform with the rest of fifteenth-century Ottoman historiography; Menage showed that the menakib ought to be identified as the passages that are unique to Apz.

13. Inalcik, "How to Read," 36–37.

14. Kafadar, *Between Two Worlds*, 100.

15. Ibid., 102–3. See also Menage, *Neshri's History*, and Paul Wittek, "The Taking of the Aydos Castle: A Gazi Legend and Its Transformation," in *Arabic and Islamic Studies in Honor of Hamilton A. R. Gibb*, ed. George Makdisi (Cambridge, Mass.: Harvard University, Dept. of Near Eastern Languages and Literatures, 1965), 662–72.

16. Colin Imber, "The Ottoman Dynastic Myth," *Turcica* 29 (1987): 15.

17. Cited in Kafadar, *Between Two Worlds*, 114.

18. Fleischer, *Bureaucrat and Intellectual*, 241.

19. Kafadar, *Between Two Worlds*, 97.

20. Fleischer, *Bureaucrat and Intellectual*, 239.

21. Christine Woodhead, "Perspectives on Süleyman," in *Süleyman the Magnificent and His Age*, ed. Metin Kunt and Christine Woodhead (New York: Longman, 1995), 164–91.

22. Ibid., 166.

23. Woodhead, "Perspectives on Süleyman," 170–71, and Fleischer, *Bureaucrat and Intellectual*, 239–41.

24. Woodhead, "Perspectives on Süleyman," 172.

25. Ibid., 172–75.

26. Fleischer, *Bureaucrat and Intellectual*, 238, shares this view.

27. Ibid., 240–42.

28. Ibid., 247–49.

29. On the extent of the development of Ottoman prose and historiography in particular at the turn of the sixteenth century, see Christine Woodhead, "Ottoman İnşa and the Art of Letter-Writing: Influences upon the Career of the Nişancı and Prose Stylist Okçuzade (d. 1630)," *Osmanlı Araştırmaları* 7–8 (1988): 143–59.

30. Fleischer, *Bureaucrat and Intellectual*, 250.

31. Jan Schmidt, *Pure Waters for Thirsty Muslims: A Study of Mustafa Ali of Gallipoli's Künhü l-Ahbar* (Leiden, the Netherlands: Het Oosters Insti-

tuut, 1991). See also the book's review by Gabriel Piterberg, *Turcica* 26 (1994): 388–91.

32. Schmidt, *Pure Waters*, 106–8.

33. Ibid., 195–213. See also Cornell H. Fleischer, "Royal Authority, Dynastic Cyclism, and 'Ibn Khaldunism' in Sixteenth-Century Ottoman Letters," *Journal of Asian and African Studies* 18, nos. 3 and 4 (1983): 198–220.

34. Ibid., 191–207.

35. Ibid., 274–77.

36. Ibid., 228.

37. Woodhead, "Ottoman Inşa," 143.

38. The brief survey of this process is based on Fleischer, *Bureaucrat and Intellectual* (chap. 8); Woodhead, "Ottoman Inşa"; and Christine Woodhead, "Research on the Ottoman Scribal Service, c. 1574–1630," *Islamkundlische Untersuchungen* 150 (1992): 311–28.

39. I am well aware of the *Şikk-i Sani*, the "Second Branch," which was headed by a defterdar and was responsible for the imperial properties in the capital and its vicinity. I choose not to dwell on it here because my chief interest is historiography, not the bureaucracy in itself. See Linda T. Darling, *Revenue-Raising and Legitimacy* (Leiden, the Netherlands: E. J. Brill, 1996), 49–81.

40. For this section, in addition to the pertinent entries in *Encyclopaedia of Islam*, new ed. (Leiden, the Netherlands: E. J. Brill, 1954–2002), and *Islam Ansiklopedisi* (Istanbul: Milli Eğitim Basimevi, 1940–88), see Baki Tezcan, "1622 Military Rebellion in Istanbul: A Historiographical Journey," paper presented at the Conference on Mutiny: Narrative, Event, and Context, Ohio State University, Columbus, 10–11 October 1998 (I am deeply grateful to Baki Tezcan for permitting me to cite his paper); Baki Tezcan, "II. Osman Örneğinde 'Ilerlemeci' Tarih ve Osmanlı Tarih Yazıcılığı," in *Osmanlı Düşünce*, vol. 7, ed. Güler Eren, 658–68 (Ankara: Yeni Türkiye Yayınları, 1999) ; introduction to Katip Çelebi, *The Balance of Truth (Mizan ül-Hakk)*, trans. and ed. Geoffrey L. Lewis (London: Allen and Unwin, 1957); Bekir Kütükoğlu, *Vekayi'nüvis Makaleler* (Istanbul: Fetih Cemiyeti, 1994), 25–85 and 103–39; Faroqhi, *Approaching Ottoman History*, 152–53; and Lewis V. Thomas, *A Study of Naima* (New York: New York University Press, 1972), 5–53.

41. Ehud R. Toledano, "The Emergence of Ottoman-Local Elites (1700–1900): A Framework for Research," in *Middle Eastern Politics and Ideas: A History from Within*, ed. Ilan Pappé and Moshe Ma'oz (New York: I. B. Tauris, 1997), 145–63.

3: AN INTERPRETIVE FRAMEWORK

1. See Lynn Hunt, ed., *The New Cultural History* (Berkeley: University of California Press, 1989), and Victoria Bonnel and Lynn Hunt, eds., *Beyond the Cultural Turn* (Berkeley: University of California Press, 1999).

2. Dominick LaCapra, *History and Criticism* (Ithaca, N.Y.: Cornell University Press, 1985), 18.

3. Colin Imber's work on this issue is a good illustration: the starting point was an attempt to show that Wittek's thesis had suspect informational foundations, but it developed into using the pertinent historiography to capture the ideological atmosphere of the era in which it was composed. See "Paul Wittek's 'De la défate d'Ankara à la prise de Constantinople,'" *Osmanlı Araştırmaları* 5 (1986): 65–81; "The Ottoman Dynastic Myth," *Turcica* 19 (1987): 7–27; and "Ideals of Legitimation in Early Ottoman History," in *Süleyman the Magnificent and His Age*, ed. Metin Kunt and Christine Woodhead (New York: Longman, 1995), 138–54. See also V. L. Menage, *Neshri's History of the Ottomans: The Sources and Development of the Text* (New York: Oxford University Press, 1964); "The Beginnings of Ottoman Historiography," in *Historians of the Middle East*, ed. Bernard Lewis and P. M. Holt (New York: Oxford University Press, 1962), 168–79; and "The Menaqib of Yakhshi Faqih," *Bulletin of the School of Oriental and African Studies* 26 (1963): 50–74.

4. See again Suraiya Faroqhi's survey in *Approaching Ottoman History: An Introduction to the Sources* (New York: Cambridge University Press, 1999), 144–74.

5. John R. Walsh, "The Historiography of Ottoman-Safavid Relations in the Sixteenth and Seventeenth Centuries," in *Historians of the Middle East*, ed. Bernard Lewis and P. M. Holt (New York: Oxford University Press, 1962), 197–212. See also Christine Woodhead, "John R. Walsh," *Osmanlı Araştırmaları* 7–8 (1988): 1–9.

6. Walsh, "Historiography," 197.

7. Ibid., 200.

8. Ibid.

9. See further Gabriel Piterberg, "Albert Hourani and Orientalism," in *Middle Eastern Politics and Ideas*, ed. Ilan Pappé and Moshe Ma'oz (New York: I. B. Tauris, 1997), 75–89.

10. Walsh, "Historiography," 200.

11. Mark Philp, "Michel Foucault," in *The Return of Grand Theory in the Human Sciences*, ed. Quentin Skinner (New York: Cambridge University Press, 1985), 68–69.

12. For a related use of the inclusion/exclusion continuum, see Ehud R. Toledano, "The Emergence of Ottoman-Local Elites (1700–1900): A Framework for Research," in *Middle Eastern Politics and Ideas: A History from Within*, ed. Ilan Pappé and Moshe Ma'oz (New York: I. B. Tauris, 1997), 145–63.

13. Reluctantly, I do not deal here with the ethical and political implications of White's theory. For a discussion of this sort, see Saul Friedlander, ed., *Probing the Limits of Representation* (Cambridge, Mass.: Harvard University Press, 1992), where Carlo Ginzburg's essay, "Only One Witness," is especially pertinent.

14. For more systematic and thorough presentations of White's theory, see Lloyd S. Kramer, "Literature, Criticism and Historical Imagination: The Literary Challenges of Hayden White and Dominick LaCapra," in *The New Cultural*

History, ed. Lynn Hunt (Berkeley: University of California Press, 1989), 97–131; and Keith Jenkins, *On "What Is History?": From Carr and Elton to Rorty and White* (New York: Routledge, 1995), 134–80.

15. The discussion in this section is based on the following works by Hayden White: *Metahistory: The Historical Imagination in Nineteenth-Century Europe* (Baltimore: Johns Hopkins University Press, 1973); "History, Historicism and the Figurative Imagination," *History and Theory* 14 (1975): 48–67; "The Question of Narrative in Contemporary Historical Theory," in *The Content of the Form: Narrative Discourse and Historical Representation* (Baltimore: Johns Hopkins University Press, 1987), 25–57; and "Narrativity in the Representation of Reality," in White, *Content of the Form*, 1–26.

16. White, "Narrativity," 1–2.

17. Michael Oakeshott, "The Activity of Being an Historian," in *Rationalism in Politics and Other Essays* (New York: Basic Books, 1962).

18. White concisely presents this understanding, from a critical perspective, in "The Question of Narrative," 26–27.

19. In addition to *Metahistory*, this aspect of White's thought is particularly evident in "Narrativity." Most suggestive is White's title of his 1987 collection of essays, *The Content of the Form*.

20. Roger Ray, "Rhetorical Skepticism and Verisimilar Narrative in John of Salisbury's *Historia Pontificalis*," in *Classical Rhetoric and Medieval Historiography*, ed. Ernst Breisach (Kalamazoo: Western Michigan University Press, 1985), 61–62.

21. White, "Narrativity," 4–5.

22. A good illustration of this narrative is the content and structure of Jacques Le Goff's *History and Memory*, trans. Steven Rendall and Elizabeth Claman (New York: Columbia University Press, 1992).

23. White, "The Question of Narrative," 43.

24. Ibid.

25. Ibid., 42.

26. White, "Narrativity," 20.

27. Dominick LaCapra, "Poetics of Historiography: Hayden White's *Tropics of Discourse*," in *Rethinking Intellectual History: Texts, Contexts, Language* (Ithaca, N.Y.: Cornell University Press, 1983), 72–80; Dominick LaCapra, "Rhetoric and History," in *History and Criticism* (Ithaca, N.Y.: Cornell University Press, 1985), 34–35.

28. Rhoads Murphey, "Review Article: Mustafa Ali and the Politics of Cultural Despair," *International Journal of Middle East Studies* 21 (1989): 243–55.

29. Cornell Fleischer, in "Notes and Comments," *International Journal of Middle East Studies* 22 (1990): 127–28.

30. David Harlan, "Intellectual History and the Return of Literature," *American Historical Review* 94 (June 1989): 581–610; David Hollinger, "The Return of the Prodigal: The Persistence of Historical Knowing," *American*

Historical Review 94 (June 1989): 610–22; and David Harlan, "Reply to David Hollinger." *American Historical Review* 94 (June 1989): 622–27.

31. Harlan, "Intellectual History," 583–84.

32. See, e.g., Roger Chartier, *The Cultural Uses of Print in Early Modern France*, trans. Lydia G. Cochrane (Princeton, N.J.: Princeton University Press, 1987), and *On the Edge of the Cliff: History, Languages and Practices*, trans. Lydia G. Cochrane (Baltimore: Johns Hopkins University Press, 1997).

33. See the seminal essay by Quentin Skinner, "Meaning and Understanding in the History of Ideas," *History and Theory* 8 (1969): 3–53.

34. Quentin Skinner, "Hermeneutics and the Role of History," *New Literary History* 7 (1975–76): 214–16, quoted in Harlan, "Intellectual History," 584. Skinner's main methodological essays, some criticisms of them, and his reaction are conveniently assembled in James Tully, ed., *Meaning and Context: Quentin Skinner and His Critics* (Cambridge, England: Polity Press, 1988).

35. Harlan, "Intellectual History," 584.

36. For Skinner's comments on this particular criticism, see "On Meaning and Speech-Acts," in Tully, *Meaning and Context*, 235–59.

37. Harlan, "Intellectual History," 586–87.

38. Ibid., 587.

39. Paul Ricoeur, "What Is a Text? Explanation and Understanding," *Hermeneutics and the Human Sciences*, ed. and trans. J. M. Thompson (New York: Cambridge University Press, 1981), 145–65. Harlan's contention with Skinner draws heavily on Ricoeur.

40. Ibid., 146–47.

41. Ibid., 148–49.

42. Ibid., 148.

43. Ibid.

44. Ibid., 149–62, esp. 158.

45. Ibid., 161–62.

46. Both Walsh, "Historiography," 200, and Lewis V. Thomas, *A Study of Naima* (New York: New York University Press, 1972), 136–39, point out the as yet unresearched problem of the use Naima made of another Ottoman historian, Şarihülmanarzade (d. 1657). This unresolved problem, however, does not hinder my investigation, for I am interested in Naima's judgment as the official seal on seventeenth-century historiography, a function he undoubtedly fulfilled regardless of the degree to which he was an original historian or "editor" of previously existing histories.

47. White's contention is with Popper's *The Poverty of Historicism*, 3rd ed. (London: Routledge and Paul, 1961), esp. 1–55. His rejection of Popper's dichotomy is stated in *Metahistory*, xi, 20, and it constitutes the starting point of "History, Historicism," esp. 48–49.

48. For notable examples, see Donald R. Kelley, *Foundations of Modern Historical Scholarship: Language, Law and History in the French Renaissance* (New York: Columbia University Press, 1975), and Nancy Partner, *Serious En-*

tertainment: *The Writing of History in 12th Century England* (Chicago: University of Chicago Press, 1980). Kelley also offers an interesting discussion on the fortunes of the term *historicism*.

49. Halil Inalcik, "How to Read Ashik Pasha-Zade's History," in *Essays in Ottoman History* (Istanbul: Eren, 1998), 35.

50. P. M. Holt, "Al-Jabarti's Introduction to the History of Ottoman Egypt," *Bulletin of the School of Oriental and African Studies* 25, no. 1 (1962): 40–42.

51. I shall, of course, sustain the suggestion that Tuği's text was also an oral address. See Chapter 4 and the Epilogue.

4: TUĞI'S REPRESENTATION OF THE HAILE-I OSMANIYE

1. Christine Woodhead, *Ta'liki-zade's Şehname-i hümayun: A History of the Ottoman Campaign into Hungary 1593–94* (Berlin: Klaus Schwartz, 1983). I am grateful to the author for suggesting the term and for pointing out the similarities between the two texts.

2. I present a thorough discussion on the various extant manuscripts elsewhere. Here I am chiefly concerned with explaining the choice of a certain manuscript. See Gabriel Piterberg, "A Study of Ottoman Historiography in the Seventeenth Century" (D.Phil. thesis, University of Oxford, 1993), Appendix A: Excursus on Sources.

3. Midhat Sertoğlu, "Tuği Tarihi," *Belleten* 43 (June 1947): 489–514; Fahir İz, "XVII. Yüzyılnda halk dili ile yazılmış bir tarih kitabı: Hüseyin Tuği, Vak'a-i Sultan Osman Han," *Türk Dili Araştırmaları Belleten* (1967): 119–55.

4. İz, "XVII," 122–23.

5. Piterberg, "A Study."

6. This will be amply shown when, in the next chapters, Tuği's text and those of the other historians are constantly compared.

7. Gustavus Flügel, *Die arabischen, persischen und Türkischen Handschriften der K. K. Hofbiblithek zu Wien*, vol. 3 (Vienna: Hildesheim, 1865–67), 256–57.

8. Compare Tuği Çelebi, *Tarih-i Tuği*, MS Flügel 1044, Austrian National Library, Vienna, 60a–b, and Hasanbeyzade, *Tarih-i Al-i Osman*, MS Flügel 1046, Austrian National Library, Vienna, 326a.

9. İz, "XVII," 122.

10. P. M. Holt, "Al-Jabarti's Introduction to the History of Ottoman Egypt," *Bulletin of the School of Oriental and African Studies* 25, no. 1 (1962): 38–51.

11. For the latter point, see, e.g., Tuği, *Tarih-i Tuği*, MS Flügel 1044, 26b–27a.

12. İz, "XVIII," 128.

13. Tuği, *Tarih-i Tuği*, MS Flügel 1044, 8a.

14. İz, "XVII," 132, and Sertoğlu, "Tuği Tarihi," 498.

15. This formula and its function in Tuği's text might correspond to what speech act theory calls the Cooperative Principle. On its application to Middle

Eastern historiography, see Marilyn Waldman Robinson, *Toward a Theory of Historical Narrative* (Columbus: Ohio University Press, 1980), Conclusion.

16. See, e.g., Tuği, *Tarih-i Tuği*, MS Flügel 1044, 3b, 20b, 21b, and 45b.

17. See, e.g., ibid., 8a, 10a, 23a, and 34a.

18. Adapted from Freud's *The Interpretation of Dreams*, the interpretation of texts along the distinction between the *manifest* and *latent* levels at which meaning is produced by the text have become known. Thus Edward Said identifies an Orientalist discourse that is manifestly varied but latently coherent and integrated. *Orientalism* (New York: Pantheon Books, 1978). My own notion of latency is derived from Hayden White, "History, Historicism and the Figurative Imagination," *History and Theory* 14 (1975): 48–67.

19. Tuği, *Tarih-i Tuği*, MS Flügel 1044, 10a–14b.

20. G. C. Fisher and A. Fisher, "Topkapı Sarayı in the Mid-Seventeenth Century: Bobovi's Description," *Archivum Ottomanicum* 10 (1985): 5–83, and Gülru Necipoğlu, "Framing the Gaze in Ottoman, Safavid, and Mughal Palaces," *Ars Orientalis* 23 (1993): 303–42.

21. Tuği, *Tarih-i Tuği*, MS Flügel 1044, 12b.

22. Ibid., 12b–13a.

23. See again Chapter 1.

24. Ibrahim Peçevi, *Tarih-i Peçevi* (Istanbul: Matbaa-i Amire, 1863–64), vol. 2, 384–86; the fact that Peçevi submits verbatim his source's report is obvious from the beginning of his account (381), but he notes it explicitly only later.

25. Tuği, *Tarih-i Tuği*, MS Flügel 1044, 23a–b.

26. Peçevi, *Tarih-i Peçevi*, 386

27. Tuği, *Tarih-i Tuği*, MS Flügel 1044, 23b.

28. Ibid., 25a.

29. Ibid., 19b–20a.

30. Ibid., 45b–46a.

31. Ibid., 19b.

32. Ibid., 25a.

33. Ibid., 33a–b.

34. Ibid., 33b–34a.

35. Ibid.

36. Ibid., 3b.

37. Ibid., 4a. A particularly strong formulation of the chief black eunuch's reported statement against the kul appears in the Dresden MS of Tuği's text and is cited in Chapter 1.

38. Ibid., 4a–5a.

39. Ibid., 5a.

40. Ibid., 22b.

41. Ibid., 26b–27a. It should be pointed out that Tuği draws no distinction between the pre-Islamic and Islamic eras. For him a host of allegedly tyrannical rulers from both periods are all simply "padishahs."

42. Ibid., 27a.

43. Ibid., 9b–10a, 20b, and 21–22a.
44. Ibid., 5b–6a.
45. Ibid., 7a.
46. Ibid.
47. Ibid., 7b.
48. Ibid., 7b–8a.
49. Ibid., 7a.
50. Ibid.
51. Ibid., 8a.
52. See again ibid., 27a.
53. See again ibid., 7a–8a.

5: THE FORMATION OF ALTERNATIVE NARRATIVES

1. Katip Çelebi, *Keşfülzunun*, vol. 1 (Istanbul, 1941), 285; O. F. Köprülü, "Hasanbeyzade," in *Islam Ansiklopedisi*, vol. 5 (Istanbul: Milli Eğitim Basimevi, 1940–88), 334–37; V. L. Menage, "Hasanbeyzade," in *Encyclopaedia of Islam*, new ed. (Leiden, the Netherlands: E. J. Brill, 1954–2002); Lewis V. Thomas, *A Study of Naima* (New York: New York University Press, 1972), 132–36.
2. See Gabriel Piterberg, "A Study of Ottoman Historiography in the Seventeenth Century" (D. Phil. thesis, University of Oxford, 1993), Appendix A: Excursus on Sources.
3. See the presentation of this episode in Chapter 2.
4. Hasanbeyzade, *Tarih-i Al-i Osman*, MS Flügel 1046, Austrian National Library, Vienna, MS Nuruosmaniye 3106, Nuruosmaniye Library, Istanbul, and MS Flügel 1049, Austrian National Library, Vienna; Ibrahim Peçevi, *Tarih-i Peçevi*, vol. 2 (Istanbul: Matbaa-i Amire, 1864), 360–62; Katip Çelebi, *Fezleke-i Tarih*, MS Rawl. Or. 20, Bodleian Library, Oxford University, 300b, 303b–304a; Mustafa Naima, *Tarih-i Naima*, vol. 2 (Istanbul: Matbaa-i Amire, 1864–66), 154, 160–62.
5. Naima, *Tarih-i Naima*, vol. 2, 161. The citation of Hasanbeyzade's history can be found only in the first version, represented here by MS Flügel 1046.
6. Hasanbeyzade, *Tarih-i Al-i Osman*, MS Flügel 1046, 304a.
7. Hasanbeyzade, *Tarih-i Al-i Osman*, MS Nuruosmaniye 3106, 581b.
8. Naima, *Tarih-i Naima*, vol. 2, 161.
9. Katip Çelebi, *Fezleke-i Tarih*, MS Rawl. Or. 20, 303b.
10. Hasanbeyzade, *Tarih-i Al-i Osman*, MS Flügel 1046, 303b (first message), and 304a (second message).
11. Katip Çelebi, *Fezleke-i Tarih*, MS Rawl. Or. 20, 304a.
12. Peçevi, *Tarih-i Peçevi*, vol. 2, 360, 361.
13. Hasanbeyzade, *Tarih-i Al-i Osman*, MS Flügel 1046, 303b.
14. Katip Çelebi, *Fezleke-i Tarih*, MS Rawl. Or. 20, 303b.
15. Peçevi, *Tarih-i Peçevi*, vol. 2, 360.

16. Adapted from Freud's *Interpretation of Dreams*, the distinction between the manifest and latent levels of texts is used by some literary critics. My notion of latency is informed by Hayden White, "History, Historicism and the Figurative Imagination," *History and Theory* 14 (1975): 48–67. See also the discussion in Chapter Three.

17. Hasanbeyzade, *Tarih-i Al-i Osman*, MS Flügel 1046, 304a.

18. Ibid., 303b; Katip Çelebi, *Fezleke-i Tarih*, MS Rawl. Or. 20, 304a; and Peçevi, *Tarih-i Peçevi*, vol. 2, 360.

19. Hasanbeyzade, *Tarih-i Al-i Osman*, MS Flügel 1046, 304a; Katip Çelebi, *Fezleke-i Tarih*, MS Rawl. Or. 20, 303b, 304a; and Peçevi, *Tarih-i Peçevi*, vol. 2, 361, 362.

20. Şevket Pamuk, "In the Absence of Currency: Debased European Coinage in the Seventeenth-Century Ottoman Empire," *Journal of Economic History* 57 (1997): 356–57.

21. Hasanbeyzade, *Tarih-i Al-i Osman*, MS Flügel 1046, 303b, 304a.

22. Hasanbeyzade, *Tarih-i Al-i Osman*, MS Nuruosmaniye 3106, 581a (second version), and MS Flügel 1049, 75a (third version).

23. Menage, "Hasanbeyzade."

24. All four historians (including Naima) report this incident.

25. Leslie P. Peirce, *The Imperial Harem: Women and Sovereignty in the Ottoman Empire* (New York: Oxford University Press, 1993).

26. Hasanbeyzade, *Tarih-i Al-i Osman*, MS Flügel 1046, 305a, 303b respectively.

27. Thomas, *Study of Naima*, 135. Thomas further stresses Hasanbeyzade's importance for Naima on 140.

28. Ibid., 149.

29. Cf. Tuği, *Tarih-i Tuği*, MS Flügel 1044, and Hasanbeyzade, *Tarih-i Al-i Osman*, MS Flügel 1046, 304b–326a, both in the Austrian National Library in Vienna. The references are from Gustavus Flügel's catalogue for this library, *Die arabischen, persischen und Türkischen Handschriften der K. K. Hofbibliothek zu Wien*, vol. 2 (Vienna: Hildesheim, 1856–57), 254, 356.

30. See again Thomas, *Study of Naima*, 135.

31. The one case where a poem appears in both texts is Tuği, *Tarih-i Tuği*, MS Flügel 1044, 30a–b, and Hasanbeyzade, *Tarih-i Al-i Osman*, MS Flügel 1046, 318a–b.

32. Ibid.

33. Cf. Tuği, *Tarih-i Tuği*, MS Flügel 1044, 60a–b, and Hasanbeyzade, *Tarih-i Al-i Osman*, MS Flügel 1046, 326a.

34. Tuği, *Tarih-i Tuği*, MS Flügel 1044, 56a–b.

35. Ibid., 57a.

36. Hasanbeyzade, *Tarih-i Al-i Osman*, MS Flügel 1046, 326*b.

37. Tuği, *Tarih-i Tuği*, MS Flügel 1044, 54a–55a; Hasanbeyzade, *Tarih-i Al-i Osman*, MS Flügel 1046, 323b–324a.

38. K. Schippmann, "Artanabus," and J. Wiesehofer, "Ardaşir I," both in *Encyclopaedia Iranica* (New York: Oxford University Press, 1987), vol. 2, 647–

50 and 371–76 respectively; R. N. Frye, "The Political History of Iran under the Sassanians," in *The Cambridge History of Iran*, vol. 3, ed. Ehsan Yarshater (New York: Cambridge University Press, 1983), 116–18.

39. Hasanbeyzade, *Tarih-i Al-i Osman*, MS Flügel 1046, 324a–325b.

40. Firdausi, *The Epic of Kings: Shah-nama*, trans. Reuben Levy (New York: Mazda, 1996), translator's prologue.

41. Cf. Hasanbeyzade, *Tarih-i Al-i Osman*, MS Flügel 1046, 324a–325b, and Firdausi, *Epic of Kings*, 270–76.

42. Hasanbeyzade, *Tarih-i Al-i Osman*, MS Flügel 1046, 324a.

43. Ibid., 325b.

44. Cf. Firdausi, *Epic of Kings*, 270, and Hasanbeyzade, *Tarih-i Al-i Osman*, MS Flügel 1046, 324a–b.

45. Firdausi, *Epic of Kings*, 271; Hasanbeyzade, *Tarih-i Al-i Osman*, MS Flügel 1046, 324a.

46. Firdausi, *Epic of Kings*, 275; Hasanbeyzade, *Tarih-i Al-i Osman*, MS Flügel 1046, 325b.

47. In addition to Chapter 3, see Tuği, *Tarih-i Tuği*, MS Flügel 1044, 26b–27a, and Hasanbeyzade, *Tarih-i Al-i Osman*, MS Flügel 1046, 314a–b.

48. On Hasanbeyzade's bias against the black eunuchship, see again Chapter 5 and specifically *Tarih-i Al-i Osman*, MS Flügel 1046, 303b–304a and 304b–305a.

49. Peçevi, *Tarih-i Peçevi*, vol. 1, 3; see also Ibrahim Peçevi, *Tarih-i Peçevi*, MS Add. 18,071, British Library, 28a.

50. Peçevi, *Tarih-i Peçevi*, vol. 2, 383. For the year of Esad Efendi's death being 1625, see Mehmed Süreyya, *Sicill-i Osmanı*, vol. 1 (Istanbul: Matbaa-i Amire, 1890), 330.

51. See two such occasions by comparing Peçevi, *Tarih-i Peçevi*, vol. 2, 382, and *Peçevi Tarihi*, vol. 2, ed. and trans. Bekir Sıtkı Baykal (Ankara: Kültür Bakanlığı, 1982), 357.

52. Peçevi, *Tarih-i Peçevi*, vol. 2, 380–81.

53. Ibid., 380.

54. Tuği, *Tarih-i Tuği*, MS Flügel 1044, 3b–5b.

55. Ibid.

56. Peçevi, *Tarih-i Peçevi*, vol. 2, 380.

57. Ibid.

58. Ibid., 378.

59. For Peçevi, see ibid., 389.

60. Tuği, *Tarih-i Tuği*, MS Flügel 1044, 45b–46a, 47b–48b, 55a–b, and 56a–b. As a young man, Abaza Pasha participated in the *celali* revolts. He was taken captive by the Ottoman army and recruited by Halil Pasha to his household. It is not unreasonable that Abaza owed his ümera career to Halil Pasha.

61. Peçevi, *Tarih-i Peçevi*, vol. 2, 389–90.

62. Cf. Tuği, *Tarih-i Tuği*, MS Flügel 1044, 32a, 56a–b, and Peçevi, *Tarih-i Peçevi*, vol. 2, 390.

63. Tuği, *Tarih-i Tuği*, MS Flügel 1044, 56b. An *odabaşı* was an officer in command of a janissary *oda* (lit. chamber or barrack), roughly a company.

64. Jane Hathaway, *The Politics of Households in Ottoman Egypt* (New York: Cambridge University Press, 1997), 5–52. Though commending Hathaway's ability to identify the barracks groupings, Ehud Toledano disagrees that they may be called households. See his "Review of Jane Hathaway, *The Politics of Households in Ottoman Egypt*," *Journal of the American Oriental Society* 120 (2000): 449–53.

65. See the Dresden MS of Tuği, *Tarih-i Tuği*, in Fahir İz, "XVII. Yüzyılnda halk dili ile yazılmış bir tarih kitabı: Hüseyin Tuği, *Vak'a-i Sultan Osman Han*," *Türk Dili Araştırmaları Belleten* (1967): 143–44.

66. Tuği, *Tarih-i Tuği*, MS Flügel 1044, 33b–34a.

67. See again ibid., 57a, and the second section in the present chapter.

68. Ibid., 58a–59a.

69. Peçevi, *Tarih-i Peçevi*, vol. 2, 390.

70. Ibid., 390–91.

71. Hasanbeyzade, *Tarih-i Al-i Osman*, MS Flügel 1049, 108a–110a.

72. Peçevi, *Tarih-i Peçevi*, vol. 2, 397.

73. Ibid., 397–98.

6: THE CONCEPTION OF THE STATE NARRATIVE

1. For a detailed study of Katip Çelebi's *Fezleke*, see Bekir Kütükoğlu, "Katip Çelebi 'Fezleke'sinin Kaynakları," *Vekayi'nüvis Makalaler* (Istanbul: Fetih Cemiyeti, 1994), 25–85.

2. Katip Çelebi, *Fezleke-i Tarih*, Ms. Rawl. Or. 20, Bodleian Library, Oxford University, 327a. All quotations and references are from this manuscript. For the published version, see Katip Çelebi, *Fezleke-i Tarih*, vol. 2 (Istanbul, 1870), 5–34. I prefer in this case the manuscripts because the published version leaves much to be desired.

3. Ibid.

4. Cf. Tuği, *Tarih-i Tuği*, MS Flügel 1044, Austrian National Library, Vienna, and Katip Çelebi, *Fezleke-i Tarih*, 327a–348b.

5. See again note 2 above.

6. Lewis V. Thomas, *A Study of Naima* (New York: New York University Press, 1972), 132–36, 139–40.

7. See Chapter 5.

8. Cf. Tuği, *Tarih-i Tuği*, MS Flügel 1044, 25a–b, and Katip Çelebi, *Fezleke-i Tarih*, Ms. Rawl. Or. 20, 338b–339a.

9. Cf. Katip Çelebi, *Fezleke-i Tarih*, 348a–361b, and Hasanbeyzade, *Tarih-i Al-i Osman*, MS Flügel 1049 (third version), 104a–116b.

10. Katip Çelebi, *Fezleke-i Tarih*, 327a–328a.

11. Ibid., 327a.

12. Cf. Katip Çelebi, *Fezleke-i Tarih*, 327a–328a, to Ibrahim Peçevi, *Tarih-*

i Peçevi, vol. 2 (Istanbul: Matbaa-i Amire, 1863–64), 380–81, and Tuği, *Tarih-i Tuği*, MS Flügel 1044, 3b–5b.

13. Katip Çelebi, *Fezleke-i Tarih*, 327a.
14. Cf. Peçevi, *Tarih-i Peçevi*, vol. 2, 384, and Katip Çelebi, *Fezleke-i Tarih*, 335a–b.
15. Cf. Peçevi, *Tarih-i Peçevi*, vol. 2, 386, and Katip Çelebi, *Fezleke-i Tarih*, 336a.
16. Cf. Peçevi, *Tarih-i Peçevi*, vol. 2, 386–87, and Katip Çelebi, *Fezleke-i Tarih*, 336a–338a.
17. Katip Çelebi, *Fezleke-i Tarih*, 341b.
18. Bekir Kütükoğlu, "Katip Çelebi," 50–55, and Suraiya Faroqhi, *Approaching Ottoman History* (New York: Cambridge University Press), 153.
19. The two explanations are in Katip Çelebi, *Fezleke-i Tarih*, 327a–328a, and Tuği, *Tarih-i Tuği*, MS Flügel 1044, 3b–5b. For a detailed discussion of Tuği's explanation, see again Chapter 4.
20. Katip Çelebi, *Fezleke-i Tarih*, 327a–328a.
21. Ibid., 27a.
22. Ibid., 327b.
23. Ibid.
24. Ibid., 328a.
25. Ibid.
26. Tuği, *Tarih-i Tuği*, MS Flügel 1044, 3b; for a detailed examination of Tuği's explanation, see Chapter 4.
27. This assertion is not exclusive to Tuği's explicit explanation but it is especially emphasized there.
28. Katip Çelebi, *Fezleke-i Tarih*, 327b.
29. Ibid., 327b–328a.
30. Ibid., 327b.
31. Tuği, *Tarih-i Tuği*, MS Flügel 1044, 3b–5b.
32. Katip Çelebi, *Fezleke-i Tarih*, 339a–340a.
33. Ibid., 340a.
34. Ibid.
35. There are several options for what *ma'nevi* denotes, and it is difficult to be decisive as to which is most appropriate in the context of this sentence. My choice, "spiritual," should not be deemed finite.
36. Katip Çelebi, *Fezleke-i Tarih*, 340a.
37. Tuği, *Tarih-i Tuği*, MS Flugel 1044, 3b–8a. For the analysis of this digression, see Chapter 4.
38. Katip Çelebi, *Fezleke-i Tarih*, 327a–330b.
39. See under the heading "The Padishah's Dream," 328b–329a.
40. Cf. again Katip Çelebi, *Fezleke-i Tarih*, 348a–361b, and Hasanbeyzade, *Tarih-i Al-i Osman*, MS Flügel 1049 (third version), 104a–116b.
41. See Chapter 5.
42. Hasanbeyzade, *Tarih-i Al-i Osman*, MS Flügel 1049, 104a–b.
43. Ibid.

44. Ibid.
45. Ibid.
46. Ibid.
47. Ibid.
48. Ibid., 104b–107a, and Peçevi, *Tarih-i Peçevi*, vol. 2, 390–91.
49. Katip Çelebi, *Fezleke-i Tarih*, 349b.
50. See also ibid., 349b–351a.
51. Hasanbeyzade, *Tarih-i Al-i Osman*, MS Flügel 1049, 108a–110a.
52. See Gabriel Piterberg, "A Study of Ottoman Historiography in the Seventeenth Century" (D.Phil. thesis, Oxford University, 1993), Appendix A: Excursus on Sources.
53. Cf. Hasanbeyzade, *Tarih-i Al-i Osman*, MS Flügel 1049, 104a, and Katip Çelebi, *Fezleke-i Tarih*, 348a–b (for the first two points); Hasanbeyzade, *Tarih-i Al-i Osman*, MS Flügel 1049, 104a–107b, and Katip Çelebi, *Fezleke-i Tarih*, 349b–351a (for the incident); Hasanbeyzade, *Tarih-i Al-i Osman*, MS Flügel 1049, 108a–110a, and Katip Çelebi, *Fezleke-i Tarih*, 361a–b (for Mere's dismissal).
54. Mustafa Naima, *Tarih-i Naima* (Istanbul: Matbaa-i Amire, 1867), vol. 2, 252.
55. See again Hasanbeyzade, *Tarih-i Al-i Osman*, MS Flügel 1049, 104a.
56. This is clearly the case with the manuscripts published by (and abundantly referred to in this study) Midhat Sertoğlu and Fahir İz.
57. For discussion of and references to White's work, see Chapter 3.

7: THE EARLY MODERN OTTOMAN STATE

1. A useful survey of the various schools of thought on the state can be found in Philip G. Cerny, *The Changing Architecture of Politics: Structure, Agency and the Future of the State* (Newbury Park, Calif.: Sage, 1990), 3–56.
2. See Timothy Mitchell, "The Limits of the State: Beyond Statist Approaches and Their Critics," *American Political Science Review* 85, no. 1 (1991): 77–96. I am indebted to Mitchell on two accounts: his critical insights on several schools of thought on the state, and his alternative concept.
3. Ibid., 79, 80, 82.
4. Philip Abrams, "Notes on the Difficulty of Studying the State," *Journal of Historical Sociology* 1 (March 1988): 58–89.
5. Ibid., 69. Regarding Abrams's commentary on Marxist scholars, see the editorial note (89). Although posthumously published in 1988, the essay was written in 1977. Meanwhile, Nicos Poulantzas published a book, *State, Power Socialism*, trans. Patrick Camiller (London: Verso, 1980), in which, drawing on Foucault, he revised his earlier work in the way Abrams had suggested.
6. For an example of the stimulating impact of Abrams's essay, see Claude Denis, "The Genesis of American Capitalism: An Historical Inquiry into State Theory," *Journal of Historical Sociology* 2 (December 1989): 328–56. Denis's article is, simultaneously, an illustration of the path opened by Abrams and the

persistence of dichotomous thinking in the social sciences. On the one hand, he skillfully deconstructs the state as a reified thing. On the other hand, his own proposal reproduces the state/society dichotomy by falling into the trap of an analogous dichotomy, between form (the state and its legislation) and content (the economy) (see esp. 347–51).

7. Abrams, "Notes," 79. It should be clarified that by *idea* Abrams means what since the spread of Foucault's theory has been known as discourse.

8. Ibid., 80.

9. Benedict Anderson, *Imagined Communities*, rev. ed.(New York: Verso, 1991), 1–9.

10. Perry Anderson, *Lineages of the Absolutist State* (New York: Verso, 1974), 401–6. Abrams discusses this work on 80–82.

11. Ibid., 403.

12. Ibid.

13. Ibid., 406.

14. Abrams, "Notes," 81.

15. This is Mitchell's main argument in "Limits of the State."

16. Partha Chatterjee, quoted in Timothy Mitchell and Roger Owen, "Defining the State in the Middle East. II," *Middle East Studies Association Bulletin* 25 (July 1991): 27; Akhil Gupta, quoted in Mitchell and Owen, "Defining the State. II," 28. See also Timothy Mitchell and Roger Owen, "Defining the State in the Middle East. I," *Middle East Studies Association Bulletin* 24 (December 1990): 179–83.

17. Şevket Pamuk, *A Monetary History of the Ottoman Empire* (New York: Cambridge University Press, 2000), 112–49, and "The Price Revolution in the Ottoman Empire Reconsidered," *International Journal of Middle East Studies* 33 (February 2001): 69–89.

18. Pamuk, "The Price Revolution," 70.

19. See especially ibid., 70–73, where these explanations are succinctly presented.

20. For Pamuk's reconsideration of Barkan's work, see esp. *A Monetary History*, 118–30, and "The Price Revolution," 73–85.

21. Pamuk, "The Price Revolution," 72, 87 (n. 19).

22. Jack A. Goldstone, "East and West in the Seventeenth Century: Political Crises in Stuart England, Ottoman Turkey, and Ming China," *Comparative Studies in Society and History* 30 (1988): 103–42. See also his *Revolution and Rebellion in the Early Modern World* (Berkeley: University of California Press, 1991).

23. Goldstone, "East and West," esp. 103–7 and 131–34.

24. Ibid., 109.

25. See again Pamuk, "The Price Revolution," 72.

26. Goldstone, "East and West," 119–20.

27. Ibid., 129.

28. Rhoads Murphey, for instance, is critical of Goldstone's observation that

the price revolution caused a breakdown of the state. See his "Continuity and Discontinuity in Ottoman Administrative Theory and Practice during the Late Seventeenth Century," *Poetics Today* 14 (Summer 1993): 419–45.

29. Goldstone, "East and West," 129–31; quotes are from 130.

30. Ibid., 133.

31. I have already begun a comparative study of the discourses of decline in the period 1600–1700 in the Ottoman Empire and Imperial Spain.

32. Examples of this change, which is so substantial that it might be deemed paradigmatic, are plentiful. See, e.g., Linda T. Darling, *Revenue-Raising and Legitimacy* (Leiden, the Netherlands: E. J. Brill, 1996), 1–22; Suraiya Faroqhi, "Crisis and Change, 1590–1699," in *An Economic and Social History of the Ottoman Empire*, vol. 2, *1600–1914*, ed. Suraiya Faroqhi et al. (New York: Cambridge University Press, 1994), 413–637; Jane Hathaway, "Problems of Periodization in Ottoman History," *Turkish Studies Association Bulletin* 2 (Fall 1996): 25–31; and Murphey, "Continuity."

33. My critical view of Inalcik's concept of the Ottoman state, and of the paradigm of which it is part, is also indebted to Huri Islamoğlu and Çağlar Keyder, "Agenda for Ottoman History," *Review, a Journal of the Fernand Braudel Center* 1 (1977): esp. 32–37.

34. Geza David, "Administration in Ottoman Europe," in *Süleyman the Magnificent and His Age*, ed. Metin Kunt and Christine Woodhead (New York: Longman, 1995), 71–91.

35. Halil Inalcik, "Military and Fiscal Transformation in the Ottoman Empire, 1600–1700," *Archivum Ottomanicum* 6 (1980): 283–337.

36. Metin I. Kunt, *The Sultan's Servants: The Transformation of Ottoman Provincial Government, 1550–1650* (New York: Columbia University Press, 1983).

37. See summary in ibid., 95–96.

38. Ibid., 98.

39. Rifaat Ali Abou-El-Haj, "The Vezir and Paşa Households, 1683–1703: A Preliminary Report," *Journal of the American Oriental Society* 94 (1974): 438–47.

40. Jane Hathaway, "The Military Household in Ottoman Egypt," *International Journal of Middle East Studies* 27 (1995): 39–52, and *The Politics of Households in Ottoman Egypt* (New York: Cambridge University Press, 1997). For an earlier attempt to place Ottoman Egypt in an imperial context, see Gabriel Piterberg, "The Formation of an Ottoman Egyptian Elite in the 18th Century," *International Journal of Middle East Studies* 22 (1990): 275–89.

41. Tosun Aricanli and Mara Thomas, "Sidestepping Capitalism: On the Ottoman Road to Elsewhere," *Journal of Historical Sociology* 7 (1994): 25–48.

42. Ibid., 25 (abstract).

43. Ibid., 34, 35.

44. Ibid., 35.

45. Ibid., 36–37.

46. Rifaat Ali Abou-El-Haj, *Formation of the Modern State: The Ottoman Empire, Sixteenth to Eighteenth Centuries* (Albany: State University of New York Press, 1991).

47. Ibid., 2–6.

48. Ibid., 6.

49. Ibid., 54–60.

50. Ibid., 11–18.

51. Ibid., 18–52. For Naima, see 45–46. The problem with Abou-El-Haj's study is the gap, concerning the *nasihat* and historical texts, between his critique and methodological exposition on the one hand, and what he actually does with them on the other. As the latter amounts to scattered remarks on the authors and brief content analysis of some of their works, it simply leaves much to be desired. For another survey of the early modern nasihat literature, see Douglas Howard, "Ottoman Historiography and the Literature of 'Decline' in the Sixteenth and Seventeenth Centuries," *Journal of Asian History* 22 (1988): 52–76.

52. Ariel Salzmann, "An *Ancien Régime* Revisited: 'Privatization' and Political Economy in the Eighteenth-Century Ottoman Empire," *Politics and Society* 21 (December 1993): 393–423. For the way Salzmann extends her interpretation to the nineteenth century, see "Citizens in Search of a State: The Limits of Political Participation in the Late Ottoman Empire," in *Extending Citizenship, Reconfiguring States*, ed. Michael Hanagan and Charles Tilly (Lanham, Md.: Rowman and Littlefield, 1999), 37–67.

53. Salzmann, "*Ancien Régime*," 394.

54. See a manifestation of this awareness in ibid., 398.

55. Ibid., 401–2.

56. These included vezirs, the high echelons of the civil and clerical bureaucracy, and powerful janissaries.

57. Ibid., 402–5.

58. Ibid., 403.

59. Ibid., 405. This passage not coincidentally appears in a section that discusses provincial society. It was there, according to the conventional decentralization thesis, that Ottoman rule became nominal at best in the eighteenth century.

60. The following works by Karen Barkey are discussed: "Rebellious Alliances: The State and Peasant Unrest in Early Seventeenth-Century France and the Ottoman Empire," *American Sociological Review* 56 (1991): 699–715; *Bandits and Bureaucrats: The Ottoman Route to State Centralization* (Ithaca, N.Y.: Cornell University Press, 1994); "In Different Times: Scheduling and Control in the Ottoman Empire, 1550–1650," *Comparative Studies in Society and History* 38 (1996): 460–83.

61. To avoid repetition, I do not bring Timothy Mitchell to bear on the present discussion (see "Limits of the State"). It should be clearly stated, however, that my critique of Barkey's approach is indebted to Mitchell's disapproval of the idealist/statist school in general.

62. Barkey, *Bandits and Bureaucrats*, 141.

63. A telling example is the comparison, itself interesting, between France and the Ottoman Empire in the seventeenth century in terms of the weaknesses and strengths of these states and the degree of their autonomy vis-à-vis the respective societies. See Barkey, "Rebellious Alliances."

64. See Barkey, *Bandits and Bureaucrats*, chaps. 5 and 6, esp. 220–29, and "Scheduling."

65. Barkey, *Bandits and Bureaucrats*, 60.

66. Ibid., 27.

67. Barkey, "Scheduling," 471, 472.

68. Chap. 6 in Barkey, *Bandits and Bureaucrats*, is a notable example.

69. Salzmann, "An *Ancien Régime* Revisited," 405. For an insightful application of this framework to another provincial setting, see Dina Khoury, *State and Provincial Society in the Ottoman Empire: Mosul, 1540–1834* (New York: Cambridge University Press, 1997).

8: THE OTTOMAN STATE AS A DISCURSIVELY CONTESTED FIELD

1. Cemal Kafadar, *Between Two Worlds: The Construction of the Ottoman State*, (Berkeley: University of California Press, 1995).

2. Ibid., 140.

3. This basic rift runs through Kafadar's argument, *Between Two Worlds*, 138–54. For a neat illustration, see his comparison between the historical representations of the conquest of Aydos Castle by Aşık Paşazade (gazi milieu) and Neşri (ulema), 103.

4. Ibid., 143. For other, most stimulating observations on the loci of power in the political imagination of the Ottomans, esp. in the seventeenth century, see Gülru Necipoğlu, "Framing the Gaze in Ottoman, Safavid and Mughal Palaces," *Ars Orientalis* 23 (1993): 303–42, and Leslie Peirce, *The Imperial Harem: Women and Sovereignty in the Ottoman Empire* (New York: Oxford University Press, 1993), 6–12. These observations can be seen in conjunction with Kafadar's "schizoid mental topography" *(Between Two Worlds)*.

5. For this pivotal process in Ottoman history, see Halil Inalcik, *Fatih Devri üzerinde Tetkikler ve Vesikalar* (Ankara: Türk Tarih Kurumu Basimevi, 1954). For its historiographical expression, see Victor L. Menage, "Some Notes on the Devşirme," *Bulletin of the School of Oriental and African Studies* 29 (1966): 64–78.

6. Kafadar, *Between Two Worlds*, 147–48.

7. Ibid., 149.

8. Suraiya Faroqhi places the Abaza affair with the larger phenomenon of "The Age of Rebellious Governors." See her "Crisis and Change, 1590–1699," in *An Economic and Social History of the Ottoman Empire*, vol. 2, *1600–1914*, ed. Suraiya Faroqhi et al. (New York: Cambridge University Press, 1994), 418–19.

9. The best study on the ümera in the early modern period is still Metin I. Kunt, *The Sultan's Servants: The Transformation of Ottoman Provincial Government, 1550–1650* (New York: Columbia University Press, 1983). Kunt, however, does not discuss the sociopolitical significance of governors such as Abaza Mehmed Pasha.

10. The history and textual relations of the historiographical discourse are thoroughly presented in Part II.

11. Tuği, *Tarih-i Tuği*, MS Flügel 1044, Austrian National Library, Vienna, 41b–42a, 55a–60a.

12. Ibid., 45b, 55a, 59b.

13. Ibid., 41b–42a, 60a.

14. Ibid., 41b.

15. Ibid., 41b–42a.

16. Ibid., 60a.

17. For an incident in the eighteenth century, Virginia H. Aksan interprets *isyan* identically, but *fitne* as "mutiny." See her "Mutiny in the Eighteenth Century Ottoman Army," *Turkish Studies Association Bulletin* 22 (Spring 1998): 116.

18. See, e.g., Tuği, *Tarih-i Tuği*, MS Flügel 1044, 55a, 56a.

19. Ibid., 46a.

20. Like Kafadar, *Between Two Worlds* (105, 118), I think that *huruc* and *ihrac* denote "making a political bid" or "coming out" rather than "rebelling."

21. Ibrahim Peçevi, *Tarih-i Peçevi*, vol. 2 (Istanbul: Matbaa-i Amire, 1864–66), 389–91.

22. Barkey, *Bandits and Bureaucrats: The Ottoman Route to State Centralization* (Ithaca, N.Y.: Cornell University Press, 1994), chap. 6.

23. Kafadar, *Between Two Worlds*, 112–13.

24. See again Halil Inalcik, "Military and Fiscal Transformation in the Ottoman Empire, 1600–1700," *Archivum Ottomanicum* 6 (1980): 283–337. For an innovative interpretation of the early modern Ottoman military institution, see Rhoads Murphey, *Ottoman Warfare, 1500–1700* (New Brunswick, N.J.: Rutgers University Press, 1999). Although Murphey mentions the sekban corps (190–91), he does not discuss it thoroughly.

25. The exposition on the celali revolts and the formation of the bandits/sekban complex is based on Mustafa Akdağ, "Celali Isyanlarından Büyük Kaçgunluk, 1603–1606," *Tarih Araştırmaları Dergisi* 2 (1964): 1–49. Mustafa Cezar, *Osmanlı Tarihinde Levendler* (Istanbul: Celikcilt Matbaasi, 1965). The more recent literature used is Barkey, *Bandits and Bureaucrats*, chap. 5, and Faroqhi, "Crisis and Change," 433–41.

26. Barkey, *Bandits and Bureaucrats*, 150.

27. Ibid., 165.

28. Faroqhi also emphasizes this conflict in "Crisis and Change," 436–48.

29. Barkey, *Bandits and Bureaucrats*, 175.

30. Rifaat Ali Abou-El-Hajj, "The Vezir and Paşa Households, 1683–1703: A Preliminary Report," *Journal of the American Oriental Society* 94 (1974):

Notes to Pages 174–185 / 229

439, is the one who brings this episode to the fore and interprets it in a similar way, though he does not use the same terminology.

31. Linda T. Darling, *Revenue-Raising and Legitimacy* (Leiden: E. J. Brill, 1996), 78–79.
32. Ibid., 79.
33. Barkey, *Bandits and Bureaucrats*, 176–87.
34. Ibid., 183.
35. Tuği, *Tarih-i Tuği*, MS Flügel 1044, 45b–46a, 47b–48b, 55a–b, 56a–b.
36. Cf. Katip Çelebi, *Fezleke-i Tarih*, Ms. Rawl Or. 20, Bodleian Library, Oxford University, 327a–361b, and Mustafa Naima, *Tarih-i Naima* (Istanbul: Matbaa-i Amire, 1864–66), vol. 2, 208–63, both under the general heading *Zikir Vak'a-i Haile-i Osmaniye*.
37. Naima, *Tarih-i Naima*, 209.
38. Ibid., 231–34.
39. Ibid., 231.
40. All quotations in this paragraph are from ibid., 231–32.
41. Metin I. Kunt, "Ethnic-Regional *(Cins)* Solidarity in the Seventeenth-Century Ottoman Establishment," *International Journal of Middle East Studies* 5 (1974): 233–39.
42. Ibid., 235.
43. Ibid., 237–39.
44. On the structure of *Tarih-i Naima*, see Lewis V. Thomas, *A Study of Naima* (New York University Press, 1972), 126–32.
45. On Naima's intisap to the Köprülüs, see ibid., 31–34, 78–79.
46. See, e.g., Rifaat Ali Abou-El-Haj, *Formation of the Modern State: The Ottoman Empire, Sixteenth to Eighteenth Centuries* (Albany: State University of New York Press, 1991); Rhoads Murphey, "Continuity and Discontinuity in Ottoman Administrative Theory and Practice during the Late Seventeenth Century," *Poetics Today* 14 (Summer 1993): 419–45; and Ariel Salzmann, "An *Ancien Régime* Revisited: 'Privatization' and Political Economy in the Eighteenth-Century Ottoman Empire," *Politics and Society* 21 (December 1993): 393–423.
47. Philip Abrams, "Notes on the Difficulty of Studying the State," *Journal of Historical Sociology* 1 (March 1988): 79.
48. Baki Tezcan, "1622 Military Rebellion in Istanbul: A Historiographical Journey," paper presented at the Conference on Mutiny: Narrative, Event and Content in Cross-Cultural Perspective, Ohio State University, Columbus, 10–11 October 1998. I am deeply grateful to the author for permission to cite his paper.

EPILOGUE: POETICS OF OTTOMAN HISTORIOGRAPHY

1. Beyond the references below, I wish to express deep gratitude to Professor Walter Andrews for his kind encouragement and insightful help in thinking about the questions addressed in the Epilogue.

2. See, e.g., a thoughtful essay by Dror Ze'evi, "The Use of Ottoman Shari'a Court Records as a Source for Middle Eastern Social History: A Reappraisal," *Islamic Law and Society* 5 (1998): 35–56.

3. Sir James Redhouse, *Redhouse Çağdaş Türkçe-Inglizce Sözlüğü* (Istanbul, 1983), 154.

4. Sir James Redhouse, *Redhouse Yeni Türkçe-Inglizce Sözlük* (1968; reprint, Istanbul, 1979), 435.

5. Mehmet Zeki Pakalın, *Tarih Deyimleri ve Terimleri Sözlüğü*, vol. 1 (Istanbul: Milli Eğitim Basimevi, 1946), 704.

6. Sir James Redhouse, *A Turkish and English Lexicon* (1890; reprint, Istanbul, 1978), 2156.

7. Alessio Bombaci, *Storia della letteratura turca* (Milan: Nuova Accademia, 1956), 438–46.

8. Johann Christian Clodius, *Compendiosvm lexicon latino-tvercico-germanicvm* (Leipzig, 1730). See "*Comoedia*" (138) and "*Theatrum*" (812).

9. Franciszek Meninski, *Thesaurus linguarum orientalum turcicae, arabicae, persicae*, vol. 3 (Vienna, 1680), 5432.

10. In ibid., Meninski referred the illustration to "Sa.," which is fully presented in vol. 1 as Hoca Sadüddin Efendi's work *(Pro Oe Minum)* and described it as "Chronici turcici elegantissimo stylo conscripti."

11. Hoca Sadüddin Efendi, *Tacüttevarih*, vol. 1 (Istanbul: Tabhane-i Amire, 1872), 347–55 (Ottoman Turkish), and *Tacüttevarih*, ed. and trans. Ismet Parmaksızoğlu (Eskişehir: Anatolia University Press, 1992), vol. 2, 176–86 (modern Turkish).

12. Firdausi, *The Epic of Kings*, trans. Reuben Levy (New York: Mazda, 1996), 67–80.

13. Ibid., 79.

14. Jorge Luis Borges, "Averroës' Search," in *Collected Fictions*, trans. Andrew Hurley (New York: Viking Books, 1998), 236.

15. Ibid., 241.

16. Hayden White, *Metahistory: The Historical Imagination in Nineteenth-Century Europe* (Baltimore: Johns Hopkins University Press, 1973). The citation is from 34, and the presentation of the theory of tropes from 31–38.

17. Ibid., 34–35.

18. Walter G. Andrews, *Poetry's Voice, Society's Song: Ottoman Lyric Poetry* (Seattle: University of Washington Press, 1985); Walter G. Andrews and Irene Markoff, "Poetry, the Arts, and Group Ethos in the Ideology of the Ottoman Empire," *Edebiyat n.s.* 1, no. 1 (1987): 28–71; Walter G. Andrews, "Singing the Alienated 'I': Guttari, Deleuze, and Lyrical Decodings of the Subject in Ottoman *Divan* Poetry," *Yale Journal of Criticism* 6 (1993): 191–219.

19. Andrews, *Poetry's Voice*, 143–74, and Andrews and Markoff, "Poetry, the Arts," especially 34–38.

20. For the lover and the beloved and the ruler as the beloved in the lyric poetry, see Andrews, *Poetry's Voice*, under "beloved" and "lover" in the Index.

21. Ibid., 158–59.
22. Ibid., 163.
23. Ibid., 159.
24. Andrews, "Singing the Alienated 'I,'," 199.
25. Ibid.
26. Ibid.
27. Herwig Wolfram, *The Roman Empire and Its Germanic Peoples*, trans. Thomas Dunlap (1990; reprint, Berkeley: University of California Press, 1997), esp. 31–34. I am grateful to Professor Patrick Geary for his help on the subject of medieval myths of origin in Europe.
28. Ibid., 33.
29. Nicholas Howe, *Migration and Mythmaking in Anglo-Saxon England* (New Haven, Conn.: Yale University Press, 1989). I noticed Howe's stimulating study thanks to another discussion—equally stimulating but with completely different concerns—Jonathan Boyarin, *Palestine and Jewish History* (Minneapolis: University of Minnesota Press, 1996), 52–55.
30. Howe, *Migration and Mythmaking*, 50.
31. Ibid., 51.
32. Ibid., 61–62.
33. Ibid., 81.
34. Ibid., 102.
35. Colin Imber, "The Ottoman Dynastic Myth," *Turcica: Revue D'Études Turques* 29 (1987): 7–27.

Bibliography

OTTOMAN TEXTS

Hasanbeyzade. *Tarih-i Al-i Osman*. MS Flügel 1046, Austrian National Library, Vienna.
———. *Tarih-i Al-i Osman*. MS Flügel 1049, Austrian National Library, Vienna.
———. *Tarih-i Al-i Osman*. MS Nuruosmaniye 3106, Nuruosmaniye Library, Istanbul.
Hoca Sadüddin Efendi. *Tacüttevarih*. 2 vols. Istanbul: Tabhane-i Amire, 1872.
———. *Tacüttevarih*. 5 vols. Translated to modern Turkish by Ismet Parmaksızoğlu. Eskişehir: Anatolia University Press, 1992.
Ibrahim Peçevi. *Peçevi Tarihi*. 2 vols. Translated to modern Turkish by Sıtkı Bekir Sıtkı Baykal. Ankara: Kültür Bakanlığı, 1982.
———. *Tarih-i Peçevi*. 2 vols. Istanbul: Matbaa-i Amire, 1863–64.
———. *Tarih-i Peçevi*. MS Add. 18,701, British Library, London.
Katip Çelebi. *The Balance of Truth (Mizan ül-Hakk)*. Translated and edited by Geoffrey L. Lewis. London: Allen and Unwin, 1957.
———. *Fezleke-i Tarih*. 2 vols. Istanbul, 1869–70.
———. *Fezleke-i Tarih*. MS Rawl. Or. 20, Bodleian Library, Oxford University.
———.*Fezleke-i Tarih*. MS Sale 62, Bodleian Library, Oxford University.
———. *Keşfülzunun*. 2 vols. Istanbul, 1941.
———. *Keşfülzunun*. 7 vols. Edited by G. Flugel. Leipzig, 1858.
Mustafa Naima. *Tarih-i Naima*. 6 vols. Istanbul: Matbaa-i Amire, 1864–66.
Tuği Çelebi (Hüseyin bin Sefer). *Tarih-i Tuği*. No reference to MS. Translated by Midhat Sertoğlu and published as "Tuği Tarihi." *Belleten* 43 (1947): 489–514.
———. *Tarih-i Tuği*. Dresden MS. Translated by Fahir İz and published as "XVII. Yüzyılında halk dili ile yazılmış bir tarih kitabı: Hüseyin Tuği, "Vak'a-i Sultan Osman Han." *Türk Dili Araştırmaları Belleten* (1967): 119–55.
———. *Tarih-i Tuği*. MS Flügel 1044, Austrian National Library, Vienna.

IMPORTANT DICTIONARIES

Bayerle, Gustav. *Pashas, Begs and Efendis: A Historical Dictionary of Titles and Terms in the Ottoman Empire.* Istanbul: Isis Press, 1997.
Clodius, Johann Christian. *Compendiosvm lexicon latino-tvercico-germanicvm.* Leipzig, 1730.
Meninski, Franciszek. *Thesaurus linguarum orientalum turcicae, arabicae, persicae.* Vienna, 1680.
Pakalın, Mehmet Zeki. *Tarih Deyimleri ve Terimleri Sözlüğü.* 3 vols. Istanbul: Milli Eğitim Basimevi, 1946.
Redhouse, Sir James. *Redhouse Çağdaş Türkçe-Inglizce Sözlüğü.* Istanbul, 1983.
———. *Redhouse Yeni Türkçe-Inglizce Sözlük.* 1968. Reprint, Istanbul, 1979.
———. *A Turkish and English Lexicon.* 1890. Reprint, Istanbul, 1978.

BOOKS AND ARTICLES

Abou-El-Haj, Rifaat Ali. *Formation of the Modern State: The Ottoman Empire, Sixteenth to Eighteenth Centuries.* Albany: State University of New York Press, 1991.
———. "Review Article: Metin Kunt, *The Sultan's Servants.*" *Osmanlı Araştırmaları* 6 (1986): 221–46.
———. "The Vezir and Paşa Households, 1683–1703: A Preliminary Report." *Journal of the American Oriental Society* 94 (1974): 438–47.
Abrams, Philip. "Notes on the Difficulty of Studying the State." *Journal of Historical Sociology* 1 (March 1988): 58–89.
Akdağ, Mustafa. "Celali Isyanlarından Büyük Kaçgunluk, 1603–1606." *Tarih Araştırmaları Dergisi* 2 (1964): 1–49.
Aksan, Virginia. "Mutiny in the Eighteenth-Century Ottoman Army." *Turkish Studies Association Bulletin* 22 (Spring 1998): 113–35.
Aktepe, Munir. "Mustafa I." In *Islam Ansiklopedisi*, vol. 7, 692–95. Istanbul: Milli Eğitim Basimevi, 1940–88.
Alderson, A. D. *The Structure of the Ottoman Dynasty.* New York: Oxford University Press, 1956.
Altundağ, Şinası. "Osman II." In *Islam Ansiklopedisi*, vol. 9, 443–47. Istanbul: Milli Eğitim Basimevi, 1940–88.
Anderson, Benedict. *Imagined Communities.* Rev. ed. New York: Verso, 1991.
Anderson, Perry. *Lineages of the Absolutist State.* New York: Verso, 1974.
Andrews, Walter G. *Poetry's Voice, Society's Song: Ottoman Lyric Poetry.* Seattle: University of Washington Press, 1985.
———. "Singing the Alienated 'I': Guttari, Deleuze, and Lyrical Decodings of the Subject in Ottoman *Divan* Poetry." *Yale Journal of Criticism* 6 (1993): 191–219.
Andrews, Walter G., and Irene Markoff. "Poetry, the Arts, and Group Ethos in the Ideology of the Ottoman Empire." *Edebiyat* n.s. 1, no. 1 (1987): 28–71.

Aricanli, Tosun, and Mara Thomas. "Sidestepping Capitalism: On the Ottoman Road to Elsewhere." *Journal of Historical Sociology* 7 (1994): 25–48.

Babinger, Franz. *Die Geschichtesschriber der Osmanen und ihre Werke*. Leipzig: O. Harrassowitz, 1927.

Barkey, Karen. *Bandits and Bureaucrats: The Ottoman Route to State Centralization*. Ithaca, N.Y.: Cornell University Press, 1994.

———. "In Different Times: Scheduling and Control in the Ottoman Empire, 1550–1650." *Comparative Studies in Society and History* 38 (1996): 460–83.

———. "Rebellious Alliances: The State and Peasant Unrest in Early Seventeenth-Century France and the Ottoman Empire." *American Sociological Review* 56 (1991): 699–715.

Bombaci, Alessio. *Storia della letteratura turca*. Milan: Nuova Accademia, 1956.

Bonnel, Victoria, and Lynn Hunt, eds. *Beyond the Cultural Turn*. Berkeley: University of California Press, 1999.

Borges, Jorge Luis. "Averroës' Search." In *Collected Fictions*, translated by Andrew Hurley, 235–41. New York: Viking Books, 1998.

Boyarin, Jonathan. *Palestine and Jewish History*. Minneapolis: University of Minnesota Press, 1996.

Cerny, Philip G. *The Changing Architecture of Politics: Structure, Agency and the Future of the State*. Newbury Park, Calif.: Sage, 1990.

Cezar, Mustafa. *Osmanlı Tarihinde Levendler*. Istanbul: Celikcilt Matbaasi, 1965.

Danişmend, Ismail Hami. *Izhali Osmanlı Tarihi Kronolojisi*. 5 vols. Istanbul: Türkiye Yayinevi, 1971–72.

Darling, Linda T. *Revenue-Raising and Legitimacy*. Leiden, the Netherlands: E. J. Brill, 1996.

David, Geza. "Administration in Ottoman Europe." In *Süleyman the Magnificent and His Age*, edited by Metin Kunt and Christine Woodhead, 71–91. New York: Longman, 1995.

Denis, Claude. "The Genesis of American Capitalism: An Historical Inquiry into State Theory." *Journal of Historical Sociology* 2 (December 1989): 328–56.

Faroqhi, Suraiya. *Approaching Ottoman History: An Introduction to the Sources*. New York: Cambridge University Press, 1999.

———. "Crisis and Change, 1590–1699." In *An Economic and Social History of the Ottoman Empire*, vol. 2, 1600–1914, edited by Suraiya Faroqhi et al., pp. 413–637. New York: Cambridge University Press, 1994.

Firdausi. *The Epic of Kings: Shah-nama*. Translated by Reuben Levy. New York: Mazda, 1996.

Fisher, G. C., and A. Fisher. "Topkapı Sarayı in the Mid-Seventeenth Century: Bobovi's Description." *Archivum Ottomanicum* 10 (1985): 5–83.

Fleischer, Cornell H. *Bureaucrat and Intellectual in the Ottoman Empire: The Historian Mustafa Ali*. Princeton, N.J.: Princeton University Press, 1986.

———. "Reply to Rhoads Murphey." *International Journal of Middle East Studies* 22 (1990): 127–28.

———. "Royal Authority, Dynastic Cyclism, and 'Ibn Khaldunism' in Sixteenth-Century Ottoman Letters." *Journal of Asian and African Studies* 18, nos. 3 and 4 (1983): 198–220.

Flügel, Gustavus. *Die arabischen, persischen und Türkischen Handschriften der K. K. Hofbibliothek zu Wien.* 3 vols. Vienna: Hildesheim, 1856–57.

Friedlander, Saul, ed. *Probing the Limits of Representation: Nazism and the Final Solution.* Cambridge, Mass.: Harvard University Press, 1992.

Frye, R. N. "The Political History of Iran under the Sassanians." In *The Cambridge History of Iran,* vol. 3, edited by Ehsan Yarshater, 126–51. New York: Cambridge University Press, 1983.

Ginzburg, Carlo. *History, Rhetoric, and Proof: The Menahem Stern Jerusalem Lectures.* Hanover, N.H.: University Press of New England, 1999.

Goldstone, Jack A. "East and West in the Seventeenth Century: Political Crises in Stuart England, Ottoman Turkey, and Ming China." *Comparative Studies in Society and History* 30 (1988): 103–42.

———. *Revolution and Rebellion in the Early Modern World.* Berkeley: University of California Press, 1991.

Harlan, David. "Intellectual History and the Return of Literature." *American Historical Review* 94 (1989): 581–610.

Hathaway, Jane. "The Military Household in Ottoman Egypt." *International Journal of Middle East Studies* 27 (1995): 39–52.

———. *The Politics of Households in Ottoman Egypt.* New York: Cambridge University Press, 1997.

———. "Problems of Periodization in Ottoman History." *Turkish Studies Association Bulletin* 2 (1996): 25–31.

———. "The Role of the Kızlar Ağası in Seventeenth-Eighteenth Century Ottoman Egypt." *Studia Islamica* 75 (1992): 141–58.

Hollinger, David. "The Return of the Prodigal: The Persistence of Historical Knowing." *American Historical Review* 94 (1989): 610–22.

Holt, P. M.. "Al-Jabarti's Introduction to the History of Ottoman Egypt." *Bulletin of the School of Oriental and African Studies* 25, no. 1 (1962): 38–51.

Howard, Douglas. "Ottoman Historiography and the Literature of 'Decline' in the Sixteenth and Seventeenth Centuries." *Journal of Asian History* 22 (1988): 52–76.

Howe, Nicholas. *Migration and Mythmaking in Anglo-Saxon England.* New Haven, Conn.: Yale University Press, 1989.

Hunt, Lynn, ed. *The New Cultural History.* Berkeley: University of California Press, 1989.

Imber, Colin. "Ideals of Legitimation in Early Ottoman History." In *Süleyman the Magnificent and His Age,* edited by Metin Kunt and Christine Woodhead, 138–54. New York: Longman: 1995.

———. "The Ottoman Dynastic Myth." *Turcica: Revue D'Études Turques* 19 (1987): 7–27.
———. *The Ottoman Empire, 1300–1481.* Istanbul: Isis Press, 1990.
———. "Paul Wittek's 'De la défate d'Ankara à la prise de Constantinople,'" *Osmanlı Araştırmaları* 5 (1986): 65–81.
Inalcik, Halil. *Fatih Devri üzerinde Tetkikler ve Vesikalar.* Ankara: Türk Tarih Kurumu Basimevi, 1954.
———. "How to Read Ashik Pasha-Zade's History." In *Essays in Ottoman History*, 31–55. Istanbul: Eren, 1998.
———. "Military and Fiscal Transformation in the Ottoman Empire, 1600–1700." *Archivum Ottomanicum* 6 (1980): 283–337.
———. *The Ottoman Empire: The Classical Age, 1300–1600.* Translated by Norman Itzkowitz and Colin Imber. New York: Praeger, 1973.
———. "The Rise of Ottoman Historiography." In *Historians of the Middle East*, edited by Bernard Lewis and P. M. Holt, 152–67. New York: Oxford University Press.
Islamoğlu, Huri, and Çağlar Keyder. "Agenda for Ottoman History." *Review, a Journal of the Fernand Braudel Center* 1 (1977): 31–55.
Jenkins, Keith. *On "What Is History?": From Carr and Elton to Rorty and White.* New York: Routledge, 1995.
Kafadar, Cemal. *Between Two Worlds: The Construction of the Ottoman State.* Berkeley: University of California Press, 1995.
Kelley, Donald R.. *Foundations of Modern Historical Scholarship: Language, Law and History in the French Renaissance.* New York: Columbia University Press, 1975.
Khoury, Dina Rizk. *State and Provincial Society in the Ottoman Empire: Mosul, 1540–1834.* New York: Cambridge University Press, 1997.
Köprülü, Orhan F. "Hasanbeyzade." In *Islam Ansiklopedisi*, vol. 5, 334–37. Istanbul: Milli Eğitim Basimevi, 1940–88.
Kramer, Lloyd S. "Literature, Criticism and Historical Imagination: The Literary Challenges of Hayden White and Dominick LaCapra." In *The New Cultural History*, edited by Lynn Hunt, 97–131. Berkeley: University of California Press, 1989.
Kunt, Metin. "Ethnic-Regional *(Cins)* Solidarity in the Seventeenth-Century Ottoman Establishment." *International Journal of Middle East Studies* 5 (1974): 233–39.
———. *The Sultan's Servants: The Transformation of Ottoman Provincial Government, 1550–1650.* New York: Columbia University Press, 1983.
Kütükoğlu, Bekir. "Katip Çelebi 'Fezleke'sinin Kaynakları." In *Vekayi'nüvis Makaleler*, 25–85. Istanbul: Fetih Cemiyeti, 1994.
LaCapra, Dominick. "Poetics of Historiography: Hayden White's *Tropics of Discourse.*" In *Rethinking Intellectual History: Texts, Contexts, Language*, 72–80. Ithaca, N.Y.: Cornell University Press, 1983.
———. "Rethinking Intellectual History and Reading Texts." In *Modern Eu-*

ropean Intellectual History, edited by Dominick LaCapra and Steven Kaplan, 47–86. Ithaca, N.Y.: Cornell University Press, 1982.

———. "Rhetoric and History." In *History and Criticism*, 15–45. Ithaca, N.Y.: Cornell University Press, 1985.

Le Goff, Jacques. *History and Memory*. Translated by Steven Rendall and Elizabeth Claman. New York: Columbia University Press, 1992.

Lindner, Rudi P. *Nomads and Ottomans in Medieval Anatolia*. Bloomington: Indiana University, Research Institute for Inner Asian Studies, 1983.

———. "Stimulus and Justification in Early Ottoman History." *Greek Orthodox Theological Review* 27 (1982): 207–24.

Menage, Victor L.. "The Beginnings of Ottoman Historiography." In *Historians of the Middle East*, edited by Bernard Lewis and P. M. Holt, 168–79. New York: Oxford University Press.

———. "Hasanbeyzade." In *Encyclopaedia of Islam*, new ed. Leiden, the Netherlands: E. J. Brill, 1954–2002.

———. "The Menaqib of Yakhshi Faqih." *Bulletin of the School of Oriental and African Studies* 26 (1963): 50–54.

———. *Neshri's History of the Ottomans: The Sources and Development of the Text*. New York: Oxford University Press, 1964.

———. "Some Notes on the Devşirme." *Bulletin of the School of Oriental and African Studies* 29 (1966): 64–78.

Mitchell, Timothy. "The Limits of the State: Beyond Statist Approaches and Their Critics." *American Political Science Review* 85, no. 1 (1991): 77–96.

Mitchell, Timothy, and Roger Owen. "Defining the State in the Middle East. I." *Middle East Studies Association Bulletin* 24 (December 1990): 179–83.

———. "Defining the State in the Middle East. II." *Middle East Studies Association Bulletin* 25 (July 1991): 25–29.

Murphey, Rhoads. "Continuity and Discontinuity in Ottoman Administrative Theory and Practice during the Late Seventeenth Century." *Poetics Today* 14 (Summer 1993): 419–45.

———. "The Functioning of the Ottoman Army under Murad IV (1623–1639)." Ph.D. diss., University of Chicago, 1979.

———. *Ottoman Warfare, 1500–1700*. New Brunswick, N.J.: Rutgers University Press, 1999.

———. "Review Article: Mustafa Ali and the Politics of Cultural Despair." *International Journal of Middle East Studies* 21 (1989): 243–55.

Necipoğlu, Gülru. "Framing the Gaze in Ottoman, Safavid, and Mughal Palaces." *Ars Orientalis* 23 (1993): 303–42.

Oakeshott, Michael. "The Activity of Being an Historian." In *Rationalism in Politics and Other Essays*. New York: Basic Books, 1962.

Pamuk, Şevket. "In the Absence of Domestic Currency: Debased European Coinage in the Seventeenth-Century Ottoman Empire." *Journal of Economic History* 57 (1997): 345–66.

———. *A Monetary History of the Ottoman Empire*. New York: Cambridge University Press, 2000.

———. "The Price Revolution in the Ottoman Empire Reconsidered." *International Journal of Middle East Studies* 33 (February 2001): 69–89.

Partner, Nancy F. "Hayden White (and the Content of the Form and Everyone Else) at the AHA." *History and Theory* 36 (December 1997): 96–106.

———. "The New Cornificius." In *Classical Rhetoric and Medieval Historiography*, edited by Ernst Breisach, 5–59. Kalamazoo: Western Michigan University Press, 1985.

———. *Serious Entertainment: The Writing of History in 12th Century England*. Chicago: University of Chicago Press, 1980.

Peirce, Leslie P. *The Imperial Harem: Women and Sovereignty in the Ottoman Empire*. New York: Oxford University Press, 1993.

Philp, Mark. "Michel Foucault." In *The Return of Grand Theory in the Human Sciences*, edited by Quentin Skinner, 66–87. New York: Cambridge University Press, 1985.

Piterberg, Gabriel. "Albert Hourani and Orientalism." In *Middle Eastern Politics and Ideas: A History from Within*, edited by Ilan Pappé and Moshe Ma'oz, 75–89. New York: I. B. Tauris, 1997.

———. "The Formation of an Ottoman Egyptian Elite in the 18th Century." *International Journal of Middle East Studies* 22 (1990): 275–89.

———. "Speech Acts and Written Texts: A Reading of a Seventeenth-Century Ottoman Historiographic Episode." *Poetics Today* 14 (1993): 387–419.

———. "A Study of Ottoman Historiography in the Seventeenth Century." D.Phil. thesis, Oxford University, 1993.

Popper, Karl. *The Poverty of Historicism*. 3d ed. London: Routledge and Kegan Paul, 1961.

Ray, Roger. "Rhetorical Skepticism and Verisimilar Narrative in John of Salisbury's *Historia Pontificalis*." In *Classical Rhetoric and Medieval Historiography*, edited by Ernst Breisach, 61–85. Kalamazoo: Western Michigan University Press, 1985.

Repp, Richard C. *The Mufti of Istanbul: A Study in the Development of the Ottoman Learned Hierarchy*. London: Ithaca Press, 1986.

Ricoeur, Paul. "What Is a Text? Explanation and Understanding." In *Hermeneutics and the Human Sciences*, edited and translated by J. M. Thompson, 145–65. New York: Cambridge University Press, 1981.

Robinson, Marilyn Waldman. *Toward a Theory of Historical Narrative*. Columbus: Ohio University Press, 1980.

Salzmann, Ariel. "An *Ancien Régime* Revisited: 'Privatization' and Political Economy in the Eighteenth-Century Ottoman Empire." *Politics and Society* 21 (December 1993): 393–423.

———. "Citizens in Search of a State: The Limits of Political Participation in the Late Ottoman Empire." In *Extending Citizenship, Reconfiguring States*, edited by Michael Hanagan and Charles Tilly, 37–67. Lanham, Md.: Rowman and Littlefield, 1999.

Schippman, K. "Artanabus [Ardavan]." In *Encyclopaedia Iranica*, vol. 2, 647–50. Boston: Routledge and Kegan Paul, 1983–90.

Schmidt, Jan. *Pure Waters for Thirsty Muslims: A Study of Mustafa Ali of Gallipoli's Künhü l-Ahbar.* Leiden, the Netherlands: Het Oosters Instituut, 1991.

Skinner, Quentin. "Hermeneutics and the Role of History." *New Literary History* 7 (1975–76): 209–32.

———. "Meaning and Understanding in the History of Ideas." *History and Theory* 8 (1969): 3–53.

———. "On Meaning and Speech-Acts." In *Meaning and Context: Quentin Skinner and His Critics,* edited by James Tully, 235–59. Cambridge, England: Polity Press, 1988.

Spiegel, Gabrielle. *The Past as Text.* Baltimore: Johns Hopkins University Press, 1997.

Süreyya, Mehmed. *Sicill-i Osmanı.* 4 vols. Istanbul: Matbaa-i Amire, 1890–98.

Tezcan, Baki. "1622 Military Rebellion in Istanbul: A Historiographical Journey." Paper presented at the Conference on Mutiny: Narrative, Event and Context in Cross-Cultural Perspective, Ohio State University, Columbus, 10–11 October 1998.

———. "II. Osman Örneğinde 'Ilerlemeci' Tarih ve Osmanlı Tarih Yazıcılığı." In *Osmanlı Düşünce,* vol. 7, edited by Güler Eren, 658–68. Ankara: Yeni Türkiye Yayınları, 1999.

Thomas, Lewis V. *A Study of Naima.* New York: New York University Press, 1972.

Toledano, Ehud. "The Emergence of Ottoman-Local Elites (1700–1900): A Framework for Research." In *Middle Eastern Politics and Ideas: A History from Within,* edited by Ilan Pappé and Moshe Ma'oz, 145–63. New York: I. B. Tauris, 1997.

———. "Review of Jane Hathaway, *The Politics of Households in Ottoman Egypt.*" *Journal of the American Oriental Society* 120 (2000): 449–53.

Walsh, John R.. "The Historiography of Ottoman-Safavid Relations in the Sixteenth and Seventeenth Centuries." In *Historians of the Middle East,* edited by Bernard Lewis and P. M. Holt, 197–212. New York: Oxford University Press, 1962.

White, Hayden. *The Content of the Form: Narrative Discourse and Historical Representation.* Baltimore: Johns Hopkins University Press, 1987.

———. "History, Historicism and the Figurative Imagination." *History and Theory* 14 (1975): 48–67.

———. *Metahistory: The Historical Imagination in Nineteenth-Century Europe.* Baltimore: Johns Hopkins University Press, 1973.

Wiesehofer, J. "Ardaşir I." In *Encyclopaedia Iranica,* vol. 2, 371–76. Boston: Routledge and Kegan Paul, 1983–90.

Wittek, Paul. "The Taking of the Aydos Castle: A Gazi Legend and Its Transformation." In *Arabic and Islamic Studies in Honor of Hamilton A. R. Gibb,* edited by George Makdisi, 662–72. Cambridge, Mass.: Harvard University Dept. of Near Eastern Languages and Literatures, 1965.

Wolfram, Herwig. *The Roman Empire and Its Germanic Peoples*. Translated by Thomas Dunlap. Berkeley: University of California Press, 1997.

Woodhead, Christine. "John R. Walsh." *Osmanlı Araştırmaları* 7–8 (1988): 1–9.

———. "Ottoman İnşa and the Art of Letter-Writing: Influences upon the Career of the Nişancı and Prose Stylist Okçuzade (d. 1630)." *Osmanlı Araştırmaları* 7–8 (1988): 143–59.

———. "Perspectives on Süleyman." In *Süleyman the Magnificent and His Age*, edited by Metin Kunt and Christine Woodhead, 146–91. New York: Longman, 1995.

———. "Research on the Ottoman Scribal Service, c. 1574–1630." *Islamkundliche Untersuchungen* 150 (1992): 311–28.

———.*Ta'liki-zade's şehname-i hümayun: A History of the Ottoman Campaign into Hungary 1593–94*. Berlin: Klaus Schwartz, 1983.

Ze'evi, Dror. "The Use of Ottoman Shari'a Court Records as a Source for Middle Eastern Social History: A Reappraisal." *Islamic Law and Society* 5 (1998): 35–56.

Index

ağa (commanding officer), 45
Ağa Kapısı, 26, 78, 129, 167, 194
Aşık Paşazade. *See* Apz
Abaza Mehmed Pasha, 29, 131, 165–76; Halil Pasha and, 109, 220n60; Katip Çelebi and, 47; Naima on, 183; Peçevi and, 46, 107, 112–13, 118; Tuği on, 74, 80, 100, 127, 194, 195
Abkhasians, 181
Abou-El-Haj, Rifaat Ali, 149, 152–54, 156, 226n51, 228–29n30
Abrams, Philip, 137, 139–41, 160–61, 183, 223–24nn5–6
Abu Ayyub al-Ansari, 11
Academy movement, 145–46
accession ceremonies, 10–11, 20, 96–97, 208n3
adalet, 111
administrative inspections. *See* yoklama
advice literature. *See* nasihat
Afrasiyab, 190
Ahmed I, 10–16, 18, 27, 28, 29, 94–96, 166, 170
Ahmed III, 165
Akdağ, Mustafa, 228n25
Akile, 18–19, 20, 24
Akkoyunlu, 37
Aksan, Virginia, 228n17
Albania, 131, 180–81, 182

"Alcove, The" (Hamid), 187
Alderson, A.D., 9, 208n3
Aleppo, 47
Ali, Mustafa, 36, 38–43, 51–52, 56–57, 64
Ali Ağa, 26
Al-i Osman, 164
Ali Pasha, 16, 97, 177
altı bölük, 19, 178. *See also* kul
Altuncuoğlu, 27
aman, 81
Amedeo of Savoy, 164
American Historical Review, 60
Anatolia: Abaza Pasha affair in, 1, 29, 67, 74, 76, 165–68, 170, 175; Hasanbeyzade in, 46; Kafadar on, 164; Katip Çelebi in, 47, 118; military transformation and, 171–73, 176, 178; Peçevi in, 46; "to move into," 23–24, 25, 86, 178–80, 182, 191–93, 196–200
Anatolian irregulars. *See* sekban
Anderson, Benedict, 138
Anderson, Perry, 138–41, 152, 160
Andrews, Walter, 193–94, 196, 197, 229n1, 230n20
Ankara, 35, 165
Annales, 50, 61
apprentices, 44, 47
Apz, 33–35, 37, 210n9, 211n12

Index

Arabic culture, 36–37
Arabic historiography, 75
Arabic language, 47, 97, 102–3
Arabic Thought in the Liberal Age (Hourani), 53
archival documents, 50, 51, 185–86, 213n3
Ardaşir I, 101–5
Ardavan IV, 101–2, 105
Aricanli, Tosun, 150–52
Arit, 38
Armenians, 156
Army of Islam. *See* kul
arz defter, 99
Arz Odası, 11
asılar. *See* rebels
astrological signs, 123–24, 177, 189
At Meydanı (Hippodrome), 25
Augustine, 198
Austrian National Library (Vienna), 72–73, 93, 131, 219n29
authenticity, 52–53
authorial intention, 60–64, 66–68, 106, 132
Averroës (Ibn Rushd), 191
Ayşe, 18
Aya Sofya, 12
Aydos Castle, 34, 227n3
Aziz al-Azmeh, 40

başdefterdar, 43, 44, 46, 174
Bab-i Ali, 173
Babüsaadet, 11, 19
Baghdad, 21, 168
bahşiş, 22
Bahman, 101
Baki Efendi, 168
Baki Pasha, 46
Balkans, 45, 147, 149, 177
bandits. *See* celali
banishment, 15–16
Barkan, Ömer Lütfi, 142, 148, 224n20
Barkey, Karen, 157–60, 170–73, 174, 176, 226n61, 228n25
barracks households, 110, 181, 221n64. *See also* Yeni Odalar

Barthes, Roland, 61
base/superstructure, 138–39
batın, 89
Bayezid I, 35, 211n11
Bayezid II, 33–34, 35, 36–37, 164
Baykal, 107
Bayram Pasha, 112
Bede, 198–99
Bekir Sıtkı-Baykal, 107
Bektaşi order, 47, 196
Belgrade, 45, 177
beloved, 193–95, 197, 230n20
Bethlen Gabor, 21
beylerbeyi, 29, 46, 148–49, 151, 168. *See also* names of beylerbeyi
biat, 11, 26
Bildisi, Idris-i, 37, 39
biological metaphor, 145, 154, 182
black eunuchs, 15. *See also* chief black eunuchs
Black Sea, 124
Blue Mosque, 15
Bombaci, Alessio, 187
bonuses, 11, 22, 107, 117, 120
book of Süleyman. *See Süleymanname*
Borges, Jorge Luis, 191
Bosnia, 46, 166, 181, 182
bostancıs, 19, 83, 120
boundaries of knowledge, 48, 54
brigands. *See* celali
Budapest, 46
bureaucracy, 42–45, 212nn38–39. *See also* sedentary state; celali vs., 157–59; gaza vs., 35–36; Naima and, 154, 182; patrimony vs., 149–50, 173–74; scribal service vs., 31, 42–43
Bureaucrat and Intellectual (Fleischer), 36
Bursa, 23, 165, 166, 179

Cairo, 23, 107, 165
Caliph Umar, 11
Cambridge Group, 61
camera. *See* perspective
Canbulad, 27

Canbuladoğlu Ali Pasha, 175
Çandarlı dynasty, 35
Çandarlı Kara Halil, 171
canon, 39
capitalism, 137, 139, 143, 150, 153
Catholic League, 21
"Cause[s] of the Event, The" (Katip Çelebi), 117
celali, 27, 54, 157–59, 166, 170–76, 220n60, 228n25
Celalzade, 37, 39, 45
Cem (Prince), 36, 164, 165, 180
centralization, 154–56, 157
centripetal decentralization, 154–56, 226n59
Chamber of Petition, 11
chancellors, 43, 44–45
chancery, 43, 44
Chartier, Roger, 61
Chatterjee, Partha, 140
chief black eunuchs, 10–12, 15–16, 18, 26–27, 93–98. See also names of chief black eunuchs; Naima on, 178; Peçevi on, 107–8; Tuği on, 77, 82–85, 87, 122–23, 125–26, 195, 217n37
China, 142, 145
Christians, 45, 46, 56, 149
chronicles, 56–58, 67, 73, 75
chronology, 65, 76, 79–88, 121–27, 175
cins, 177, 180–83
Circassians, 181
classical age, 146–50, 154, 176
coinage, 11, 27
Cold War, 136
comparative history, 152–53
conceptualization of state, 3, 136–41, 146–54
conflictuality, 30, 31, 34, 35, 48–49
consorts, 15, 18. See also haseki sultan
Constantinople, 34, 164
content/form dichotomy, 55–57, 58, 65
contested field. See discursive battle

contextual meaning, 4, 60–62; in Hasanbeyzade, 97, 103; in Tuği, 67–68, 73–74, 88, 89, 194
Cooperative Principle, 216–17n15
Corneille, Pierre, 187
countercrossing, 200
coup d'état, 169–70, 209n42
crisis of seventeenth century, 3, 55, 96, 141–46, 153, 155, 157, 172
Cronica (Gervase), 56
cronici, 56
Crown of Histories (Hoca Sadüddin Efendi), 39, 92, 188
cultural signifiers, 98, 175
cülus akçesi, 11

damad, 14, 28, 29, 80
Damascus, 23, 165
Darling, Linda, 174
darüssaade ağası. See chief black eunuchs
dava, 111
David, Geza, 147
Davud Pasha, 29, 80–81, 109, 209n42; Hasanbeyzade on, 100–104, 106; Katip Çelebi on, 118; Peçevi on, 28, 209n42; Tuği on, 78
daye hatun, 18, 79
decentralization, 154–56, 226n59
decision making, 136, 159
decline paradigm, 142, 145–50, 154, 157, 176, 185–86, 225nn31–32
defterdar, 43, 44, 46, 170, 212n39
Defterdar Kapısı, 174
defter emini, 43
defters, 6, 99
Deleuze, Gilles, 197
Deli Sultan Ibrahim. See Ibrahim I
demographic changes, 141–44
Denis, Claude, 223–24n6
Derviş Ağa, 81, 100, 111
devşirme, 149, 172–73, 180
Devlet-i Aliye, 171
dictionaries, 187–88
digressions, 65; in Hasanbeyzade, 101–6; in Tuği, 76, 80–89, 125–27, 169, 189

Dilaver Pasha, 24, 80
dirlik, 149, 151
discursive battle, 48–49, 54, 152, 163–84
distribution of surplus, 151–52, 162
divinely ordained fate. *See* preordained destiny
divine majesty, 102–3
Diyarbekir, 46, 170
Diyyak Mehmed Pasha, 109
documentary model of knowledge, 5–6, 42, 50, 99, 148, 185–86
donative, 22
dramatic tragedy, 188–91
dreams, 24, 86–87, 89–90, 126–27, 189
Dresden manuscript, 22, 74, 75, 111, 209n30, 217n37
dua, 20, 85, 89, 189, 196, 209n26
dynastic household. *See* royal household
dynastic state. *See* sedentary state

Eğerliname, 38
eşkiya, 169
easterners, 181
Ebusuud, 45
Ede Bali, 19
Edirne, 164, 165, 178, 188
editorial approach, 119, 122, 124–27, 132
Egypt, 15–16, 23, 83, 110, 150, 178
Eight Paradises (Bildisi), 37
ekberiyet, 10, 12–15, 20
elite households: Abou-El-Haj on, 149; celali and, 172–75; Hathaway on, 150; Kunt on, 148; malikâne maqataa and, 155, 226n56; royal household and, 110, 195
elites, 47, 144, 153
embeddedness, 104–5, 151
emirler, 24, 168
empiricist historiography, 41, 59
encodation, 57
enderun, 148
England, 145, 151

English medieval historiography, 4, 207n6
English Revolution, 143
erbab-i zahir, 84, 89, 196
Erzurum, 29, 67, 74, 80, 107, 165, 167–69, 176
Esad Efendi, 10, 18–19, 24, 85, 106
Essence (Ali), 39–41
essentialism, 144, 145, 210n8. *See also* Hegelian essentialism
ethnic-regional affiliation. *See* cins
eunuchs, 15, 105. *See also* chief black eunuchs
Eurasia, 2, 55, 96, 141, 143, 148–49, 153, 154
Eurocentric bias, 150
Eurocentric models, 2, 141–42, 143
Evliya Çelebi, 195
exclusion. *See* inclusion/exclusion
Exodus, Book of, 199
Eyüp, 10, 11, 15

Faroqhi, Suraiya, 119, 210n1
farr, 102–3
Fars, 101
fate. *See* preordained destiny
Fatih Sultan Mehmed. *See* Mehmed II
Fatma, 187
Ferhad Pasha, 46
ferman, 13
fethname, 38, 72
fetish of the defter, 6, 186
fetva, 24, 25, 75–76, 85, 86, 101, 125
feudalism, 138, 151–52
Fezleke-i Tarih (Katip Çelebi), 91–92, 114–17, 119, 121–27, 130, 131, 177–78, 208n14, 222n19
figurative language, 95–96
filmmaking, 66, 77–79
finance directorship, 43, 44, 174
Firdausi, 38, 102, 190
fisc, 155
fiscal crises, 143–44
fiscal system, 154–56
fitne ü fesad, 168–69, 194, 228n17
Fleischer, Cornell, 31, 36–37, 38–41, 45, 48, 51, 60, 212n38

Flügel, Gustavus, 73, 219n29. *See also* MS Flügel 1044; MS Flügel 1046; MS Flügel 1049
form. *See* content/form dichotomy
Foucault, Michel, 48, 54, 64, 141, 223n5
foundational text. *See* urtext
France, 157, 227n63
fratricide, 10, 12–15, 20–21, 106
Freud, Sigmund, 179, 217n18, 219n16
Friday prayer, 11, 27
frontier, 10, 17; Hasanbeyzade and, 92; Kafadar on, 4, 19, 32, 35, 164–65, 179–80, 193, 197, 210n8; pencik and, 171–72
Fünfkirchen, 46
"fusion of horizons," 60

Galata, 34
Gallipoli, 164, 171–72, 199
garden party, 193–94, 196–98
garlic metaphor, 32–34
Gate of Felicity, 11
gaza, 17–18, 32, 33–36, 171–72, 198, 203, 210n8
gazaname, 38, 72
gaza tales, 33, 211n12
gazi-dervish milieu, 19, 31–32, 33, 35–36, 163–65, 227n3
gazi/kul resentment, 164, 172, 179
gazis: Apz and, 33, 35; Bayezid II and, 36; Menage on, 35–36
gazi-sultan image: fratricide and, 20–21; of Osman II, 17–18, 19, 24–25, 208n16, 209n21; of Süleyman, 38
"gelmek," 167–68
Genç Osman. *See* Osman II
genealogies, 150
"Genesis of American Capitalism, The" (Denis), 223–24n6
Georgians, 181
Gervase, 56–57
Gibb, H. A. R., 185–86
"gitmek," 167–68, 178
"golden cage." *See* kafes
Golden Horn, 10, 11

Goldstone, Jack, 143–46, 157, 224–25n28
governors. *See* beylerbeyi
Gramsci, Antonio, 137
grand vezirs, 26–29, 35. *See also* names of grand vezirs; Bab-i Ali as residence of, 173–74, 228–29n30; Hasanbeyzade and, 97, 101–6; Naima and, 47; Peçevi on, 107, 109–10, 112; Tuği on, 80, 100, 125–26
Greek drama, 190
Greeks, 156
Grosseteste, Robert, 55
Guattari, Félix, 197
Gupta, Akhil, 140
Gürcü Mehmed Pasha, 29, 80, 100, 109–10, 116, 119; in Abaza Pasha affair, 175, 176; alternative narratives about, 127–29, 130; Naima on, 181–83

Haci Bektaş, 36
Haci Halife. *See* Katip Çelebi
Hafız Pasha, 46, 170
"haile," 1, 186–88
Haile (Hamid), 187
Haile-i Osmaniye, 1–3, 24–25, 165; Hasanbeyzade on, 91–106; interpretive framework of, 53–54, 64, 66–67; Katip Çelebi on, 114–32; Peçevi on, 106–12; plot of, 9–29; state and, 176–84; tragedy and, 186–91; Tuği on, 45, 71–90
hajj, 23, 24, 75, 86, 107, 120, 179
Halil Pasha, 109, 175, 220n60
Hamid Tarhan, Abulhak, 187
Hapsburgs, 182
Harem-i Has. *See* imperial harem
Harlan, David, 60–63, 66
Hasan al-Kafi, 97
Hasanbeyzade, 2, 45–46; as Katip Çelebi source, 114–18, 120, 127–30, 178, 208n14; on Mustafa Ağa, 16, 93–98, 208n14; as Naima source, 98, 182, 208n14, 219n27; as Peçevi source, 106–9; Tuği as

Hasanbeyzade *(continued)*
    source for, 72–73, 91, 98–106, 111, 112, 115–16
haseki sultan, 10, 13–14, 18, 38
Hasht Bihisht (Eight Paradises) (Bildisi), 37
Hathaway, Jane, 110, 150, 221n64
hatime, 99–100
hatt-i şerif, 101
Hegelian essentialism, 2, 42, 58, 136–37, 140, 146
Herder, Johann Gottfried, 61
hermeneutic arc, 63, 67
high culture, 36–39, 43, 186
Hippodrome (At Meydanı), 25
histoire événementielle, 1, 21
Historia Ecclesiastica (Bede), 198–99
Historia Pontificalis (John of Salisbury), 56
historical consciousness, 34–37, 58, 164, 180, 183
historical narrative, 53, 55–60, 73, 226n51
historicity, 2, 66, 68, 147, 159, 161, 172
historiographical corpus, 52–54, 59, 66, 132
"historiographical explosion," 38
historiography. *See* Ottoman historiography
History and Memory (Le Goff), 214n22
history/historiography distinction, 4–5
History of the House of Osman (Paşazade), 37
History of the Year 1000, 98
history writing, 31, 39–41, 51, 60–64, 131, 182, 210n1
hoca, 23, 25, 82, 84, 125–26
Hoca Ömer Efendi, 23–24, 83, 86, 90, 108, 122
Hoca Sadüddin Efendi, 19, 39, 56, 92, 188, 230n10
Hollinger, David, 60
Holt, P. M., 67–68, 75–76

Homizdagan, battle of, 101
horoscope. *See* astrological signs
Hotin siege, 21, 22–23, 83–84, 107–8, 120, 122, 126, 189
Hourani, Albert, 53
House of Osman, 31, 35, 37, 94, 163–64, 169
Howe, Nicholas, 198–99
Hungarian campaign, 46, 72, 147
Hurrem Sultan, 14, 38, 208n6
"huruc," 228n20
Hüseyin bin Sefer. *See* Tuği Çelebi
Hüseyin Köprülü Pasha, 47
Hüseyin Pasha. *See* Mere Hüseyin Pasha
Hüsrev Pasha, 166

Ibn Khaldun, 40–41, 64
Ibn Rushd (Averroës), 191
Ibrahim I, 14, 97
idealist state, 136, 140, 147, 148, 154
idealist statism, 157–60, 171, 174, 226n61
Ideengeschichte, 36
"ihrac," 228n20
ilmiye hierarchy, 44, 45, 46
iltizam, 155–56
imaginary narrative, 55–56
imam, 24, 90
Imber, Colin, 35, 51, 199, 213n3
immobility, 153
imperial cavalry. *See* sipahis
Imperial Divan, 11, 109
imperial harem, 9, 14–15, 18, 26, 194–95, 208n6, 209n19; Hasanbeyzade on, 106; Tuği on, 77
Imperial Treasury, 35, 43–44, 85, 94, 96–97
inşa, 41, 44
Inalcik, Halil, 31, 67–68, 146–48, 172, 225n33
incentives. *See* bonuses
"Incident of the *Abu'lfeth*, The," 129
inclusion/exclusion, 2, 49, 54, 135, 158, 161, 193, 213n12; of Abaza,

175–76; of celali, 171; of sekban, 173
inevitability, 88–90, 123–24, 189
informational documents, 5, 51, 213n3
insanity, 11, 12–13, 14, 29, 94–97
intellectual history, 60–61
intentionality, 60–64, 147, 158–60
interpretation, 63–64, 68, 193–96
Interpretation of Dreams, The (Freud), 179, 217n18, 219n16
interpretive framework, 50–68
Interregnum (1403–13), 33, 211n11
intertextuality, 61, 63
intisap: of Abaza, 109, 175–76; of Davud Pasha, 80; of Hasanbeyzade, 97; of Naima, 47; of Tuği, 45
irregular troops. *See* sekban
Islamic state, 17, 146
Islamoğlu, Huri, 225n33
Istanbul: Abaza Pasha affair and, 166–68, 170; Apz in, 34; Bethlen Gabor in, 21; Kafadar on, 164, 165; Katip Çelebi in, 46; Naima in, 47; natural disasters in, 124; Osman II and, 19–20, 23, 25, 107, 178–80; Pamuk on, 96–97; political public in, 11, 25
İstanköylü Ali Pasha, 16, 97, 177
isyan, 169–70, 194, 228n17, 228n20
İz, Fahir, 72–73, 74–75

janissaries, 1, 19, 25, 28. *See also* kul; in Abaza Pasha affair, 165–68, 170; Hasanbeyzade on, 129, 130; Katip Çelebi on, 118, 120; military transformation and, 172–73; Naima and, 47, 178; Peçevi on, 107; Tuği and, 45, 67, 73, 77, 83, 131, 181, 196
janissary barracks (Istanbul). *See* Yeni Odalar
Jews, 156
John of Salisbury, 56
Journal of Historical Sociology, 137
jurisconsult. *See* sheyhülislam

kılıç kuşanması, 11
kızlar ağası. *See* chief black eunuchs
Ka'be, 75, 86

kadi, 23, 83, 159
Kafadar, Cemal: on early Ottoman historiography, 4, 31–34, 36, 51, 210n3, 210n6, 210n8; on gaza, 17, 19, 32–33; on political imagination, 163–65, 176–77, 180, 191, 197, 227nn3–4
kafes, 11, 26, 77–78
kalem, 42
kalemiye, 42, 45, 46, 47
Kalenderoğlu, 27
kanun, 45
Kanuni Sultan Süleyman. *See* Süleyman
kapı, 110, 148, 149, 150, 155, 158–59
kapı halkı, 173
kapı kulları. *See* kul
kapudan pasha, 109, 175
Kara Davud Pasha. *See* Davud Pasha
Karakaş Pasha, 22, 108, 117
Kara Mizak, 28, 78–79, 112, 118–19, 217n24
Kara Rüstem, 171–72, 190
Kar-Namak-i Artakhshir Papakan (Pahlavi), 103
Katip Çelebi, 2, 46–47; on Abaza Pasha affair, 166; Hasanbeyzade as source for, 208n14; on Mustafa Ağa, 11, 93–98; as Naima source, 177–78, 182; Peirce on, 208n14; on preordained destiny, 89; state narrative and, 113, 114–32, 186, 188–89, 222n19; Tuği as source for, 72–73, 83, 91–92; Walsh on, 52
Kawakibi, 186
kaymakam, 110
kazasker, 171
Kemal, Namik, 187
Kemal Paşazade, 37, 39, 67, 227n3
Kemankeş Ali Pasha, 29, 112, 130
Keyder, Çağalar, 225n33
Khalid ibn Walid, 11
"kiyas ettirdi," 95
knowledge, boundaries of, 48, 54
Koçu Bey, 154
Köprülü household, 13, 181, 182
Kösem Sultan, 14–15, 18, 20

Küçük Ali Ağa, 47
Küçük Hasanbey, 45
Kuhn, Thomas, 41
kul, 19, 21–23, 25–27, 29; in Abaza Pasha affair, 165, 168–70, 175–76; Barkey on, 159; bureaucracy and, 35, 44, 150; Hasanbeyzade and, 46, 99–100, 128–29, 177; Kafadar on, 31, 164–65; Katip Çelebi on, 117–18, 120–21, 130; military transformation and, 172–73; Naima and, 177–78; Peçevi on, 107–10, 220n51; Tuği and, 45, 67, 73–88, 100, 110–12, 125–27, 130–31, 177, 181, 193–96
kul-centrism, 74, 88, 112, 126, 168–70, 179
Künhü'l-ahbar (Ali), 39–41
Kunt, Metin, 148–49, 175, 180–82, 228n9
Kuran, 24, 86
Kütükoğlu, Bekir, 119
Kuyucu Murad Pasha, 159, 166, 175

LaCapra, Dominick, 4–5, 50, 58, 185
lala, 105–6
Lala Mehmed Pasha, 46
latent meaning, 132, 217n18, 219n16; in Hasanbeyzade, 95–96, 104–6; in Katip Çelebi, 120, 121–22; in Peçevi, 112; in Tuği, 77–87, 123
Lefkeli Mustafa Pasha, 29, 80, 100
Le Goff, Jacques, 214n22
Levels (Celalzade), 37
life-term revenue tax farm, 155–56, 226n56
Lindner, Rudy, 32–33, 35, 210n6, 210n8
Lineages of the Absolutist State (Anderson), 138
linguistic turn, 50–51, 59–60
literary sources, 52, 98–99, 186
literature, 39–41, 46
litterateurs, 39
localized janissaries. *See* yerliye
location. *See* perspective

Lokman, Seyyid, 39
lover-beloved relationship, 193–95, 197, 230n20
Low Countries, 142
lyric poetry, 193–94, 197

ma'nevi, 124, 222n35
madness. *See* insanity
Mahfiruz, 15, 18
Mahmud Efendi, 24
Mahmud II, 165, 184
Mahmud (Prince), 12
malikâne muqataa, 155–56, 226n56
manifest meaning, 217n18, 219n16; in Hasanbeyzade, 95–96, 104, 106; in Katip Çelebi, 120, 121; in Peçevi, 107; in Tuği, 77, 80, 84–85
manuscripts, 72–75, 92–93, 131, 216n2, 216n6, 223n56
marginalization, 32, 34, 164
Marxist scholarship, 137, 138–39, 141, 146, 150, 152, 160, 223n5
materialism, 152, 154
Mecca, 23–24, 75, 83, 86
medievalists, 4, 6
medreses, 35, 38
Mehmed Ağa, 47, 120
Mehmed I, 33
Mehmed II, 13, 31, 34, 35, 36, 164, 208n6
Mehmed III, 12, 14, 17–18, 106
Mehmed II mosque. *See* Sultan Mehmed Mosque
Mehmed (Prince), 20–21, 84, 85, 89, 105, 189, 196
Mehmet Genç, 154
Melek Ahmed Pasha, 195
Menage, Victor L., 33, 34–35, 51, 211n12
menakib, 33, 211n12
Meninski, Franciszek, 188
Mere Hüseyin Pasha, 29, 80–81, 100–101, 106, 109–12, 183; alternative narratives about, 127–31; Hasanbeyzade on, 116; Katip Çelebi

on, 115–16, 119–20; Naima on, 181–83; Tuği on, 115, 180–82
Metahistory (White), 56, 65
Metin I, 228n9
metonymy, 179, 191–92
Middle East, 47, 150
Mihaloğlu Mehmed Bey, 33
Mihrimah, 14
military transformation, 172–73, 174, 228n24
mimesis, 56
Ming China, 143–46
misinterpretation, 193–96
Mitchell, Timothy, 140–41, 160–61, 162, 173, 223n2, 224n15, 226n61
modernist bias, 41, 42, 57, 58–60, 64, 214n22
monetarist theory, 141–44
monetarization, 149, 155
Moralı Hasan Pasha, 47
MS Flügel 1044, 72–73, 75, 130, 131
MS Flügel 1046, 93
MS Flügel 1049, 93
MS Nuruosmaniye 3106, 93
mufti of şeriat, 45
Muhasebe department, 47
mühimme defterleri, 99
mufti of kanun, 45
Muqaddima (Ibn Khaldun), 40
Murad I, 164, 171
Murad II, 188
Murad III, 12, 13, 38
Murad IV, 2, 13, 14, 21, 29, 45, 116, 166, 171
Murphey, Rhoads, 17, 25, 60, 224–25n28, 228n24
Muslims, 19, 85, 156, 186, 210n8
Mustafa Ağa, 11, 15–16, 93–98, 108–9, 208n14, 219n24
Mustafa bin Abdallah. *See* Katip Çelebi
Mustafa I, 1, 10–16, 18, 20, 21, 26, 27–29, 165, 208n3, 209n42; in Abaza Pasha affair, 175; alternative narratives about, 93–101, 108–10; Katip Çelebi on, 116, 118; Peçevi on, 107; Tuği on, 74, 76, 77–81, 85, 194–95
Mustafa III, 165
"müttefikan," 130
mythic migration, 198–200

Naima, Mustafa, 2, 47; Şarihülmanarzade as source for, 215n46; on Abaza Pasha affair, 166; Abou-El-Haj on, 154; Hasanbeyzade as source for, 208n14; history writing and, 64; Katip Çelebi as source for, 130; on Mustafa Ağa, 93–94; on Osman II, 16, 20, 209n26; Peçevi as source for, 209n42; on preordained destiny, 89; state narrative and, 92, 113, 114, 131, 176–84; Thomas on, 51, 98, 219n27; Tuği as source for, 72
narrative discourse, 54, 56–58, 64–65, 132, 135
nasihat, 40, 145, 153–54, 157, 176, 226n51
nation-states, 42, 153, 154–55, 180
natural disasters, 124
Neşri, 33, 34, 37
"neo-Mamluk," 150
New Palace, 208n6
Newtonian mechanical physics, 154
nişancı, 43, 44–45
niyet, 86, 90, 169
nonconformism, 17, 18, 21
North Africa, 47, 150
Nurbanu, 14
Nuruosmaniye Library (Istanbul), 93

Oğuz, 164
Oakeshott, Michael, 55
oath of allegiance (biat), 11
odabaşı, 110, 112, 128, 130
Ohrili Hüseyin Pasha, 26, 78, 80, 84, 118
Okçuzade Mehmed şah Bey, 43
Old Palace, 14, 15, 18, 26, 47, 78, 208n6
Ömer Efendi. *See* Hoca Ömer Efendi

onion metaphor, 32–33
oral address, 67–68, 71, 73–77, 84, 86–88, 130, 132, 193–95, 216–17n15
Orhan Gazi, 33
Orientalists, 14, 41, 52, 72, 150, 154, 185–86, 217n18
Origo Gentis, 198
Orta Cami, 26–28, 78, 79, 112, 118, 194, 209n42
Osman Bey, 32
Osman Gazi, 19, 209n21
Osman II, 45, 46, 165; accession, deposition, and assassination of, 1, 11, 12–13, 14–15, 16–28, 209n19; alternative narratives about, 127–29; Barkey on, 170–71, 173; countercrossing and, 199–200; Hasanbeyzade on, 93, 96, 97–98, 99, 101, 103, 105–6; Katip Çelebi on, 116–27; Naima on, 177–78, 182; Peçevi on, 107–8, 170; Tezcan on, 183–84; Tuği on, 74–75, 77–90, 111, 116, 165–69, 189–92, 194–97
Osmanlı sociopolitical identity, 18–19, 49, 54, 171, 175–76
Ottoman Empire: The Classical Age, 1300–1600, The (Inalcik), 146
Ottoman historians, 2, 41, 45–47, 219n24. *See also* names of Ottoman historians; Kafadar on, 4; manuscripts and, 71–72, 216n6; on Mustafa Ağa, 15; on Osman II, 16, 19, 178; sources and, 119; on succession, 12–13, 20
Ottoman historiography: formation of, 30–49, 210n3, 211n29; interpretive framework for, 50–68; poetics of, 185–200
Ottomanists, 6, 50, 144
Ottoman Turkish language, 38, 47, 97, 187
Owen, Roger, 140

padishah. *See names of Ottoman sultans*
Pahlavi, 103
Pakalın, Mehmet Zeki, 187
Pamuk, Şevket, 96–97, 141, 142–43, 144, 224n20
Papak, 101
particularism, 144, 153
Partner, Nancy, 4, 6, 50, 207n6
patrimony, 149–50, 173–74
patronage, 39, 110, 149; of Süleyman, 37–38
patron-client relationships, 45, 47, 81, 193–94, 230n20
Pazanoğlu, 27
Peçevi, Ibrahim, 2, 46; on Abaza Pasha affair, 166, 169–70, 176; alternative narrative of, 16, 22, 106–12; alternative narratives of, 220n51; as Katip Çelebi source, 91–92, 114–19, 127–29; on Mustafa Ağa, 11, 93–98; as Naima source, 177, 209n42; on Orta Cami scene, 28, 78–79, 209n42, 217n24; state narrative and, 176; Tuği as source for, 72, 91; Walsh on, 52
Peirce, Leslie, 9, 12–15, 17, 27, 98, 208n14, 209n26, 209n42, 209n45
pencik, 35, 171, 173
pencik emini, 172
Persian culture, 36–37, 38
Persian language, 47, 102–3
Persis, 101
personal prayer. *See* dua
perspective, 66; in Abaza Pasha affair, 166–68; in Hasanbeyzade, 97–98; in Katip Çelebi, 118; in Peçevi, 107, 112, 169–70, 176; in Tuği, 74, 77–79, 112, 166–69, 176
petitions, 25–26, 46, 85, 167, 194
plagiarism, 52–53, 99, 119
Pocock, J. G. A., 61
poetics, 3, 58, 65, 185–200
poetry, 74–75, 84, 99–100, 111, 116, 193–94, 197, 219n31
Poetry's Voice (Andrews), 230n20
Polish campaign, 19, 20–21, 105, 107–9, 117, 120
political households. *See* kapı

political imagination, 163–65, 177, 183, 197, 227n4
political public, 11, 25
"politicized rhetoric," 171, 176
Popper, Karl, 64, 215n47
popular chronicles, 75
popular literature, 145
positivist polarities, 2, 55–56, 157–59, 171
"postclassical" period, 147
postmodernism, 4, 6, 51
poststructuralism, 60–63
Poulantzas, Nicos, 137, 223n5
prebendal land grants, 46, 149
precapitalist formations, 152
prejudices, 98, 181
preordained destiny, 88–90, 123–24, 190
price revolution, 141–46, 148, 172, 224nn19–20, 224–25n28
primary sources, 119
primus inter pares, 19, 35, 164
private property, 151
private/public dichotomy, 173–74
privatization, 155
production, 150–52
the Prophet, 11, 24, 86, 182
prose: of Ali's Essence, 39–41; chancery and, 44–45; Okçuzade on, 43; in Tuği's text, 74, 76, 80, 99; Walsh on, 52; White on, 58, 65; Woodhead on, 211n29
Protestant Union, 21
provincial administration. See ümera
public humiliation, 26–27
public/private dichotomy, 173–74
Pure Waters for Thirsty Muslims (Schmidt), 40–41
Puritan movement, 145–46

quantity theory of money, 141–42
queen mother. See valide sultan
Quellenkritik, 40, 72, 135, 160

Ranke, Leopold von, 42
Ray, Roger, 56
reaya families, 44

rebels, 12, 27, 54, 107, 166–69, 175, 220n51
reconstruction, 5, 59–60, 145, 186
recruitment system. See devşirme
Redhouse, James, Sir, 186–87
referents, 4, 31, 51, 57, 61–63, 65, 119
reification of state, 2–3, 42, 135–41, 157–58, 161, 165, 176, 223–24n6
reisülkuttab, 43, 44, 45, 46
repetition, 53, 76, 84
Ricoeur, Paul, 3, 62–64, 66–68
Roe, Thomas, Sir, 20
Rousseau, Jean-Jacques, 61
royal household, 3, 9, 13, 15, 208n6, 208n16; bureaucracy and, 173–74; devşirme and, 149–50; elite households and, 110, 175, 195; of Ibrahim I, 97; pencik and, 35
royal tutor. See hoca
Rumelia, 43, 46, 147, 171–72

şagirdan, 44
Şapur (Prince), 102, 104, 105
Şarihülmanarzade, 215n46
şehname, 38
şehnameci, 38, 39
şeriat, 24, 45, 85, 128, 186
şerif, 24, 83
şikk-i sani, 212n39
Sıdkı Çelebi, 78, 112, 118–19
sınıf, 178
Safavids, 12, 21
Safiye, 14
sahn-i seman, 43
Said, Edward, 217n18
Salzmann, Ariel, 154–56, 161–62
sancak, 148
Saray-i Atık. See Old Palace
Saray-i Cedid. See New Palace
Sassanian story, 101–6, 115
"schizoid mental topography," 164–65, 176, 179–83, 191, 197, 227n4
Schmidt, Jan, 40–42
scientific historiography, 57
scientificity, 40–42
scribal services, 31, 42, 43, 46, 47, 99. See also bureaucracy

Sebeb-i vak'a (Katip Çelebi), 117
secondary sources, 119
sedentary state, 10, 12, 17, 20, 35, 149, 163, 208n16, 227n3
sekban, 22–23, 27; in Abaza Pasha affair, 167, 169, 175; Kafadar on, 180; military transformation and, 171–73, 174, 178–79, 228nn24–25; Tuği on, 22–23, 83, 195
Selim I, 11, 92
Selimname, 72
seniority, 10, 12–15, 20
sermons, 11, 27
Sertoğlu, Midhat, 72–73
shahanshah, 101
Shahname (Firdausi), 38, 102–5, 190
Shakespeare, William, 187, 190
Sheyh Mahmud, 87
sheyhülislam, 10, 16, 18. *See also* names of *sheyhülislam;* Hasanbeyzade on, 101, 129; Peçevi on, 106; Tuği on, 75, 85, 125
"Sidestepping Capitalism: On the Ottoman Road to Elsewhere" (Aricanli and Thomas), 150
sikke ve hutbe, 11, 27
Silahdar Mehmed Ağa, 181
silsila, 39
Sinan Pasha, 46
sipahis, 19, 22, 25, 27; Hasanbeyzade on, 129, 130; Katip Çelebi on, 117; Peçevi on, 108, 112; Tuği and, 67, 73, 77, 83, 111
siyakat, 47
Skinner, Quentin, 61–62, 66, 68
social history, 50, 60
"Social Logic of the Text" (Spiegel), 4
social networks. *See* intisap
society/state polarity. *See* state/society polarity
socioeconomic revolution, 153
sociopolitical groups, 32, 34–35, 43, 49, 166, 171. *See also* Osmanlı sociopolitical identity
Sohrab, 190
Sokollu (Serbian Sokoloviş), 46

sons-in-law. *See* damad
sources, 4, 41–42, 50–51, 64, 98–99, 152, 210n3. *See also* manuscripts; Abou-El-Haj on, 153; Katip Çelebi on, 115, 118–19; Kunt on, 148; Peçevi on, 106
sovereignty, 17, 19, 20, 27, 35, 208n16
Spain, 225n31
"special event" histories, 71–72, 216n1
speech act theory, 61–62, 216–17n15
speech/writing dichotomy, 62–64, 66–68
Spiegel, Gabrielle, 4
stagnation, 151
standing army. *See* kul
State, Power, Socialism (Poulantzas), 223n5
state historian. *See* vakanüvis
state ideology, 32, 35
state narrative, 2, 64, 176–84, 215n46; conception of, 47, 53, 114–32; discursive battle over, 48–49, 54
state/society polarity, 136–41, 152, 154, 157–62, 174, 176, 223–24n6, 227n63
statist approach, 136–37, 140, 223n2
Structure of Scientific Revolutions, The (Kuhn), 41
Stuart England, 143–46
succession mechanism, 10, 12–15, 20–21
Sufi sheyh, 19, 24
Sufism, 145, 193–95, 196
suhtes, 172
Süleyman, 13–14, 37–39, 45, 72, 171, 208n6
Süleyman Ağa, 22–24, 25, 83, 98, 108–9, 196
Süleymaniye mosque, 25, 125
Süleymanname, 38, 72
Sultan Ahmed Mosque, 15
sultanic household. *See* royal household
Sultan Mehmed Mosque, 112, 129–30, 131
superstructure, 138–39, 152

supply of money, 141–44
surplus, distribution of, 151–52, 162
symbols of sovereignty, 11, 27
synecdoche, 191–200
Syria, 23, 83, 175, 178, 180

Ta'likizade, 72, 216n1
Tacüttevarih (Hoca Sadüddin Efendi), 39, 92, 188
Tahmina (Princess), 190
taklid-i seyf, 11
Tanzimat, 147
Tarih-i Al-i Osman, 31, 38, 48, 56, 64, 71, 75, 78, 91–92, 169
Tarih-i Al-i Osman (Hasanbeyzade), 99; as Katip Çelebi source, 115; as Peçevi source, 106
Tarih-i Naima, 177–78, 181
Tarih-i Peçevi, 107, 114, 115, 117, 119, 178, 220n51
Tarih-i sene-i elf, 98
Tarih-i Tuği, 66–68, 115, 222n19
tax farming, 155–56
Tebakatü'l-memalik ve deracatü'l mesalik (Celalzade), 37
teleological narratives, 35, 42, 154
telhis, 99
Tevarih-i Al-i Osman (Paşazade), 37
textual tiers, 58–59
Tezcan, Baki, 183
tezkereci, 46
theoretical purity, 66, 68
"Theory of the Middle Ground" (Spiegel), 4
Thirty Years' War, 21
Thomas, Lewis V., 51, 98–99, 219n27
Thomas, Mara, 150–52
Thrace, 164
thugs. *See* zorbas
timar, 46, 149
time. *See* chronology
Toledano, Ehud, 47, 221n64
Topkapı palace, 10, 12, 15, 16, 18, 26, 77, 173–74, 195, 208n6
trading networks, 141
"tragedy," 1, 186–88

tragic plot, 188–91
treasury. *See* Imperial Treasury
tribalism, 32, 210n6
Tuği Çelebi, 2, 45–46, 222n19; on Abaza Pasha affair, 166–70, 173, 175–76, 228n10; as Hasanbeyzade source, 91, 98–106; as Katip Çelebi source, 91, 114–32, 178; on Mere Hüseyin Pasha, 110–12; on Osman II, 20, 24, 121, 209n26, 222n27; as Peçevi source, 91, 106–12, 119; perspective and, 75–79; on preordained destiny, 88–90; state narrative and, 71, 176–83; text as defense of kul, 21–23, 26–27, 79–88, 217n41; text as oral address, 71, 73–77; text as synecdoche, 191–98; text as tragedy, 189; text as urtext, 2, 66–68, 88, 92, 93, 191
Turhan, 14
Turkish and English Lexicon (Redhouse), 187–88
Turkish and English Lexicon (Redhouse and Pakalın), 187–88
Turkish Republic, 165
tutor, royal. *See* hoca; lala
tyrants, 85, 89, 105, 196, 217n41

uc. *See* frontier
ulema, 25–26, 31–32, 34, 35, 164. *See also* sheyhülislam; Hasanbeyzade on, 98, 129; Peçevi on, 112
ulema lineages, 18–19
Umar (Caliph), 11
ümera, 1, 24; in Abaza Pasha affair, 166, 170, 175–76, 220n60, 228n9; Barkey on, 159, 174; Kafadar on, 180; Kunt on, 148–49; Peçevi in, 46
Umm al-Qura (Kawakibi), 186
Unkapanı, 34
urbanization, 141–43
urtext, 2, 66, 88, 191
Üsküdar, 25, 179
Üsküdari Mahmud Efendi, 24, 86, 90, 170
Usul al-Hikam fi Nizam al-'Alam (Hasan al-Kafi), 97

Vak'a-i Hayriye, 184
vakanüvis, 38, 47, 182
valide sultan, 10, 12, 13–16, 18, 26–29, 98; Peçevi on, 79; Tuği on, 78
vantage point. *See* perspective
"varmak," 167
velocity of money circulation, 141–44
verbs, 95, 167, 178
Veysi, 181
vezir/pasha household, 149, 156
via dolorosa, 26–27
Vico, 68
Vienna manuscript, 111
viewpoint. *See* perspective
vizirieal firm, 156
von Grunebaum, Gustav, 185–86

Walsh, John R., 52–53
Weberian terminology, 42–43, 137, 182
westerners, 181–82
wet nurse, 18, 79
White, Hayden, 55–60, 64–68, 131–32, 192, 213–14nn13–15, 214n19, 215n47, 219n16, 223n57

white eunuchs, 15
wilderness, 197–98
Wittek, Paul, 34, 51, 210n6, 210n8, 213n3
Wolfram, Herwig, 198
Woodhead, Christine, 37, 44, 72, 211n29, 212n38, 216n1

Yıldırım Sultan Bayezid. *See* Bayezid I
Yahşi Fakih, 33, 211n12
Yavuz Sultan Selim. *See* Selim I
Yeğen Osman Pasha, 172
Yedikule, 79, 189
Yeni Odalar, 25, 110, 167, 194
yerliye, 47, 165, 167
yoklama, 22, 45, 107–8, 117
Yusuf Ağa, 120

zahir, 89
Zikir Vaka-i Haile-i Osmaniye (Katip Çelebi), 186
zorbas, 27, 109–10, 112, 128–29
zübde-i Al-i Osman (Süleyman), 37

STUDIES ON THE HISTORY OF SOCIETY AND CULTURE

Victoria E. Bonnell and Lynn Hunt, Editors

1. *Politics, Culture, and Class in the French Revolution,* by Lynn Hunt
2. *The People of Paris: An Essay in Popular Culture in the Eighteenth Century,* by Daniel Roche
3. *Pont-St-Pierre, 1398–1789: Lordship, Community, and Capitalism in Early Modern France,* by Jonathan Dewald
4. *The Wedding of the Dead: Ritual, Poetics, and Popular Culture in Transylvania,* by Gail Kligman
5. *Students, Professors, and the State in Tsarist Russia,* by Samuel D. Kassow
6. *The New Cultural History,* edited by Lynn Hunt
7. *Art Nouveau in Fin-de-Siècle France: Politics, Psychology, and Style,* by Debora L. Silverman
8. *Histories of a Plague Year: The Social and the Imaginary in Baroque Florence,* by Giulia Calvi
9. *Culture of the Future: The Proletkult Movement in Revolutionary Russia,* by Lynn Mally
10. *Bread and Authority in Russia, 1914–1921,* by Lars T. Lih
11. *Territories of Grace: Cultural Change in the Seventeenth-Century Diocese of Grenoble,* by Keith P. Luria
12. *Publishing and Cultural Politics in Revolutionary Paris, 1789–1810,* by Carla Hesse
13. *Limited Livelihoods: Gender and Class in Nineteenth-Century England,* by Sonya O. Rose
14. *Moral Communities: The Culture of Class Relations in the Russian Printing Industry, 1867–1907,* by Mark Steinberg
15. *Bolshevik Festivals, 1917–1920,* by James von Geldern
16. *Venice's Hidden Enemies: Italian Heretics in a Renaissance City,* by John Martin
17. *Wondrous in His Saints: Counter-Reformation Propaganda in Bavaria,* by Philip M. Soergel
18. *Private Lives and Public Affairs: The Causes Célèbres of Prerevolutionary France,* by Sarah Maza
19. *Hooliganism: Crime, Culture, and Power in St. Petersburg, 1900–1914,* by Joan Neuberger

20. *Possessing Nature: Museums, Collecting, and Scientific Culture in Early Modern Italy*, by Paula Findlen
21. *Listening in Paris: A Cultural History*, by James H. Johnson
22. *The Fabrication of Labor: Germany and Britain, 1640–1914*, by Richard Biernacki
23. *The Struggle for the Breeches: Gender and the Making of the British Working Class*, by Anna Clark
24. *Taste and Power: Furnishing Modern France*, by Leora Auslander
25. *Cholera in Post-Revolutionary Paris: A Cultural History*, by Catherine J. Kudlick
26. *The Women of Paris and Their French Revolution*, by Dominique Godineau
27. *Iconography of Power: Soviet Political Posters under Lenin and Stalin*, by Victoria E. Bonnell
28. *Fascist Spectacle: The Aesthetics of Power in Mussolini's Italy*, by Simonetta Falasca-Zamponi
29. *Passions of the Tongue: Language Devotion in Tamil India, 1891–1970*, by Sumathi Ramaswamy
30. *Crescendo of the Virtuoso: Spectacle, Skill, and Self-Promotion in Paris during the Age of Revolution*, by Paul Metzner
31. *Crime, Cultural Conflict, and Justice in Rural Russia, 1856–1914*, by Stephen P. Frank
32. *The Collective and the Individual in Russia: A Study in Practices*, by Oleg Kharkhordin
33. *What Difference Does a Husband Make? Women and Marital Status in Germany*, by Elizabeth Heineman
34. *Beyond the Cultural Turn: New Directions in the Study of Society and Culture*, edited by Victoria E. Bonnell and Lynn Hunt
35. *Jazz, Rock, and Rebels: Cold War Politics and American Culture in a Divided Germany*, by Uta G. Poiger
36. *The Frail Social Body and Other Fantasies in Interwar France*, by Carolyn J. Dean
37. *Blood and Fire: Rumor and History in East and Central Africa*, by Luise White
38. *The New Biography: Performing Femininity in Nineteenth-Century France*, edited by Jo Burr Margadant
39. *France and the Cult of the Sacred Heart: An Epic Tale for Modern Times*, by Raymond Jonas

40. *Politics and Theater: The Crisis of Legitimacy in Restoration France, 1815–1830*, by Sheryl Kroen
41. *Provisional Notes on the Postcolony*, by Achille Mbembe
42. *Fascist Modernities: Italy, 1922–1945*, by Ruth Ben-Ghiat
43. *Women Writing Opera: Creativity and Controversy in the Age of the French Revolution*, by Jacqueline Letzter and Robert Adelson
44. *Popular Theater and Society in Tsarist Russia*, by E. Anthony Swift
45. *Beyond the Pale: The Jewish Encounter with Late Imperial Russia*, by Benjamin Nathans
46. *The View from Vesuvius: Italian Culture and the Southern Question*, by Nelson Moe
47. *The Three-Piece Suit and Modern Masculinity: England, 1550–1850*, by David Kuchta
48. *The Emancipation of Writing: German Civil Society in the Making, 1790s-1820s*, by Ian F. McNeely
49. *Obstinate Hebrews: Representations of Jews in France, 1715–1815*, by Ronald Schechter
50. *An Ottoman Tragedy: History and Historiography at Play*, by Gabriel Piterberg

Compositor:	G & S Typesetters, Inc.
Text:	10/13 Aldus
Display:	Aldus
Printer and Binder:	Integrated Book Technology, Inc.